GET YOUR
DUCKS
IN A ROW

THE BABY BOOMERS GUIDE
TO ESTATE PLANNING

HARRY S. MARGOLIS

GET YOUR DUCKS IN A ROW
THE BABY BOOMERS GUIDE TO ESTATE PLANNING
HARRY S. MARGOLIS

Ducks in a Row Publishing

Published by Ducks in a Row Publishing
Wellesley, Massachusetts

Copyeditor: Julie Hills
Cover and Interior design: Yvonne Parks, www.pearcreative.ca
Cover copy: Lisa Canfield, www.gethipcreative.com
Proofreading: Clarisa Marcee, www.avenuecmedia.com
Index: Elena Gwynne, www.quillandinkindexing.com

Library of Congress Control Number: 2019903953

ISBN: 978-1-7339310-0-7 (paperback)
         978-1-7339310-1-4 (Kindle)
         978-1-7339310-2-1 (ePub)

DEDICATION

To Susan for her unflagging support
no matter the windmills at which I tilt.

CONTENTS

PREFACE

HOW TO USE THIS BOOK

One of my great pleasures from more than three decades practicing elder law and estate planning has been hearing the stories of thousands of families. When Leo Tolstoy suggested that all happy families are alike, he missed the mark: all families have both happy and sad times and all are different in their own way. This book is about families, their stories, and how they care for one another. I hope it helps you better care for yourself and your family by answering your questions about estate planning and removing hurdles that might be preventing you from moving forward with your own plan.

This book is designed to be useful whether you are in the active process of preparing your estate plan, you're still formulating ideas, or you have questions about the estate planning documents you have already signed. You may read it from beginning to end, or dip into it to get answers to specific questions. This book will help explain your choices, answer questions, demystify terms, and narrow down your decisions.

While I've attempted to be comprehensive, you might have questions that this book doesn't answer or for which the answer is not clear. In that case, you can visit my website, www.AskHarry.info, where you will find answers to estate planning questions posted by other consumers, or can post your own question. If your question is more specific or complex, and particularly in situations involving local law or local interpretation of federal law, then I recommend that you consult with a local elder law, special needs, or estate planning attorney.

The book starts with a description of the many reasons most people don't engage in estate planning with the hope that once we've discussed these obstacles, they will lose their power and no longer stand in the way of taking the steps to protect yourself and your family.

The substance of the book describes the five essential estate planning documents everyone should have and the decisions that clients must make around them. These basic documents might be sufficient for your situation and with this book and a DIY program, you might be able to execute these documents on your own. However, many specialized issues require attorney involvement. The second half of the book describes these more complex issues, and will help you determine whether you wish to pursue planning in one or more of these intricate areas that require the guidance of an experienced attorney.

We will also follow the estate planning of a typical couple and the events during their lives that cause them to change their plans. Meet our avatars:

THE JORGENSONS

John and Joyce Jorgenson are both 60 years old and in good health. They both continue to work but are thinking about retirement. They have three children, Jack, Jill and Jennifer, all out of college and working. Jack and Jill are both married. Jack has two children and Jill has one.

John and Joyce's financial picture is as follows:

Income (annual)
John $135,000
Joyce $70,000

Savings and Investments

Checking	$15,000
Savings	$25,000
Investments	$235,000
John's IRA	$400,000
Joyce's IRA	$225,000
Total	$900,000

House	$500,000 fair market value, no mortgage

Life Insurance

John	$500,000
Joyce	$250,000

Both are term policies with no cash value.

We will learn more about John, Joyce and their children and grandchildren as the details become relevant to our planning discussion. And their situation will morph over time to fit the estate planning concepts we will be discussing.

I should say a few words about why this book is aimed at Baby Boomers. First of all, I'm one. So I'm in the same boat as you are in many ways. Second, as a Baby Boomer you are at a stage of life when you need to concern yourself about estate planning. You might be one of many who signed a will as a younger adult and have not reviewed it since. Now, the will is out of date. If you have children, probably they are grown. You might have grandchildren. You might have divorced and remarried. You have more assets than you did back when you were starting out. You have retired or are hoping to. And, to be blunt, you can't be certain that you'll be healthy—or even alive—for another three or 30 years. You want to make sure your money lasts as long as you do and that you have decent care if you become incapacitated. In short, it's time for you to do estate planning and now that it's time, you're more likely to follow through.

That said, if you're not a Baby Boomer, you're still welcome to read this book. You too will face these decisions sooner or later (and need to be prepared for the unknown), and I hope you will find it to be of assistance.

INTRODUCTION

BARRIERS TO ESTATE PLANNING

Everyone needs an estate plan and few people have one. As they say, the only certainty in life, other than taxes, is death. Almost as certain is some period of disability before death. Without planning, both of these eventualities— disability and death—can cause undue stress and cost to family members. Yet, most Americans do no planning or fail to update old documents they might have executed at an earlier time, such as after the birth of a child.

We keep our clients' original estate planning documents in successively numbered files stored in fireproof and waterproof safes. As I prepared for a meeting with a high school friend and his wife to update their estate plan, I was surprised (and delighted) to learn that their safe files were numbered 1 and 2. This means that they were among my first clients. But it also meant that they had not updated their plans since 1987, 28 years earlier. Now their children are grown and, fortunately, they have substantially more assets. Also fortunately, it didn't matter that they had not updated their documents since they've both remained in good health (and my friend's recent bicycle accident was not debilitating). But the facts that their family situation has changed, that they're not so sure about the ability of their young adult children to manage money, and that in Massachusetts they have a taxable estate, still mean that they now need a more comprehensive plan than they did three decades ago.

In most cases, putting off estate planning until you are older does not present a problem. Anyone under 50 has a very small chance of becoming ill or passing away during any 10-year period. Unfortunately for Baby Boomers, the chances of dying in the next 10 years increases dramatically after age 50. This can be seen from the following (somewhat morbid) table I developed from Social Security Administration actuarial data for Americans.

LIKELIHOOD OF DYING DURING THE NEXT DECADE*

Age	Males	Females
0 to 10	.8%	.7%
10 to 20	.4%	.2%
20 to 30	1.3%	.5%
30 to 40	1.6%	.9%
40 to 50	3.2%	2.0%
50 to 60	7.4%	4.4%
60 to 70	14.5%	9.5%
70 to 80	31.5%	26.9%
80 to 90	65.4%	54.8%
90 to 100	94.9%	90.9%
100 to 110	99.8%	99.5%
	2 out of 100,000 American men survive to 110	13 out of 100,000 American women survive to age 110

* The percentages indicate the statistical chance that an individual at any given age will die during the coming decade. For instance, a 40-year-old man has a 3.2% chance of dying before age 50 and a 60-year-old woman has a 9.5% chance of dying before age 70. These are population-wide statistics, so they do not reflect any particular individual's health or risk in terms of lifestyle or the community in which they live.

So it's not totally irrational for Baby Boomers to have delayed estate planning until now—especially for women whose survival rate is significantly higher than that of men. But, as the chart indicates, Baby Boomers (those born between 1946 and 1964) shouldn't wait any longer to do their estate planning. And these numbers don't reflect the chances of illness or disability, which also increase dramatically after age 60, and again after age 70.

I recently met with two women in one week whose husbands were both in their early 60s and were suffering from dementia. These encounters reflect the greater risk of illness and incapacity, as age increases, than the risk of death in the statistics above.

Yet the likelihood of good health, at least through age 50, is only one of many reasons people hesitate to execute new or updated estate plans. Here are some more:

1. They don't see a need.
2. The cost feels prohibitive and unclear.
3. Fear of lawyers.
4. Thoughts of death and incapacity are disturbing.
5. Difficulty making decisions.
6. The need is not "pressing."
7. Availability of other means to avoid probate (the court process of conveying property to one's heirs).
8. Anxiety about using DIY alternatives.
9. Inertia.
10. It feels like a foreign language.

Let's address each of these in turn with the hope that doing so will drain their power to deter your estate planning.

1. THEY DON'T SEE A NEED

In addition to anticipation of good health, many people don't see a need to do estate planning because they don't have an "estate." If an "estate" means a mansion with expansive grounds, estate planning is only for the rich. In the context of estate planning, however, "estate" simply means whatever you own, whether it's a little or a lot. While those with smaller estates may not have to concern themselves with tax issues, they still need to say who will receive their stuff, who will manage the process, and who will protect their minor children, if any (not an issue for most Baby Boomers). As important as providing for the distribution of your property after you pass away, your estate plan will also provide for one or more people you choose to step in and take care of you and your family in the event you become incapacitated.

Estate planning is for everyone. Without taking the basic steps described in this book, your family can be forced to take control through the court system, which can be expensive and cumbersome, and can lead to infighting among family members. Putting a plan in place will save them time, stress, and money and make their lives much easier in the event of your incapacity. In addition, it can save you substantial money and put the person or persons *you choose* in charge of making decisions for you.

2. COST AND UNCERTAINTY

No one wants to spend money. And yes: legal fees are expensive, and often unknown, to the extent that lawyers charge by the hour and clients often don't know in advance what the fee will be. One of the goals for this book is to save money for its readers. If you know exactly what you need, you will spend less of your attorney's time and reduce the fee. And at the end of the book, you'll find a discussion about whether to use an attorney at all and how to find the right lawyer for your needs. But the bottom line is that the cost of *not* doing planning can be substantially higher than the cost of hiring an attorney. Additional expenses can pile up in higher legal fees down the road, care costs that could have been reduced by qualifying for Medicaid or Veterans benefits, or taxes that might have been avoided. The non-monetary costs, in the form of wasted time spent by family members or avoidable family conflict, may be harder to measure, but are significantly even more important.

3. FEAR OF LAWYERS

Lawyers themselves play a huge role in discouraging clients from planning. Along with cost uncertainty and alienating legal jargon, there's often a sense that lawyers make the process more complicated than it needs to be. Sometimes that sense is accurate and sometimes it's not, but it can be difficult for a client to discern whether the source of complication is their own situation or the lawyer's approach.

Unavoidably, while most attorneys care about the best interests of their clients, they also have a vested interest in the client doing more planning as opposed to less. It is difficult to extract this vested interest from the recommendations. Is the attorney recommending the more complicated and expensive plan because she will earn more, or because she has seen dozens of cases where it has made a significant difference for her clients and their families? In addition, the attorney's viewpoint may be skewed by experience. An attorney who frequently deals with challenging estate matters may think that all clients should take the necessary steps to avoid them, while the attorney who has never run into these issues, and sees their likelihood as slim, may not see the need for certain planning measures. Thus an attorney's advocacy for doing more, rather than less planning may well not be nefarious or driven by the desire for higher fees, but simply based on that attorney's experience. This book will help readers pick apart what planning is necessary and what is optional so that they can make informed choices about their own planning.

But for some people, all lawyers are terrifying. They've seen tough lawyers battling in court on television or in the movies, or have an image of lawyers as slick and seedy. Yet just like people in every other occupation, these stereotypes do not hold. Lawyers come with all temperaments and personalities. Those who become estate planners are as likely as their clients to be uncomfortable with legal battles—perhaps that's why they chose this specialty. They are more likely to value their relationship with their clients and the experience of meeting and working with them should be pleasant, or even enjoyable.

4. DISTURBING TOPICS

Of course, no one relishes contemplating his own death or disability, or that of loved ones. Since such events are unlikely to happen tomorrow, next week, or even next year, we often put off considering them and deal with much more pressing everyday issues: work, family, recreation, friends, house maintenance, etc. Yet, without planning, the stress and potential family conflicts that can arise can be even more unpleasant than contemplating our death and incapacity. Many of our clients express great relief once they sign their documents. The relief is not because they're done working with us (we hope), but because they know that they have taken an important step to care for themselves and their families.

5. DIFFICULTY MAKING DECISIONS

The estate planning process will involve many decisions. You will need to choose who to name to important roles and how your assets will be divided. You might have to decide who to name as a guardian of minor children, or who will make decisions in your stead if you are no longer able to make them for yourself. For some, this will be easy, and for others this will be quite difficult. Often it is easier to simply put off the decisions.

For those with tough decisions to make, both the estate planning process and receiving input from experienced attorneys can actually help. Often, seeing names on draft documents gives clients the opportunity to feel whether or not the choice is right. Based on their experience with hundreds or thousands of prior clients, experienced estate planning attorneys can usually walk clients through the tough decisions.

When embarking on the planning process, remember that few estate planning steps are irrevocable. In almost all cases, if you change your mind you can change your estate plan. (Yes, it's possible you will incur extra cost, so of course we recommend trying to "get it right" the first time. The point is to know that there's a safety hatch in the event you do change your mind.) Don't let less than complete certainty prevent you from creating a plan.

6. THE NEED IS NOT "PRESSING"

If you're (relatively) young and healthy, you are unlikely to need an estate plan any time soon since your chances of becoming incapacitated or passing away in the near future are quite low, as the statistics cited above demonstrate. That's why life insurance and disability insurance are much cheaper for younger adults than for older ones. It's true that the 20-year-old is much *less likely* to need estate planning documents than a 60-year-old. But the possibility of injury, illness or death is not zero, even for a 20-year-old. One in 76 male and one in 200 female 20-year-olds will die before age 30. For 40-year-olds, one in 30 men and one in 50 women will die before age 50. And these numbers do not even account for the possibility of illness, incapacity or disability. So, it's important at any age to have at least a basic estate plan in place (even when your major asset is yourself).

Often, people take up estate planning at two times in their lives: when they have children and when they retire. These are good times to take this step. When you have children you become responsible for people other than just yourself. When you retire, your circumstances have changed: you might move, and given that you're older, the odds of becoming incapacitated or passing away have increased greatly. It is also at these times that your old document likely will be out of date. In your youth, you might have named siblings or close friends to important roles that can now be filled by adult children, or by other friends, colleagues, or family members who are in the best position *now* to take them on.

While having children and retirement are the prime times that most people plan their estates, we recommend reviewing your plan more often. Your circumstances and the laws are both likely to change during the intervening decades. Sit down with your estate planner once a decade, or any time your circumstances change, such as if you move from one state to another.

7. OTHER WAYS TO PASS ON PROPERTY

The reality today is that wills govern a relatively small part of how people's assets are passed on. Anything owned in joint names with someone else passes to the surviving owner at death. Life insurance and retirement plans pass to designated beneficiaries. Many investment and bank accounts permit owners to name who will receive their accounts at death. With these alternative methods of directing who will receive one's assets, many people feel that they have no need for a will or further estate planning. That might be largely true with respect to investable assets, but it might not apply to any real estate you own and definitely does not preclude the necessity of putting durable powers of attorney and health care directives in place. Alternative methods of passing on property and assets will be discussed in more detail later in this book.

8. ANXIETY ABOUT DIY OPTIONS

For those who want to avoid the trouble and expense of working with an attorney, a number of do-it-yourself options exist, including LegalZoom, RocketLawyer, Willing and financial pundit Suze Orman's "Must Have Documents" online program. These offer well-crafted estate planning instruments without the involvement of a lawyer, avoiding high legal fees and overcomplication. Many people avoid using these simple programs because they fear (for good reason) that they might miss something important because they "don't know what they don't know." I hope that this book will help fill in those gaps, permitting those with simple estate situations to use a DIY program with more assurance, and directing readers with more complex situations to be more comfortable discussing them with an attorney.

9. INERTIA

Inertia, n. lack of movement or activity especially when movement or activity is wanted or needed

Like many of the other tasks we know we need to complete, estate planning gets put on the back burner as we deal with the more immediate everyday concerns and responsibilities. To those of us in this position, let me report what a client said to me the other day after signing her estate planning documents: "It is such a relief to have signed my documents. Now I can rest easy." We all just need to get it done. If inertia is getting in your way, it's okay to acknowledge that so you can figure out what you need to do to get the ball rolling!

10. IT FEELS LIKE A FOREIGN LANGUAGE

The language of estate planning creates many of its problems. Legal terms that mean little or nothing to non-lawyers can discourage many from moving ahead. What's an "estate?" Or "probate?" Or an "executor?" Why is a will called a "Last Will and Testament?" Isn't "will" enough? Lawyers bandy these words about because once you've gone to law school you don't remember what you didn't know before that first day of Torts class. (And does anyone who is not a lawyer know what "torts" means?)

Since these words are second nature to estate planning attorneys, they often don't think to explain them (a curse of many professions with their own arcane nomenclature), which can result in clients not being clear about how estate planning truly applies to them. In this book I'll define the terms and then avoid using them as much as possible.

Now that you know what's holding you back, please use this book to move ahead.

PART 1

THE FIVE (OR SIX OR SEVEN) ESSENTIAL DOCUMENTS

In the book *5@55,* my colleague Judith Grimaldi describes the five essential estate planning documents everyone needs by the time they reach age 55. And financial planning guru Suze Orman recommends four "Must Have Documents" in her online planning program. My list of essential documents includes five:

- Durable power of attorney
- Health care directive
- HIPAA release
- Will
- Revocable trust

Although most people think of estate planning as taking care of what happens after death, four of the five documents on my list cover planning for incapacity during your lifetime. They make it easy for people you trust to step in, handle your finances and make both legal and health care decisions for you. Only two of the documents, your will and revocable trust (which also has lifetime benefits), affect what happens to your property after your death. In another way, these two may be thought of as lifetime documents as well—the lifetimes of your children rather than your lifetime—since they greatly influence how your children, grandchildren and other heirs live their lives.

The following chapters outline, in detail, the purposes of these five essential documents, definitions of associated terms, and considerations of the various choices you will need to make when completing them.

CHAPTER 1

DURABLE POWER OF ATTORNEY

Through a durable power of attorney you can appoint another person (or two people)—your "attorney-in-fact"— to step in and manage your financial and legal affairs if and when you ever become incapacitated.

Many estate planners consider the durable power of attorney to be the most important estate planning instrument— even more important than a will. What happens if you don't have a durable power of attorney? If you became incapacitated without one, your family members would have difficulty paying your bills, accessing your accounts, and dealing with your business interests. They might not be able to pay for the medical care you need, to maintain your house, or to care for your loved ones.

Without this relatively simple document, your family would have to go to court to appoint a conservator or guardian to manage your affairs. That court process takes time, costs money, and the judge might not choose the person you would have preferred. In addition, once a guardianship or conservatorship is in place, the assigned representative may still have to seek court permission to take planning steps that could have been immediately implemented under a simple durable power of attorney.

CASE STUDY

My client, a successful accountant, unfortunately became demented prior to retirement. He could no longer manage his business, which involved many complicated matters. This included a dispute with a key employee and concerns by his major client about the confidentiality of its records. Fortunately, my client had executed a durable power of attorney several years earlier naming his son as attorney-in-fact. Using the power of attorney, the son was able to get himself appointed as the key corporate officer for the accounting firm and to fund the client's revocable trust to be managed by a respected trust company. As corporate officer, the son could oversee the winding down of the business, work out matters with the client and former employee, and take care of his father's living arrangements, including cleaning out his apartment and authorizing placement in a chosen assisted living facility. Without this one document, the son would have had to seek court authority, not only causing delay and added legal expenses, but also making his father's situation public and having to serve his father with papers establishing his incapacity, potentially causing a dispute between them.

GUARDIANSHIP & CONSERVATORSHIP

Parents are natural guardians of their minor children, meaning that until age 18 they can make decisions about their children's health care, where they live, and how they invest and spend their money. At age 18, the children become adults (at least in the eye of the law) and can make these decisions themselves. (It's always seemed odd to me that in the United States 18-year-olds have full legal rights to vote, handle their money, get married, and join the military, but they can't buy a drink. A topic for another book.)

Without a durable power of attorney and health care proxy in place, the only way after age 18 that one person can step in and make a choice for another is to become their court-appointed guardian or conservator. In most states now, the guardian is responsible for personal and health care decisions and the conservator for legal and financial ones. In the past, guardianship encompassed both roles. The same person or people can serve as both guardian and conservator, but the roles are now separate. The person seeking appointment must petition the local probate court, give notice to the individual believed not able to handle his affairs as well as all next of kin, get a doctor to write an opinion that the individual does not have capacity, and have a court hearing on the appointment. If she is successful, then she must periodically report to the court on her actions and for some purposes (such as the administration of extraordinary medical care or the sale of real estate), seek specific court permission in advance.

All of this means delay, hiring a lawyer for each step, and cumbersome recordkeeping. It also means taking away the protected person's rights since after the appointment he can no longer make medical, financial or legal decisions himself. In some instances, he can no longer vote. If family members disagree on who should serve as guardian or conservator, protracted litigation can cause huge costs and the severing of ties between brothers and sisters.

Assigning durable power of attorney and health care proxy can ensure that the person who has lost their capacity to make decisions for themself has the opportunity to appoint someone they trust to this important position, and communicate with that person about their values and wishes.

On the positive side, guardianship and conservatorship provide for court oversight that can often provide important protections for the person with incapacity, protecting theft or misuse of property.

DURABILITY

In this discussion of powers of attorney, I have sometimes used the word "durable" to describe the document. To be "durable," a power of attorney must contain wording directing that it continue after the principal—the person creating the power of attorney—becomes incapacitated. Formerly, under the so-called "common law"—the traditional law created by centuries of court decisions—powers of attorney ended upon the incapacity of the principal, the legal theory being that the attorney-in-fact steps into the shoes of the principal to act in her place, so if the principal is legally incompetent, so is the attorney-in-fact. Every state has now adopted laws permitting the creation of "durable" powers of

> attorney that survive the incapacity of the principal and today almost all powers of attorney are "durable."

CHOICES

In theory, the durable power of attorney is a relatively simple document. All it should need to say is the following:

I, Joe Schmoe, hereby appoint Janet Planet to step in for me in the event of my incapacity to handle my financial and legal matters.

But in fact, most durable powers of attorney run to several pages and involve a number of important decisions. Two nationally-known estate planners, Jonathan Blattmachr and Martin Shenkman, have even written an entire ebook just on powers of attorney: *Powers of Attorney: The Essential Guide to Protecting Your Family's Wealth.* While most of the issues covered in an entire book devoted to the topic are of greatest interest only to practitioners in the field, you will face some important choices when drawing up documents.

Here are some of the decisions you will need to make for your durable power of attorney:

1. WHO TO APPOINT.

Of course, you need to appoint someone you trust to have your best interests in mind. The person also needs to be organized and responsible, and have the time (or be able to make the time) to carry out the functions of paying bills, guiding investments and handling any legal matters that might arise. Generally, people appoint family members to this role, but in the case that no family members are appropriate, they might appoint a friend or even an accountant, attorney or clergy person. If there is no one suitable to appoint, despite the benefits of the power of attorney, you might need to resort to a court-appointed conservator in the event of incapacity.

2. HOW MANY AGENTS TO APPOINT.

You may appoint one or more agents on your power of attorney. Having multiple agents allows more than one person to share the responsibility and permits them to divvy up tasks. If you appoint more than one, however, make sure that the document permits each to act on his or her own. Requiring them to act together provides checks and balances, but it could become very cumbersome if all of your agents have to sign every check or other document. Also, if you appoint more than one agent, make sure they get along and communicate well. If not, difficult misunderstandings can arise. This is why we generally advise against naming more than two agents, though it's not unusual for parents with three children to name them all so as not to leave one out. We have seen some attorneys prepare two separate powers of attorney naming different agents rather than name two agents on the same document. This makes us uncomfortable since anyone dealing with either agent might not know that the other document exists and it might discourage communication between the agents.

3. ALTERNATES.

In case the first person or people you appoint to be your attorney-in-fact cannot serve, you can name one (or more) alternates. For instance, you might name your spouse as your agent and your children as alternates. If you do appoint alternates, make sure the document is very clear about when the alternate takes over and what evidence he or she will need to present when using the power of attorney. Otherwise, a bank or other financial institution might deny access to an account if it's not certain that the alternate has indeed taken over.

For this reason, we often advise clients to appoint multiple agents, for instance a spouse and a child, rather than one and then an alternate. This avoids any question of proof when the second agent steps in.

4. "SPRINGING" OR CURRENT.

A power of attorney might be either immediate (current) or "springing."

The idea behind powers of attorney is that they will be used only when the person who creates it becomes incapacitated. Interestingly, traditionally powers of attorney expired when the principal became incompetent, the theory being that the attorney-in-fact stands in his shoes and can only do what he can do: if he's incompetent, then so is his agent. Every state has passed laws providing for "durable" powers of attorney that survive the incapacity of the principal. But when should they take effect? One would think only upon incapacity—a so-called "springing" power of attorney, springing into effect upon incapacity.

Yet, in almost all cases, we recommend that our clients execute immediately effective powers of attorney. We advise against creating springing powers of attorney because they create a hurdle for the agent to get over to use the document. When presented with a springing power of attorney, a financial institution will require proof that the incapacity has occurred, often in the form of a letter from a doctor. Obtaining that letter will be one more task the attorney-in-fact will have to carry out, often when already overwhelmed dealing with a parent's illness while still trying to stay employed and care for children. It can also mean a delay in access to funds needed to pay for care or to maintain a home. In most cases, if a client trusts someone enough to name her as his agent, he also trusts her not to use the document until the appropriate time. And if he learns that this trust was misplaced, then he can always revoke the appointment.

A final argument for executing a current, rather than a springing, power of attorney is that it may be needed when the principal is competent, but unavailable. For instance, a financial or legal matter may come up while you are vacationing in Europe. It could be important that the attorney-in-fact can step in and act while you are out of the country.

5. GIFTING.

Often, powers of attorney authorize the agent to make gifts on the principal's behalf, even though strictly speaking that might not be in her best interest—isn't it always better to have more money than less? But it may well be what you would want to do if you were competent to act on your own—to support children and grandchildren or to take steps to reduce taxes or qualify for public benefits.

Power of attorney forms frequently limit these gifts to the annual gift tax exclusion—currently, $15,000 per individual per year—which with the recent evisceration of federal gift and estate taxes is meaningless for all but the 1 percenters, since you have to give away $5.49 million (in 2019) to be subject to any gift taxes. So, there's no tax reason to have this limitation.

On the other hand, you might want to include it simply to limit the amount of gifts your attorney-in-fact can make each year. This can make sense for financial management purposes, but can tie your attorney-in-fact's hands in terms of planning. For instance, it might make sense to transfer your house into a trust or a life estate for long-term care planning purposes, but this would be impossible if gifts in excess of $15,000 per recipient per year were barred. So, we generally exclude such limitations in our documents. In addition, in order to avoid any charges of self-dealing, we explicitly empower attorneys-in-fact to make gifts to themselves. (Some argue that the power to make gifts to oneself can have adverse tax consequences if the attorney-in-fact were to pass away. Without going into details, we both disagree with this reasoning and feel that even if we were wrong it would affect few people under the current tax regime.)

6. TRUST POWERS.

Similar to the power to make gifts, it can be important to authorize the attorney-in-fact to make, amend, and fund trusts on your behalf. Power of attorney forms often permit the funding of preexisting trusts but not their modification, or the creation of new trusts. These additional powers can be extremely important in the context of long-term care, asset protection or special-needs planning for spouses, children, and grandchildren of the principal.

7. COPIES AND STORAGE.

Once the agents and the wording of your power of attorney have been determined, how many originals should you execute and who should keep them? Most powers of attorney include language saying that a copy should be treated like an original, but this is not always honored by third parties. In addition, an original may be inaccessible at some time. For instance, in transactions involving real estate, an original must be recorded with the deed. It will be returned, but perhaps not for several months. Our practice is to prepare three originals for our clients to execute, generally keeping one original in our safe and giving two to the client. I can't tell you how many times over the years clients have misplaced original documents.

Clients generally hold onto their originals and tell their agents where the documents are located, for when they are needed. We also create paper and digital copies of the powers of attorney (and other estate planning documents) that the client may keep or provide to agents and other family members, for when an original document is not needed.

8. FINANCIAL INSTITUTION FORMS.

Even with an immediate power of attorney, clients sometimes have difficulty getting banks or other financial institutions to recognize the authority of the attorney-in-fact. A certain amount of caution on the part of financial institutions is understandable: when someone steps forward claiming to represent the account holder, the financial institution wants to verify that the attorney-in-fact indeed has the authority to act for the principal. Still, some institutions go overboard, for example requiring that the attorney-in-fact indemnify them against any loss or that the lawyer who drew up the document certify that it is still in effect, even though they might not have communicated with the client for years.

Many banks or other financial institutions have their own standard power of attorney forms. To avoid problems, ask the ones where you have accounts if they have such forms and execute them along with a general durable power of attorney. Revocable or "living" trusts (discussed below) can also help avoid this sort of problem with powers of attorney.

THE JORGENSONS

John and Joyce name each other on their durable powers of attorney, but have some trouble deciding who to name as alternates. We advise them not to name all three of their children because that could cause confusion, and they don't want to name two, since leaving one child out could create hurt feelings. Even though being named on a power of attorney may be more of a burden than an honor, the child not listed may take it as a vote of no confidence. Ultimately, John and Joyce name Jill as their sole alternate because she lives closest to them; Jack and Jennifer are both living out of state.

Their powers of attorney are immediately effective and have broad gifting and estate planning powers. They give their children copies, but keep the originals in a locked file cabinet with their other important legal and financial documents, letting their children know where they can find a key.

FREQUENTLY ASKED QUESTIONS

I'm afraid that the person I appoint won't manage my affairs properly.

Giving someone the potential power to manage your affairs can be frightening. This is why it is important for you to appoint someone you trust to be your attorney-in-fact. She must step into your shoes and use your financial resources as you would, for your benefit. If you do not have anyone close to you who you feel confident appointing to this role, you might be able to find a professional, such as an attorney or accountant, to step in if needed. The other alternative is not to execute a power of attorney. Then, if you become incapacitated the court can appoint a conservator to manage your affairs under its oversight. This will be more expensive and cumbersome, but will provide protection. If you have someone who you would like to serve as conservator, you can nominate him and the court will almost certainly appoint the person you choose. Otherwise, someone will petition to be appointed or the court will choose from among attorneys and others it knows who competently act as conservators. This last alternative, while secure, will likely be the most expensive because the professional conservator will charge for her time.

Does a power of attorney take away my rights?

Absolutely not. Only a court can take away your right to manage your own affairs, through a conservatorship or guardianship proceeding. An attorney-in-fact simply has the power to act along with you, and as long as you are competent, you can revoke the power of attorney.

What if I change my mind?

You may revoke your power of attorney at any time. You simply need to send a letter to your attorney-in-fact telling her that her appointment has been revoked. From the moment the attorney-in-fact receives the letter, she can no longer act under the power of attorney. If you have any concern that she will violate this rule, then also notify your financial institutions of this change. If you have recorded the power of attorney with the land records of your county or at the probate court, you must record the revocation as well.

Can I remove my sister as attorney-in-fact for my mother?

If your mother is still legally competent, she can revoke her existing durable power of attorney and execute a new one, naming you or someone else as her new agent. If she does not have legal capacity, you will have to go to court to have a conservator or guardian appointed, who could then revoke the existing power of attorney.

Can I transfer assets to myself using my parent's power of attorney?

This is a grey area and may depend on specific state law. Generally, most attorneys would advise that the power of attorney document must explicitly authorize the gifting plan you propose. A minority opinion, however, would argue that such gifting is permitted under the general grant of powers included in almost all powers of attorney. That said, if everyone is in agreement, as a practical matter your gifting plan might be possible and not be challenged. Gifting is not uncommon as a Medicaid planning device but can have both positive and negative tax results, depending on the circumstances. It also subjects the transferred assets to your creditors (and those of your siblings), and to risk if any of you were to get divorced or pass away while holding the funds.

Does having gone through bankruptcy disqualify someone from serving as an agent under a durable power of attorney?

Not technically. The durable power of attorney law says nothing about the qualifications of the person appointed. On the other hand, the grantor of a power of attorney will want to be sure her agent is financially responsible.

Can my father execute a new power of attorney even though some consider him to be incompetent?

Competency is not black and white—in which one moment you're competent and the next you're not. The line is grey and people may cross back and forth, having legal capacity today but not doing as well tomorrow, or getting tired and failing later in the day. In addition, people can be competent for some tasks and not for others.

For instance, one would want a stronger showing of legal capacity for your father to completely change his estate plan than for him to confirm the plan he's had for years. I'd recommend that your father meet with an elder law attorney. You should not be in the room when they meet. It will be up to the attorney to determine your father's wishes, whether he is being unduly influenced by anyone, and whether he is competent to execute a new durable power of attorney.

If I execute a power of attorney, can I still maintain my own accounts?

Absolutely. Signing a power of attorney does not take away any of your rights or control. It just gives your agent the ability to step in and help out if you are ever incapacitated. You have the right to revoke the power of attorney at any time.

What should I do if the bank won't honor my father's power of attorney that appoints both me and my brother?

While banks and other financial institutions are known to refuse to accept powers of attorney for no good reason, in your case it sounds like the bank might have a point—but only so far. If the power of attorney does not specify that you and your brother can each act on your own, then the bank should still honor any check signed by both of you. If it won't, you might want to contact your state agency that regulates banks to see if it will apply some pressure on your behalf.

Can I transfer my father to another nursing home using his power of attorney?

No and yes. Generally a power of attorney provides you with the power to control your father's finances and enter into contracts for him, but does not give you the power to decide where he lives, unless it specifically grants such power. Absent a guardianship appointment, your father has the right to make his own decisions in this regard. If he is not competent to do so, you may need to seek guardianship. That's the "no" part. Practically, if your father does not object to being transferred, you can sign the paperwork with the new facility and have your father moved there. Without a guardianship, it's up to his acquiescence.

When might I need multiple originals?

We always prepare three original durable powers of attorney for our clients because their agents sometimes need more than one. If you have to deed any property, you will have to record an original. Sometimes financial institutions, timeshare corporations, and stock transfer agencies require an original. They will all return them eventually, but it's best to have a spare while the original is out of your possession. When you don't have a spare, some institutions will accept a copy certified by a notary or an attorney. If they don't, you may have to give up the original and cross your fingers that it will be returned to you on a timely basis.

As an Agent Under a POA, Can I Change the Alternative Agent Named in the POA?

No. Only the person who granted the power of attorney can change who he named. If he's not competent to do so now, your only option is to organize other family members or friends to step in in the event you become incapacitated. They would probably have to seek a court-ordered conservatorship to supersede the successor attorney-in-fact. The best answer if you feel your alternate is inappropriate to serve in this role is to stay healthy.

CHAPTER 2

HEALTH CARE DIRECTIVES

The title of this chapter is in the plural because we will be talking about two or three types of health care directives, depending on how they're counted and combined: the health care proxy (or durable power of attorney for health care), the living will and the medical directive. (The HIPAA release could be included in this chapter, but we treat it as a separate necessary document.) Each of these has a different, but related, function and each carries distinct legal significance in the various states. With a health care proxy, you appoint an agent to carry out your wishes; a living will dictates the withdrawal of life support under certain circumstances; and a medical directive provides instruction in non-life threatening situations. We will also discuss briefly Do Not Resuscitate orders and Medical Orders for Life Sustaining Treatment.

HEALTH CARE PROXY

Every state provides for the creation of a health care proxy or durable power of attorney for health care appointing an agent to make health care decisions for you if and when you are unable to do so yourself. Once a physician determines that you have lost the capacity to make or communicate health care decisions, the person you appoint stands in for you, has access to all of your medical records, and may speak with doctors and other health care providers as if he were you.

Your agent is supposed to make a "substituted judgment" decision on your behalf. This means that—at least in theory—your agent will make the same health care choices as you would make, if you had complete information about your medical status, the treatment options available, their likelihood of success, and the amount of pain and discomfort each of the treatment options might cause. Of course, standing in your shoes is easier said than done, but the more communication you have with your agent about your goals and wishes, the easier this will be for him when he has to step in.

So far, I have been speaking of a single health care agent. The health care proxy law in Massachusetts, where I practice, only permits the appointment of a single agent. You may also appoint successor agents to step in if the original agent cannot serve. While this limitation of a single agent does not exist in all states, it can make sense. Not only does it avoid disagreements between agents, it provides for a distinct point person in dealing with numerous medical teams and providers. This is especially important when a person is hospitalized. With multiple agents communicating with the treating and consulting doctors, nurses, specialists, social workers and discharge planners, it is likely that critical information will be lost. By choosing one person with the authority to talk with each member of the team, and to collect and sort all of the relevant information, it's more likely that she will be able to make decisions based on a complete picture of all of the available facts. This can reduce confusion and improve treatment and discharge decisions.

MEDICAL DIRECTIVE

While the health care proxy or durable power of attorney for health care names an individual to make decisions for an incapacitated patient, it does not—by itself—guide what decisions that agent will make. There are two types of medical directives that do so. The first is the living will, which permits you to direct that medical care be withheld or withdrawn under specific circumstances, such as an irreversible coma or terminal illness. In most states, living wills have the force of law with or without the patient naming an agent under a health care proxy. In those states without living will statutes, they simply provide guidance to the health care agent.

Even if you execute a living will, your agent likely will need to make decisions in situations that are not life and death. These may involve which medical tests to perform, when to move from one facility to another, or whether to undergo certain treatment options.

Because the concept of appointing a health care agent is that she will make the decision you would make, were you able to do so, guidance from you is critical. Without this communication, your agent will have to do their best to make these decisions based on her judgement of what would be in your best interest. Advance guidance, through conversations or a written document, makes it more likely that your wishes will be carried out. Ellen Goodman, Pulitzer Prize-winning former columnist for *The Boston Globe*, has started a website and small movement to encourage conversations about end-of-life care. The website at theconversationproject.org provides tools for getting the conversations going among family members.

While these conversations are vital, if they do not occur (or if various family members remember them differently), written medical directives are also very important. These can be general statements about your wishes and goals, for instance that you do not want extraordinary medical care to keep you alive, or that everything should be done to keep you going in case of a future medical breakthrough. Or they can be very specific about types of treatment you would want under various circumstances. For instance, would you want dialysis if you were already terminally ill? The difficulty in terms of providing specific guidance to an agent is that this type of question can be difficult to answer in the abstract, particularly for those without medical training.

A number of organizations have developed workbooks that individuals can fill out to more fully state their values, to guide their health care agents and other family members on end-of-life care. One that we use in our office is Five Wishes, from Aging With Dignity (agingwithdignity.org). It is available in both print and online versions for $5 (and attorneys and others can purchase bulk orders for $1 each).

Attorneys debate whether health care proxies and medical directives should be combined in a single document or kept separate. The main argument against combining the two is that only the appointment of the agent has legal power. Once appointed, the agent stands in for you and is to make decisions on your behalf. Your medical directive is a private communication between you and your agent.

If combined, and the proxy includes a medical directive, health care personnel may look to that rather than follow the instructions of your agent.

The argument for including a medical directive in the health care proxy is more practical and for the sake of convenience. It avoids the further proliferation of documents and makes it more likely that the agent and health care providers are aware of the medical directive. If it is left to the client to prepare as a separate document, she may never get around to completing it. Our office practice is to combine the two, though the medical directives in our documents are quite broad in nature. We then urge our clients to have conversations with their agents, and provide optional workbooks for clients to complete either on their own or together with the agents they appoint.

As with other estate planning documents, it's important that you review your health care proxy and medical directive every few years. You might change your mind about who would best serve as your agent or alternate and, more likely, your health care wishes will change over time. As a 20- or 30-year-old, you might not be able to imagine living with any disability. As a 70- or 80-year-old, you might be able to accept and adapt to various limitations that come with age. We are not the same person we were in our youth and might not want the same choices made for us.

DNRS AND MOLSTS

People often confuse health care proxies, living wills and medical directives with do not resuscitate (DNR) orders. While the former are all documents executed by the individual, DNRs are medical orders executed by a doctor or other health care provider, such as a nurse. They are typically instituted when a patient is already terminally ill and are intended to avoid resuscitation, which can be a violent procedure and—while getting the patient's heart and lungs working again—might not bring her back to where she was before her heart or breathing stopped. Many people who are not otherwise healthy want to avoid such an intervention. But to do so, you must communicate this to your doctor in advance. Otherwise, emergency and other health care providers will do what they can to keep you alive.

CASE STUDY
DNRS

In *GPSolo*, a magazine published by the American Bar Association, Los Angeles Attorney J. Anthony Vittal describes his wife's decline from terminal cancer. Though she had expressed her desire not to be resuscitated, she never asked her doctor to execute a DNR. At one point, she fell into a coma and was resuscitated against her wishes. She was intubated and it took 11 hours for her to be stabilized. Afterwards, she spent four months in a specialized respiratory hospital before telling her husband, "I didn't sign up for this, you didn't sign up for this, we didn't sign up for this, and I just want it f***ing over . . . NOW! Just MAKE IT HAPPEN!" They were able to withdraw life support and let her pass away peacefully. On the one hand, a DNR order in place may have prevented those last four difficult months. On the other hand, without the resuscitation having occurred, she would not have been able to have said goodbye to her family. So it can be difficult to know what is right, in some cases even after the fact.

DNRs have a few drawbacks. They only work if medical personnel know about them and in some states they are limited to care in the institution where the doctor writes the order. Many states have broadened their reach to apply anywhere and patients who have DNRs are often counseled to tape them to the front of their refrigerators so that emergency workers can find them. Unfortunately, even this is not foolproof. Our firm had a client whose mother had a DNR which the EMTs read when they were called. But they did not follow it because it wasn't clear on its face that the person who signed it had the authority to do so under state law, since she was not a doctor (though she did have that authority). Rather than risk liability for not resuscitating the woman, they did so against her wishes with predictable results: she died a few days later in intensive care rather than in her bed at home. The moral of this story seems to be that in order to protect against unwanted medical treatment, we need to dot every i and cross every t . . . or try to resist calling the EMTs.

The other problem with DNRs is that they only refer to resuscitation, not to other forms of treatment. A growing movement has introduced a new form: medical orders for life sustaining treatment (MOLSTs). These permit doctors to write much more specific orders for their patients who are terminally ill. This requires a more full discussion between physicians and patients, which has its own benefits in terms of making sure that the patient better understands his prognosis and treatment options and the doctor better understands the patient's wishes. (When Medicare was expanded some years back to actually compensate doctors for having these conversations, rather than only paying them for medical procedures, Sarah Palin scotched the plan with her reference to mythical "death panels." Fortunately, Medicare has more recently expanded its coverage to permit physician compensation for these all-important conversations.) After such a consultation, the doctor and patient together can execute a MOLST governing all future care. MOLSTs are not yet available in all states, but statutes authorizing them are spreading.

When the patient can no longer discuss DNRs and MOLSTs with his doctor, his health care agent can do so instead.

As you can see, while this section discusses health care directives as a single concept, it can encompass as many as four separate documents if you execute a health care proxy, a living will and a separate medical directive, and complete a workbook (not to mention a DNR or MOLST down the road). To avoid this proliferation of separate documents, in our practice we combine the health care proxy and medical directive, dispense with a living will (which is not given legal effect in Massachusetts in any case) and offer the workbook to those clients who wish to go further.

CHAPTER 3

HIPAA RELEASE

The third essential document might be classified under health care directives above, but it's a bit different and equally necessary. Under the limitations of the Health Insurance Portability and Accountability Act (HIPAA), medical personnel and institutions are not required to share information with anyone but the patient or her guardian, not even with a spouse or a child. How strictly these restrictions are followed varies greatly. Some medical providers take a practical approach and recognize tacit approval by patients to talk with family members or talk in emergency settings. However, others use HIPAA as a shield to avoid talking with family members who they see as complicating their work. This can cause a huge problem, especially in an emergency room setting where the doctors and nurses have no idea what the patient's status was before the emergency episode or what medications she might be taking. She might be confused or lethargic, but the health care providers have no way of knowing whether this is her usual status or she was driving and playing tennis the day before. Lack of knowledge can be more than inconvenient. For instance, piling on new medications to old can have adverse effects.

HIPAA permits doctors, nurses and other medical personnel to refuse to share information with family members of patients. They often say that they don't have the right to communicate with people other than the patient. That is not the law and, even if it were, in emergency rooms or other settings, medical personnel may listen to what family members tell them without imparting any information about the patient. But having a legal debate with medical providers, especially in an emergency setting, will probably accomplish little. It's better to avoid the debate and potential problem altogether.

This can be accomplished by everyone executing a HIPAA release in advance. These can be much broader than health care proxies or durable powers of attorney for health care because you can list everyone who you might want to be able to communicate with health care personnel. While only your health care agent can make decisions on your behalf, anyone might have information to tell doctors and nurses or might be able to relay information they receive to other family members.

CHAPTER 4

WILL

Two Baby Boomer cyclists have stopped at a café and their conversation turns to estate planning. One comments to the other that "My biggest concern when I die is that my wife will sell my bicycles for what she thinks I paid for them."

With the will, we are moving from documents that permit others to act for you while you're alive to those that govern what happens to your property after you pass away. The will serves a few purposes:

- Directing the distribution of your probate property
- Naming your executor or personal representative to carry out your wishes

- Appointing a guardian to your minor children

The will is quite formal, requiring two witnesses who need to watch you sign and attest to your competence. While in most states the will is valid simply with the witnesses signing, having it notarized makes it "self proving." Without the notarization, upon your death one of the witnesses would have to appear in court to validate the will. With a notarized affidavit as part of the will, it's not necessary to locate witnesses and convince them to come to court. This is why any professionally drawn will includes notarization.

As you can see, this is a formal process. In every state there are many statutes and court cases governing the process for carrying out the instructions in wills, and interpreting any ambiguities or their application in the event of unforeseen circumstances (such as the prior death of a beneficiary). But here's the irony: **these days the will has no effect on the distribution of most property.** Non-*probate* property passes without regard to what the will says, without the formality of the will execution (signing), and without the structure of the probate laws governing the process. As such, the will does not govern:

- Jointly owned property, which passes to the surviving joint owner or owners
- Property in trust, which passes as directed in the trust
- Life insurance or retirement accounts, which are

payable to designated beneficiaries

- Payable on death accounts, which also go to designated beneficiaries

Often this leaves little or no property to pass under the terms of the will. It also often means confusion and lack of coordination when the will or trust says one thing, but property ownership and beneficiary designation says something else. For instance, a father's will might direct that all of his property be divided equally among his three children, but he might have a joint account with one child and a life insurance policy payable to his ex-girlfriend. Who knows what he wanted? Did he want to favor that one child, or was her name put on the account simply to provide access in case he needed help with his finances? Did he just forget to change the beneficiary designation on his life insurance policy after he broke up with his girlfriend, or did he still have affection for her and want to support her?

CASE STUDY
COMPETING INSTRUCTIONS

In a case our office handled, we created an estate plan that left most of a mother's estate in trust for the benefit of her only son. By using a trust rather than simply having the money pass to him outright, the funds would be protected from his creditors and would not be taxed a second time at the son's death. (In Massachusetts, the threshold for taxation is $1 million, much lower than the 2019 federal threshold of $11.4 million.) Yet, when the mother passed away, we learned that a number of her accounts named her son as beneficiary, rather than the trust. This meant that these funds passed to him outright without the tax and creditor protection of the trust. This often occurs because banks and investment houses ask their clients who they want to name as beneficiary without inquiring how these designations fit in with the rest of their plans.

WHAT'S THE DIFFERENCE BETWEEN A WILL AND A LAST WILL & TESTAMENT?

You may have heard of a "last will and testament" and wondered what that means or how it's different from a will. They are actually the same thing. So why add extra words? "Last" is added because only the last will you execute counts. It's usually best to destroy old wills, so there's no confusion about which will governs. Our office was involved in a will contest where an elderly woman executed a will under quite questionable circumstances. At first, it appeared that if the will were thrown out by the court, our client (her brother) would receive half of her very large estate. Unfortunately for our client (and for us, since we took the case on a contingency fee basis), during the course of litigation a 1960 will was found that gave our client nothing. Even though a lot had changed in the woman's life over the intervening half century, once the new questionable will was thrown out, the 1960 will was her last will and it governed the distribution of her estate.

"Testament" means the same as "will." So if last will and testament is redundant, why use both words? The answer is that lawyers are a nervous and paranoid group and they use both words to make sure there's no confusion. Or at least that's part of the answer. The other part goes back to 1066 when the Normans conquered England and imported French (or whatever predecessor of today's French they spoke back then). The result was that English became a mix of the two languages, with two words for a lot of the same things. You can "get" something (Anglo Saxon) or "acquire" it (French). In general, the Anglo Saxon words are shorter and less formal while the French-derived words are longer and more formal. Thus, we have "will" (Anglo Saxon) and "testament" (French).

TANGIBLE PERSONAL PROPERTY

Estate planning attorneys think of three kinds of property: *tangible* personal property, *intangible* personal property, and *real* property. Tangible personal property is just about anything you can touch, including furniture, jewelry, clothing, artwork, stamp and other collections, and vehicles. Intangible personal property refers to cash, bank accounts, investments, and intellectual property such as copyrights in anything you may have written. And real property is real estate.

As we discussed above, much of intangible personal property and real estate often passes outside of probate to joint owners and designated beneficiaries. This is not true of tangible personal property, which technically passes under the will through probate. However, as a practical matter, it's usually not necessary to go through the probate process to transfer personal property. Instead, families handle it informally, simply delivering items to the designated recipients or deciding among themselves how to divvy up the deceased person's belongings.

In your will, you may simply leave it to your family to figure out who gets what items among themselves or decide for them through a number of different methods. Typically, wills say something like:

"I give my tangible personal property in as nearly equal shares as possible to those of my children who survive me."

This language specifically excludes children who might not survive the testator—the person writing the will, "testatrix" if she's woman—in order to avoid involving grandchildren in the distribution of personal belongings. The family can still decide to give them items from your estate, but not giving them legal rights to the property simplifies the legal process. By saying that the division should be as equal "as possible" acknowledges the fact that it's impossible to split jewelry, artwork, silverware and other items exactly equally, but asks that the personal representative make the effort to make the distribution as equal as possible. Of course, this begs the question as to whether we're talking about equal monetary or sentimental value. Also, it's possible to make the distribution equal by selling all of your personal property and distributing the proceeds. But often personal items, such as photographs, books, furniture and artwork have far greater personal than market value.

Many people specifically designate who will receive the items of most sentimental or monetary value, in order to avoid later conflicts in case family members won't agree. You can make specific bequests (legal speak for a gift given in a will), or through a side memorandum referred to in your will. Depending on the wording in the will, such a memorandum can be given the force of law or simply be advisory. The advantage of the memorandum over including the gifts in the will is that you can change it at any time without having to go back to your lawyer to modify your will. But make sure that you keep a copy of your memo or letter with your original will. Sending a copy to your lawyer is also a good idea. In all but one case in my practice, family members have followed the instructions left in such an informal memorandum whether or not they had the force of law. In that one situation, which occurred before Massachusetts law permitted making the memorandum legally enforceable, one of seven children objected to the distribution directed by her mother, forcing a resolution in court. She was totally unreasonable, but had the right to make her case, however weak it was. A psychologist later surmised that what was driving this daughter, even if she didn't know it, was a wish to stay connected to her siblings. She was already so estranged from them, that once the probate was completed she would probably never talk to them or see them again. By dragging out the probate process, she maintained a connection, no matter how contentious.

In any event, in all other cases in our experience, families have followed the written memorandum whether or not it was legally enforceable. Often clients first talk with family members to get an idea of what items they would most like to have, to help them designate who will receive which items. Some people write the names of the designated recipients on stickers on the backs of pieces of furniture, photos or artwork.

For items of tangible property not specifically provided for in the will or a side memorandum, families use a number of methods for determining who gets what. Often they draw numbers and then take turns selecting the items they want. Where the estate includes property of significant monetary value, such as antiques, jewelry, artwork or silverware, it can be useful to have them appraised in advance. This can help inform the choices each family member makes. Matters can get somewhat complicated if there are one or two items significantly more valuable than all of the rest. Then, the family might decide that whoever receives those items will skip a number of turns in selecting other property. Or it might be necessary to sell that one Jasper Johns painting and split the proceeds.

The process can also be complicated by distance. If family members don't live near the decedent, it might be difficult to choose items in a round robin fashion. The personal representative might have more work to do making lists, taking photos and boxing up items for various family members. Some families might try to avoid the extra work for the personal representative by making distributions when everyone is in town for the funeral or memorial service. But this can be premature for a number of reasons. Some family members might not be emotionally ready to take this step; it's too early to have everything appraised; and everyone might feel that they're acting like vultures, picking over the belongings of the recently deceased. On the other hand, convenience may have to trump the feeling of being rushed. Especially if the deceased left a memorandum with specific gifts, it can make sense for those in town to take whatever was left to them. The need to avoid the cost of continuing to rent an apartment can also argue for moving quickly. In short, every case is different and the personal representative will have to weigh the pros and cons of moving quickly or slowly with respect to tangible personal property.

SPECIFIC BEQUESTS

YOU CAN'T TAKE IT WITH YOU

A man calls his three closest friends—a priest, a rabbi and a lawyer—to his death bed. "Friends," he tells them, "as you know, I have no family. I've decided that what I've worked hard for all of my life should come with me when I die. I've paid off all of my debts and cashed out all of my investments. Here are three envelopes, each holding $200,000 in cash. You are my closest and most trusted friends. I'd like to give one to each of you and for you to promise to make sure that the three envelopes are buried with me." The three friends agree and take the envelopes. A few weeks later, the man passes away. The three friends attend his funeral. After his casket is lowered into the ground, each throws the envelope on top and waits for the dirt to be filled in.

As they're walking away together, the priest turns to the two other men and says, "This is weighing on my mind.

I have to confess that my envelope only contained $160,000. We needed another $40,000 for the Sunday school building fund and I'm sure our friend would have supported the cause."

Then the Rabbi says, "As long as you're coming clean, I will too. I took $60,000 out of my envelope to pay for a new roof for the synagogue."

The lawyer turns to them and says, "I'm shocked. You're both men of the cloth and gave your word to our friend. Unlike you, I wrote him a check for the full $200,000."

"Bequest" is just a fancy word for giving something at death. Often it refers to specific items or amounts. These might be to friends, family members or charities. For instance, you might give specific amounts to your grandchildren or your alma mater, with the rest—the "residue"—of your estate going to your children. However, if the bequests are large and your estate dwindles over time, you risk not having much left for your residuary beneficiaries. For instance, if your assets today total $1 million and you give $100,000 to charities, they will receive 10 percent of your estate. But if by the time you die, your estate dwindles to $500,000, the gifts to charity would constitute 20 percent, which might be a larger portion than you want to give them.

To avoid that risk, it can make sense to limit specific bequests to a percentage of your total estate. This is distinct from *giving* a percentage instead, which you could also do. But that has a couple of drawbacks. First, the total gift amount is then quite unspecific, and can vary greatly with the increasing or decreasing wealth of the testator. Second, it can be complicated to calculate since your personal representative won't know the final value of your estate until she pays all the estate expenses and taxes. The final gift amount will even be affected by investment results. And it gets really complicated if you have a taxable estate and you're making a gift to charity. The size of the gift will affect the amount of the tax deduction, and the size of the after-tax estate will affect the size of the contribution, turning this into a circular calculation. It can be a lot easier simply to write a check for a specific amount, especially if the amount is small, but to have an upper limit on the bequest in the case your estate has dwindled.

CASE STUDY
BEQUESTS

When using a percentage figure as a limit on a specific amount, be very clear. Of course, this is true of all legal writing, but here's a case in point: I represented the personal representative in an estate where the will said the following:

I give the lesser of 10 percent of my estate and $200,000 each to my two granddaughters.

Did the grandmother mean to compare 10 percent to $200,000 (so that each granddaughter should get that amount, to be cut down if each bequest exceeds 10 percent of her estate)? Or did she mean to compare 10 percent to "$200,000 each," cut down if the gifts together ($400,000) exceed 10 percent of her estate?

Given the context, that the grandmother's estate is around $2 million and was about the same size when she signed her will, I'm pretty sure that she meant the former, which is important because under that reading each granddaughter will receive approximately $200,000. Under the second reading, they would each receive about $100,000. We just had to make sure that all of the other beneficiaries agree. There would be no confusion if the will instead had said:

I give each of my two granddaughters the lesser of 10 percent of my estate and $200,000.

But even this could have presented problems. Did the grandmother mean 10 percent of her gross estate, her probate estate, her taxable estate or her net estate after payment of all taxes and costs of administration? In other words, in determining the amount to be divided by 10 are we simply including what's in the probate estate (or what is in the trust, if this were in a trust) or all property that passed at her death, including jointly owned assets and accounts with beneficiary designations? Even if this were clear—for instance if it said "net taxable estate," which would include everything the grandmother had an interest in—difficulties could arise. The first issue is who should pay the estate tax if there is any. Often wills contain "apportionment" clauses that say whether taxes should be charged proportionally to all estate assets or to the residue (see below) of the estate.

The second issue came up in a will that (I regret to say) we drafted in our office. Our client wanted to make a substantial gift to a charity but limited it to 10 percent of her net estate after taxes. The problem here is that the larger the charitable gift, the lower the taxes, but the lower the taxes, the bigger the net estate and the bigger the charitable gift. It becomes a circular calculation that had to be resolved through a dedicated computer program.

A third problem can arise if the trust or will provides for a bequest based on the taxable estate, but much of the decedent's property passes through joint ownership or beneficiary designations. The trust or will might not control enough money to fulfill the bequests.

REAL ESTATE

Real estate (sometimes called "real property" by attorneys) may be treated like other assets or separately. If the plan is for the same people to receive your entire estate, you don't need to mention real estate in your will (or trust). It will simply pass as part of the residue of your estate (see below). But if you want your real estate to pass differently from your other assets, then it merits its own paragraph or section in your will. In addition, if you have a taxable estate (unlikely federally, given the 2019 $11.4 million threshold, but more possible in particular states with lower thresholds) and you expect your real estate to be sold after your death, there can be a tax benefit to directing that it be sold. If your personal representative must sell the property under the terms of your will, then he can deduct the cost of the sale, including any broker's commission, on the estate tax return. For instance, if a house sells for $500,000, the brokerage commission is $30,000 and the estate tax rate is 6 percent, then the savings will be $1,800 ($30,000 x 6% = $1,800). This might not be a huge benefit, but it's a pretty good return for adding one sentence to your will.

RESIDUE

The residue (or remainder) of your estate is everything that is left after you provide for distribution of your tangible personal property, real estate and specific bequests. If you do not make any specific bequests or provide separately for real estate (if any), the residue will include everything but your tangible personal property. This means that it can include real estate as well as savings and investment accounts. Generally, your will and the process of probating your estate works in the following order (more or less):

- Pay debts, taxes and costs of administering your estate
- Distribute tangible personal property
- Sell or convey real estate
- Distribute any specific bequests
- Distribute the residue

Then, you're done; though each of these steps can take months or, in some rare cases, years.

PERSONAL REPRESENTATIVE

Your will permits you to choose who will be in charge of settling your estate after you pass away. This includes paying any outstanding bills, filing tax returns, cleaning out your house or apartment, distributing personal assets, filing life insurance claims, fulfilling your bequests, selling real estate if necessary, filing the appropriate papers in court, ultimately distributing the estate assets, and dealing with anything else of a legal or financial matter that might arise. It's a big job. Whether this person is called your "personal representative," "executor" or "executrix," it's the same role. But who should you choose?

Usually people name their spouse or children if they have any who they are confident can fill this role competently and fairly. Deciding among children can be difficult since clients often don't want to seem to favor one over others. As a result, they often name all of their children to this role. That can work fine if the children get along and work well together, but not if they don't. As a general rule, we encourage clients to name no more than three people to this role in order to keep the process from becoming too cumbersome. The more personal representatives, the more people who need to sign documents and the more meetings and lines of communication it entails.

Also, the more likely it will be that one of the personal representatives disagrees with the others or matters fall through the cracks when it's not clear who's responsible for what.

What about appointing a third party as personal representative, such as your accountant or attorney? We generally advise against doing so because it removes the control from the family. The family can always hire professionals to do the bulk of the required tasks, but usually they should have the power to oversee the professional's work. In addition, the more the professional does, the more she will charge. On the other hand, appointing someone who is not a family member can solve a lot of problems in some instances. It might be that no family member is competent to fill this role or can be relied upon to act impartially. Or appointing one or two children, but not others, might cause lasting resentments. If you have total confidence in someone outside of the family or a more distant relative to fill this role, he or she might be a better choice. This might add to the probate costs, but could save both money and family harmony in the long run, making it well worth the cost.

In short, there's no one-size-fits-all answer to the question of who should serve as executor. It depends on your circumstances and the available candidates for this role.

PROBATE PROCESS

Strictly speaking, "probate" refers to the court process of transferring property solely in the deceased individual's name, though this is only a piece of the work that needs to be accomplished. The "probate process," "estate administration," "trust settlement," and "estate settlement" are all different terms for the process of transferring property from the deceased to heirs and taking care of the myriad related matters. This includes paying debts, distributing tangible personal property, clearing out a house or apartment, selling real estate, paying taxes, and closing out various bank and investment accounts. In effect, closing out a legal and financial life can be complicated and take time: usually about a year, but sometimes longer.

Before the personal representative can take possession of probate property, she needs to be appointed by the probate court. This involves filing a petition with the original will and death certificate and providing notice to all the next of kin (the closest relatives of the deceased). If no objections are filed during a waiting period set by the court, the personal representative will be officially appointed and be able to take possession of bank and investment accounts. At the beginning, she will be required to file an inventory with the court, which is a list of all of the probate assets. At the end of the probate process, she must also file an account listing funds that have come into the estate and expenses and distributions that have been paid out during the course of the estate administration. Remember, the inventory and account do not include assets that pass outside of probate, such as jointly owned property or property with designated beneficiaries, such as life insurance policies, retirement accounts and some bank and investment accounts. Such non-probate property, however, will be included on estate tax returns if the estate is taxable.

CAPACITY & UNDUE INFLUENCE

In order to execute a will, you must be over age 18 and understand (1) the nature and extent of your property, (2) the natural objects of your bounty—meaning your family and loved ones, and (3) the disposition of your property set out in your will. You must also not be under someone else's undue influence. In other words, no one can be forcing you to distribute your assets in a way that is not of your own choosing. It is the lawyer's job to determine whether you meet these requirements. In most cases, no one questions either issue, but circumstances might make the attorney take notice and extra care. For instance, one child might come in to meet with the attorney and the client may say he wants to favor that child in his estate plan. Or the child might do all of the talking with the parent remaining mostly silent. In those cases, the attorney is likely to (and should) ask to speak to the client alone to determine whether he has capacity or is under the child's influence.

Capacity is often easier to identify than undue influence, since a conversation can usually reveal what the client understands. Undue influence, on the other hand, is probably occurring outside of the lawyer's office and might be difficult to ascertain in a conversation with someone who will be returning to the home. Is the client favoring his daughter because he's dependent on her and she said that if he didn't give her his house she would move out? Or is he truly thankful for the assistance she has provided and want to reward her with the house? The lawyer must make his best guess based on all of the circumstances and whatever feeling he has about the client's decision. But if the lawyer says he is uncomfortable creating the estate plan for the client, won't the daughter take her father to another attorney who might be less exacting?

CASE STUDY
UNDUE INFLUENCE

These issues were at the heart of a recent Massachusetts case involving an elderly woman and her grandnephew. The young man moved in with his great-aunt to help care for her and eventually brought her to see her longtime attorney with a request to change her estate plan. The attorney was uncomfortable with the changes and suggested they return another time. Apparently, he wanted to see if the woman was steadfast in her wish to change her plan.

Instead, the grandnephew brought his great-aunt to the office of an attorney who was doing some work for him. Even here, the first lawyer who met with them refused to prepare a new plan. But the lead partner at the firm asked another attorney in his office to meet with them and he prepared the new plan favoring the grandnephew and naming him as the woman's agent on her durable power of attorney and health care proxy.

Ultimately, all of these documents were rescinded by the probate court, but not until the woman underwent back surgery from which she never recovered. Her estate sued the second law firm for malpractice and, in a novel legal argument, for wrongful death, arguing that if the new health care proxy had not been executed, the prior agent would not have agreed to the ill-fated back surgery. Unfortunately for those of us curious about the outcome of this claim, the parties settled out of court.

Getting back to the issue of capacity, while it is stated as a single standard, in practice it is a sliding scale. If a parent is going to divide her assets equally among all of her children, no one is likely to question her capacity and the attorney is not going to be overly concerned. If, on the other hand, the parent is favoring one child over others, there is more likely to be a challenge and the attorney is going to take steps to make sure that there is no question about the client's capacity. This might include meeting with the client one-on-one, a conversation with the client's physician, or an independent examination by a psychiatrist or psychologist, all depending on the specific circumstances. We have had cases where we have felt the need to take these steps, and often there's an initial objection by the client or the favored child as to why we are questioning what they want. But usually that objection disappears when we explain that without our taking these steps, not only is the will likely to be challenged but they are more likely to lose the case. If after taking these extra steps we are confident as to the client's capacity and wishes, and we can explain to any potential challenger what measures we took to develop this confidence, it will be less likely that matters end up in court. And if they do, we will be able to testify in support of the new estate plan.

RULES OF INTESTACY

Every state has laws governing the distribution of probate assets in the event the deceased person leaves no will. These are called the rules or laws of "intestacy" and the property is called the "intestate" estate. In general, these laws have the property distributed to the surviving spouse and closest relatives, starting with children and then other descendants. If there are no surviving children or other descendants, property passes to parents, then siblings, then nieces and nephews. Depending on who the survivors are, they will receive different shares. For instance, in many states, a surviving spouse will receive a larger share if he is the father of surviving children than if it's a second marriage and the children had a different father, in which case the children would receive a larger share.

Beware relying on these rules if there's anything unusual about your family situation. For instance, you may treat a spouse's child as your own, but if you never adopted him, he will have no interest in your estate under the intestacy rules. If you never married your partner, she will have no interest in your estate.

CASE STUDY
STEIG LARSSON

This reality can be best demonstrated in the case of Steig Larsson, the author of the widely successful Millennial trilogy (now continuing with a ghost-written fourth book in the series) of crime novels starting with *The Girl with the Dragon Tattoo*. He lived with Eva Gabrielsson from 1974 until his untimely death in 2004, before the trilogy was published. They were never married and Larsson never executed a will. As a result, his large estate passed to his father and brother, with nothing going to Gabrielsson.

A few other facts make this story even more troubling. First, between the ages of one and nine, Larsson lived with his grandparents rather than his parents. Second, it has been reported that he did write a will in 1977 giving his entire estate to the Socialist party, but never executed it. Third, at least one reason that Larsson and Gabrielsson never married is that due to his reporting on extremist groups in Sweden, Steig did not want their home address to be a public record, which was required to obtain a marriage certificate under Swedish law. These circumstances almost certainly mean that the intestacy rules honored none of Larsson's likely true wishes.

MISCELLANEOUS ISSUES

A. No-Contest Clause

If you are concerned that someone might challenge either the disposition of property in your estate plan or your choice of personal representative, you can include a no-contest (or "in terrorem") clause in your will. This will penalize anyone who challenges your choices by eliminating their share of the estate if they make a claim. But the reality for many clients is that they fear a challenge from someone they are disinheriting. Thus, if they disinherit them completely, the no-contest clause doesn't work since there's no penalty. If they're getting nothing, they will lose nothing by challenging the will. So, we advise such clients to at least make a small gift to these individuals in order that they have something to lose. Sometimes clients feel so strongly that they can't even make a small gift. But at least the no-contest clause expresses their strong feelings that their wishes be carried out as stated.

B. Out-of-State Will

Don't worry if you move. Under the U.S. Constitution, a will executed in one state must be given "full faith and credit" in all other states. That said, have your estate plans reviewed if you move to another state because we never know what we don't know. There might be differences in the law or in practice in the new state, which would call for a modification of your documents.

C. Out-of-State Property

Your will covers out-of-state as well as in-state property. However, for it to be effective, your heirs will have to establish a second (or "ancillary") probate in the second state. Even if you have no probate property in your own state, in most instances, your heirs first will have to start the probate process in your state of residence so that the second probate can be ancillary to the first. While I am a strong proponent of revocable trusts in all cases, their added benefit of avoiding probate in a second state makes them virtually indispensable if you live in one state and own real estate in another state.

D. Omitted Beneficiaries

You may leave out certain beneficiaries on purpose, as we discussed above under no contest or in terrorem clauses. But testators have been known to leave beneficiaries out by mistake as well. This can happen when the person creates a will mentioning his children by name, subsequently has another child, but doesn't update his will. To correct against this, states have so-called "pretermitted heir" statutes to include spouses and children of testators even if they are not mentioned in wills. However, you are not forced to include your children in your will. You can avoid the effect of your state's pretermitted heir statute by clarifying in the will that the omission is intentional, not made by mistake.

E. Testamentary Trusts

"Testamentary trust" is a fancy (or archaic?) word for a trust in a will. Most trusts are created through separate documents, which we will discuss more fully in the next section. In most states, practitioners urge clients to create separate trusts in order to avoid the involvement of the probate court. But the practice in a few states is to include trusts in wills. Trusts in wills can also have certain benefits, especially in the area of Medicaid planning. In this arena, for reasons that no one has ever explained, Congress *created* protections for testamentary trusts that one spouse leaves for another, while explicitly *denying* these protections to separate trusts one spouse might create for the other. Others might create trusts in their wills because they welcome the oversight provided by the probate court. Wills also often contain language providing for the creation of a testamentary trust in the event that any of the beneficiaries are minors, or are incapacitated for any reason. In such cases, the likelihood might be that no trust comes into existence, so there's no reason to create a separate trust document, but the testamentary trust can come into play if the need arises.

F. Codicils

A codicil is an amendment to a will. They are rare because they require the same formalities as a will—two witnesses and a notary in most states—and it can be confusing to have to compare the original will to one or more codicils to determine the ultimate distribution of assets or appointment of fiduciaries. Further, if you have changed your mind about how you wish to distribute your estate, you might not want your heirs to be able to see how your feelings about them may have changed over time. As a result, when updating a will most people simply choose to execute a new will and revoke (and shred) the prior one

G. **Copies of Wills**

Unlike many other legal documents, which are often executed in duplicate or triplicate, there can only exist one original will. In general, copies of wills have no legal significance. However, if the original will cannot be located for any reason, states have laws for presenting and authenticating copies. In general, in the absence of the original the presumption will be that the owner destroyed it, which is treated as a revocation. But this presumption may be rebutted by testimony as to other reasons the will might be missing, for instance that the drafting attorney has retired and cannot be located. Each case depends on its facts.

H. **Handwritten or "Holographic" Wills**

Wills, of course, are formal documents with requirements about their execution and the originals often stapled to official-looking blue backing paper. But is a will you scribble on notebook paper enforceable? These are known as "holographic" wills and, yes, they are valid if executed under the requirements of state statute. In most states, there must be two witnesses who watch the individual sign her will, and also obtain acknowledgment from her that the document she is signing is her will. A notary is usually not required for the will to be valid, but it makes the process easier. The notarization makes the will "self-proving," meaning that the witnesses do not have to appear in court to attest to the will's authenticity. In about half the states, no witnesses are required for a holographic will, but proving its validity in court is more difficult without witnesses.

CASE STUDY
HOLOGRAPHIC WILLS

Early in my practice, I was appointed conservator of a woman who was hospitalized and believed to be homeless. We shortly discovered that she in fact had an apartment and substantial savings in the bank—earning no interest, which I quickly remedied, more than covering my fee. (This was when banks actually paid to borrow your money.) While going through her possessions I came across a small day diary, and leafing through it we found the following handwritten on one page:

L, W & T,

I give all of my estate to the Boston Athenaeum.

[signed with the woman's initials]

Founded in 1807, the Boston Athenaeum is one of the oldest private libraries in the country, housed in a beautiful old building in Boston's Beacon Hill

---

neighborhood. We learned that the woman had been a long-time subscriber to the library.

Massachusetts is not one of the states that allows holographic wills without witnesses and conservators do not have the power to create wills on behalf of the incapacitated person. However, the law does permit conservators to petition the probate court for authority to create an estate plan that puts the incapacitated person's wishes into effect. So, I asked the court for permission to create a trust on the woman's behalf and for her benefit, that would give whatever was left at her death to the Boston Athenaeum, which the court approved.

As an interesting aside, as part of this process, I hired a genealogical firm to try to find any relatives of the woman, who had never been married and had no children. Both of her parents, however, had many siblings. The genealogists reported to us that they couldn't find any children of those siblings. Then, after the woman passed away, three of her cousins surfaced to challenge the trust we had created. After some digging, we learned that they had been solicited to bring the suit by the genealogical firm. Needless to say, we paid them no more than a small nuisance fee to go away—and never used that genealogical firm again.

FREQUENTLY ASKED QUESTIONS

What is probate?

Probate is the process of administering and settling an estate after a person dies. The exact probate process differs from state to state, but in general, it includes the following steps:

1. *Filing the will and petition at the probate court in order to be appointed executor or personal representative.* In the absence of a will, heirs must petition the court to be appointed "administrator" of the estate.

2. *Marshaling, or collecting, the assets.* This means that the executor has to find out everything the deceased owned. He must file a list (an "inventory") with the probate court. It's generally best to consolidate all the estate funds to the fullest extent possible. Bills and bequests should be paid from a single checking account, either one established by the executor or one set up by the attorney for the estate, so that they can keep track of all expenditures.

3. *Paying bills and taxes.* If a state or federal estate tax return is needed it must be filed within nine months of the date of death. If this deadline is missed and the estate is taxable, severe penalties and interest may apply. If the executor does not have all the information available in time, she can file for an extension and pay her best estimate of the tax due.

4. *Filing tax returns.* The executor must also file a final income tax return for the decedent. If the estate earns income during the administration process, she will have to obtain a tax identification number in order to keep track of such earnings and file a return on behalf of the estate. The income will ultimately pass through to the beneficiaries, but the estate might be able to deduct certain estate expenses.

5. *Distributing property to the heirs and legatees.* Generally, executors do not pay out all of the estate assets until the period runs out for creditors to make claims, which can be as long as a year after the date of death. But once the executor understands the estate and the likely claims, he or she can distribute most of the assets, retaining a reserve for unanticipated claims and the costs of closing out the estate.

6. *Filing a final account.* The executor must file an account with the probate court listing any income to the estate since the date of death and all expenses and estate distributions. Once the court approves this final account, the executor can distribute whatever is left in the closing reserve, and finish his or her work.

What does probate cost?

The cost of probate varies depending on the size and complexity of the estate. Strictly speaking, "probate" is the court process of transferring property after someone dies. But in this context it involves everything that needs to be done financially and legally to close out the deceased's legal and financial life and pass on property to his heirs, some of which might involve the courts but much of which does not. In general, the more property and assets the deceased had, the more complicated and expensive the probate process will be, yet the cost will be a smaller percentage of the total estate since some costs apply no matter the size of the estate.

Another factor has to do with the types of assets in the estate. Bank accounts are easy to handle, while tangibles— such as furniture, artwork and silverware—are a bit more difficult, as is real estate. Most difficult, often, are "alternative" investments. We've recently had difficulty getting control over and finding a market for interests in a real estate investment trust. And often, there's no market for timeshares, yet the estate and heirs have to keep paying the annual fees.

The use of trusts can greatly reduce costs by avoiding the need to go to court. And often the act of funding of the trust during life helps consolidate accounts and reduces the amount of work necessary to "marshal" the estate.

These are some of the fees that need to be paid in order to probate an estate:

- Court fees
- Personal representative fees

- Attorney's fees
- Accounting fees
- Appraisal fees
- Bond fees

The end result is that probate costs vary greatly and can range anywhere from 1 to 10 percent of the gross estate.

Do all family members of the deceased have the right to be present at a will reading? And are they allowed to receive a copy of the supposedly new will that leaves everything to one person in the family instead of split between everyone who was named in the first will?

We've all seen movies where all the family members show up at an attorney's office for the will to be revealed and read out loud. That actually rarely happens. Instead, family members are generally simply provided with copies of the will and related documents, such as trusts. But do they have the right to such documents. Yes, in the case of the will, because it must be filed with the appropriate probate court. The personal representative does not have to provide a copy (unless required by the laws of the specific state), but it is a public record that anyone can look at. But the answer is usually no in the case of trusts. They are private and only need to be provided to beneficiaries, not to anyone who is not a beneficiary.

Is My Mother Responsible for My Deceased Brother's Debts?

My brother recently died in Texas and at the time of death he was on state aid and had no money. My mother who lives in Arizona has recently received a few bills. Is she obligated to pay his debts? There is no estate. What does she do with these bills?

Your mother is not responsible for your brother's debts out of her own funds as long as she did not guarantee any of your brother's debts. If your mother had received money from your brother's estate, she would be responsible for using those funds to pay your brother's obligations. This can become a gray area if she received non-probate funds, such as life insurance proceeds or if she was the beneficiary on an IRA. But in this case, she has no obligation and should simply let the creditors know the situation. There have been some heartbreaking stories in the news recently about parents of young adults who died unexpectedly after incurring large college loans that their parents had cosigned. In addition to mourning their losses, the parents in some states are still on the hook for paying off the college loans.

What is the best way to give money to my grandchildren?

Gifting assets to your grandchildren can do more than help your descendants get a good start in life; it can also reduce the size of your estate and the tax that will be due upon your death (assuming you have an estate that's taxable in your state or federally).

Perhaps the simplest approach to gifting is to give the grandchild an outright gift. You may give each grandchild up to $15,000 a year (in 2019) without having to report the gifts. The problem with an outright gift is that you have no way of making sure the money is spent the way you would want it spent.

The following are some other ways you can give to grandchildren:

- You can pay for educational and medical costs for your grandchildren. There's no limit on these gifts, meaning that you can pay these expenses in addition to making annual $15,000 (in 2019) gifts. But you have to be sure to pay the school or medical provider directly.
- You can make gifts to a custodial account that parents can establish for a minor child.
- You can transfer money into a trust established to benefit a grandchild or all of your grandchildren.
- You can reduce your taxable estate while earmarking funds for the higher education of a grandchild through the use of a 529 account.
- You can use other gift vehicles like IRAs and savings bonds.
- You can make a larger gift for a specific purpose, such

as to help pay for a wedding or the down payment on a house. Technically, if you give more than $15,000 in a calendar year, or $30,000 if both you and your spouse are making the gift, you are supposed to file a gift tax return reporting the gift. However, if your estate is not near the taxable threshold of $11.4 million (in 2019) there will be no penalty for not reporting the gift.

Can I Force My Brother to Close Out My Mother's Estate?

My mother died 13 years ago. My brother has been in charge of her estate. He refuses to put her home up for sale, instead using the estate's money to pay the upkeep on an empty house for 13 years. What can we do to get this estate settled? Can my brothers and sister do anything?

The short answer is that there are remedies, but you, your brothers, and your sister need to hire a probate attorney to represent you. That attorney will be able to take a number of steps to force action, depending on all of the facts and the laws and practices in your state. These steps might include actions to force your brother to provide an accounting, to remove him as executor, to charge him for losses to the estate or a partition action to force a sale of the property. Only a local attorney can properly advise you on the best strategy given all of the facts and the laws in your state.

Can I Refuse to Serve as Executor?

I no longer want to be named as executor for my mother-in-law upon her passing. How can I resign?

Just because you are named as executor in a will does not mean you are required to serve in that role. If your mother-in-law is still alive, you can inform her you no longer want the position, and she will need to amend her will to name a different executor. If she has already passed away or is no longer competent to execute a new will, you can inform the successor executor, if there is one, or the court that you do not want to serve in this capacity. If you are already serving as executor, you will need to formally resign in writing at the probate court and provide a written accounting of what you have done. If the will does not name a successor executor, the probate court will choose an executor after you resign. State law dictates who has priority to serve. The surviving spouse usually has first priority, followed by children. If no spouse or children are in line, then other family members may be chosen. If more than one person has priority and the heirs can't agree on who should serve, then the court will choose.

Is an Executor Required to Provide Beneficiaries with Financial Records?

What does the executor do with all the financial records of the deceased person after all his work is done? How long does he keep the records? Are the beneficiaries entitled to the financial records of the estate or is the executor in charge of them?

To answer your last question first, only the executor is entitled to the deceased's financial records. However, the executor has a duty to provide the beneficiaries with an inventory showing what is in the estate and an account showing how it has been managed, as well as any information they need to manage what they receive from the estate. In addition, if a dispute arises—for instance, if the beneficiaries challenge the executor's account—they would have the right to discovery, meaning that they could ask questions and get copies of all financial accounts. In general, even if the executor technically controls financial records, it is better to be transparent. Lack of transparency breeds distrust.

In terms of how long to keep records, the rule of thumb for tax records is seven years. However, this does not mean you have to keep the records in paper form. You can scan the documents. The executor can dispose of other financial records as soon as the final account is approved by the probate court. Nevertheless, it can't hurt to continue to maintain digital records in case they are needed in the future.

My sister was named executor of our parents' will. I am disabled and was living in a nursing home but met a loving woman and am now engaged and living with her—my sister has not executed the will over three years after my folks passed. Does a will have to be executed within a certain length of time or can she drag it out forever? I have a feeling she is just waiting for me to have to return to a nursing home so no monies have to be distributed to me.

While each state has its own deadline, three years is far too long in every state. You can go to court to force your sister to get moving or to have her removed as personal representative and someone else appointed who will move the process along.

THE JORGENSONS

John and Joyce execute relatively simple wills naming one another as personal representative and all three children as alternates in case the surviving parent cannot serve for any reason.

They also give all of their assets to one another, and then equally to their children when the second of them passes away. The will has separate provisions for distributing their tangible assets (things they can touch, such as clothing, furniture, artwork and silverware) and everything else, the "residue" (real estate, bank accounts and investments).

The paragraph on tangible assets says that they will be distributed as equally as possible and refers to a list either parent may leave saying who should receive which items. It also says that if one or more of their children predeceases them, his or her share of the tangible assets will go to the surviving child or children. In contrast, the paragraph regarding the residue says that the share of any child who dies before the parents will go to the child's children, if any. A further section of the will says that if anyone who might receive an inheritance is under age 25 the personal representative may continue to hold the property in trust for the grandchild's benefit until he or she reaches age 25.

CHAPTER 5

REVOCABLE TRUST

Over decades of practice, I have become a strong proponent of revocable trusts as a means to avoid probate and, more importantly, to provide for asset management in the event of incapacity. Revocable trusts are incredibly flexible and can achieve many goals, including tax, long-term care and asset-protection planning. Revocable trusts are sometimes called "living" trusts or even "loving" trusts, but these are simply terms developed by some practitioners to market a longstanding estate planning instrument.

Essentially, a revocable trust is a new financial entity that you create. As the creator, you are called the "grantor" or the "donor." You are a beneficiary of the trust and can also serve as the sole trustee or as one of a number of co-trustees. The trustees manage the assets in the trust, which can include real estate, bank accounts, investments and tangible property (such as fine art) under the terms set forth in the trust document.

In principle, a trust document can be as short and simple as this:

> I, Hillary, hereby create this trust as grantor and trustee. If I ever become incapacitated or upon my death, my husband, Bill, will step in as trustee. During my life, the trustee may distribute principal and income to me or on my behalf as the trustee, in its sole judgment, determines appropriate. After my death, all of the remaining income and principal shall be distributed to my good friend, Barack. I may amend or revoke this trust at any time by delivering a writing signed by me to any trustee.

———————————————

Hillary

Of course, trusts in fact are much longer as they cover many possible occurrences and legal matters. But before we get into those issues, let's discuss what this simple example accomplishes. First, whatever Hillary places into trust during her life will pass to Barack at her death without going through probate, avoiding the cost, delay and publicity of probate. Second, in the event of incapacity, Bill can step in and manage the trust property without any fuss. While he might also do so through a durable power of attorney, we have found that banks and other financial institutions are much more comfortable with trusts. They have been known to reject durable powers of attorney that are more than a few years old or to require that the drafting attorney certify that the power of attorney has not been revoked. (This puts the attorney in an awkward position since he cannot really know what the client did in his absence, but he wants to help out the client's family, so will probably sign the affidavit.)

Especially with older clients who are more likely to become incapacitated or to be the victims of scams aimed at seniors, we recommend that they appoint co-trustees in addition to successor trustees. If Hillary were to follow this advice, she would name Bill as her co-trustee and Chelsea as successor trustee. Bill's appointment as co-trustee would make his ability to step in in the event of Hillary's incapacity or death entirely seamless.

The secret to making revocable trusts work is to fund them. This means retitling assets, whether real estate, bank accounts or investment accounts, in the name of the trust. All too often, attorneys draw up wonderful estate planning documents, advise clients to fund their trusts, and then nothing happens. Trusts have no relation to assets that are not retitled. However, if you execute a "pour-over" will along with your trust saying that at your death all of your assets will be distributed to your trust, your wishes as to the ultimate distribution of your estate will be carried out. You just won't avoid probate and will not have as strong of protection in case of incapacity.

To place bank and investment accounts into your trust, you need to retitle them as follows:

Hillary and Bill as Trustees of The Hillary Revocable Trust created by agreement dated June 26, 2015.

Depending on the institution, you might be able to change the name on an existing account, or else you will need to open a new account in the name of the trust and then transfer the funds. The financial institution will probably require a copy of the trust, or at least of the first page and the signature page, as well as signatures of all the trustees. As long as you are serving as your own trustee or co-trustee, you can use your Social Security number for the trust. If you are not a trustee, the trust will have to obtain a separate tax identification number and file a separate 1041 tax return each year. You will still be taxed on all of the income and the trust will pay no separate tax.

You will need to execute a deed and a trustee's certificate to transfer real estate into the trust. If you have a mortgage on your property, the mortgage document might have a clause requiring notice of any change in title and perhaps even a "due on sale" clause that applies. However, we have never given notice in our practice and have never seen an issue arise as long as the clients continue to make their monthly mortgage or line of credit payments. However, if you intend to refinance your property or take out a line of credit, wait until you do so before deeding the real estate into your trust. In most instances, banks and other lenders require that you remove the property from the trust and put it back in your name before signing any new mortgage papers.

Depending on your state, you might also need to redo a homestead declaration after transferring property into a revocable trust.

Getting back to the issue as to why revocable trusts are many pages long rather than a single paragraph, here are some of the issues revocable trust documents cover, as well as decisions you might need to make.

- When does the successor trustee take over? When **all** of the original co-trustees stop serving—whether due to incapacity, death or resignation—or when **one** of them stops serving?

- How do you define the incapacity of a trustee?
- What can the trust invest in?
- May it pay the debts of your estate?
- If there's an absence of trustees for any reason and you are not available, who appoints the new trustee? Do you want to require that new trustees have any particular qualifications?
- Do you want to give anyone else the right to remove trustees?
- What accounts or statements, if any, must the trustee provide to beneficiaries?
- Do you want distributions to be made to beneficiaries under age 18, or just made on their behalf? Would you prefer the trustee to continue managing the funds until your children or other beneficiaries reach, say 25 or 30? You can also provide for partial distributions at various ages.
- What powers should the trustees have?

These and more issues need to be decided for all trusts. More complex trusts designed for tax and asset protection purposes that are discussed later in the book present even more choices and get even longer and more complex. Unfortunately, whenever an attorney faces an issue not covered in a trust document, she may add an applicable provision to her future trusts, and as these provisions accumulate, the documents get longer and longer, even when only one trust in 1,000 might face a particular problem again.

THE JORGENSONS

John and Joyce decide to change their wills to provide that the residue of their estates (everything but their tangible personal property, or the things they can touch) goes to their revocable trust—a so-called "pour over" will. They are the trustees of their trust as long as they are alive and competent. When neither can continue this role, they appoint their three children to step in as co-trustees. The children will be able to manage the property and investments for their parents if necessary. When both John and Joyce have passed away, the trust assets will be able to be distributed equally to the three children without the expense and delay of a probate process. The assets will also be readily available to pay for any expenses that come up, such as maintaining a house until it is sold, paying rent for an apartment until it is cleaned out, paying for any final bills that come through following the death of the parent, and paying funeral expenses. The trust says that if anyone who might receive a distribution is under age 25, the trustee may continue to hold the property in trust for the grandchild's benefit until he or she reaches age 25.

CHAPTER 6

"BONUS" ESSENTIALS

While the five estate planning documents described above are necessary for everyone (with some quibbles about the revocable trust) and sufficient for most, there are at least two other issues almost everyone needs to consider: beneficiary designations and digital assets.

1. BENEFICIARY DESIGNATIONS

As we discussed above, many types of property and investments pass outside of probate. In addition to jointly owned property and assets in trust, such non-probate property includes life insurance, retirement plans, and bank or investment accounts that permit the owner to designate who will receive them at his death. Often when you open up an account, the bank or investment house representative encourages you to name beneficiaries to simplify matters at your death. This action does not take into consideration the rest of your estate plan or changes in your situation that might occur in the future. Perhaps you actually do want an old life insurance policy to be payable to your ex-spouse. (Just kidding.)

The first step is to get a copy of all of your beneficiary designation forms and to review them to make sure that they are consistent with the rest of your estate plan or, if they are different, that the difference is intentional. If you make these designations online, print a copy of the page so that you also have a paper record. Once you have collected all of these forms, put them in a folder with your other estate planning documents so that you and your heirs can quickly and easily find them in the future.

In determining how to make your beneficiary designations, we need to consider each type of account separately.

a. Bank and investment accounts

If you are using a revocable trust, you can make it the owner of all of your bank and investment accounts. This way you avoid the need to name anyone as beneficiary and you still avoid probate. Then, all of the protections provided in the trust—for instance, that children do not receive their inheritance until a certain age, or provisions for who receives the funds if a beneficiary predeceases you—will apply to the accounts. If you're not using a revocable trust, simply name those who will receive your estate under the terms of your will. Or name no one. Then the terms of your will will govern and, while you won't avoid probate, you'll make sure that the people you want will receive the assets, that your personal representative will be in charge, and that any changes you make in the future—such as disinheriting your wayward nephew—will apply to the accounts.

b. Life insurance

Unlike bank and investment accounts, the ownership of many life insurance policies—especially those that come as an employment benefit—cannot be transferred to your revocable trust. And there's really no benefit to doing so in any case. (There might be some tax and long-term care planning reasons to transfer property to irrevocable trusts, which will be discussed below in the appropriate sections.) Instead, the beneficiary designation is the most important decision. If you have a revocable trust, you may name it as the beneficiary for the reasons mentioned above. Or you can name particular individuals. The beneficiary designation form will permit you to name alternates in the event that the first person or people you name predecease you.

c. Retirement plans

We have a whole chapter about planning for retirement plans—IRAs, 401(k)s, 403(b)s and Roth IRAs—below, but need to say a few words here related to these accounts.

First, don't transfer your retirement plans to your revocable trust! The only way to do so is to liquidate the plan first, which would be a taxable event. In most instances, financial planners will advise you to keep funds in your retirement plans for as long as possible—to "stretch" them—in order to delay paying taxes. Doing so permits you to make money on the taxes you defer by investing the funds and presumably when you retire and need the funds you will be in a lower tax bracket than you are in when you are working. Thus, if you wait until then to withdraw funds, you'll likely pay less tax.

Second, don't name your revocable trust as a beneficiary of your retirement funds without consulting your lawyer. Unless the trust contains necessary language to hold retirement funds, in most instances they will have to be liquidated and the taxes paid on them within five years of your death, which is inconsistent with the strategy of postponing tax payments for as long as possible. On the other hand, if you have a relatively small amount of funds in retirement accounts, this might not be a big problem. In addition, all too often estate planners go to heroic efforts to permit retirement plans to be stretched, and the beneficiaries liquidate them and pay taxes on them within five years anyways. Years ago, this happened in a case I will not soon forget.

George came to see me after his father died. To his surprise, his father had $900,000 in his retirement plan and no designated beneficiaries. This meant that the funds would have to be withdrawn and the taxes paid over five years. At that time, the threshold for federal and state estate taxes was $600,000, meaning that much of the money was subject to both income and estate taxes. Of the money above the threshold of $600,000, more than half would go to the IRS and the state revenue department. Also, at the time—this was decades ago—neither I nor the investment house involved were as familiar with inherited IRAs (more on this term below) as we all are now. So, we had some learning to do. We moved heaven and earth to set up individual accounts for George and his four siblings to permit them to stretch their shares of their father's IRA for even five years. We accomplished our goal of setting up the inherited IRAs so that the withdrawals could be spread out over the lifetimes of the beneficiaries. Yet, within a year virtually all of the siblings had liquidated their IRAs in any case and we could have saved a lot of trouble (and legal fees for the family) by liquidating them through the estate and paying the income taxes up front.

And so lastly, despite George's story, it's much more important with retirement plans than with life insurance or other investments that you designate beneficiaries. While some heirs will fail to take advantage of the ability to defer taxes, others may stretch them through their lives for their own benefit and even that of their heirs. Here, we need to discuss an important distinction. If you designate your spouse as the beneficiary, after your death she can convert the funds into her own plan and it will be treated for purposes of required minimum distributions just like the retirement plans into which she contributed her own funds. No other beneficiary may do so. Non-spouse designated beneficiaries must keep inherited retirement plans separate and begin taking distributions based on their age by the end of the calendar year after the deceased owner passed away. They can still stretch the withdrawals out during their lifetimes, but cannot wait until they reach age 70 ½ to take withdrawals.

2. DIGITAL ASSETS

The news is packed with stories about how our digital lives are subject to hacking, whether by Russian trolls or others seeking access to our financial accounts and online lives. Related to this issue of cybersecurity is the question of how you plan for these digital assets: who can stand in for you, and who should have both control and ownership of the accounts when you die. While this planning is extremely important, it's also confusing because the term "digital assets" encompasses almost as wide a variety of items as other types of assets, some of which overlap:

- Online access to bank, investment and credit card accounts
- Social media sites such as Facebook, Instagram and LinkedIn
- Dating sites
- iCloud, Dropbox and other online data storage
- Airline, hotel and other miles sites hosting travel assets or benefits
- Yelp, TripAdvisor and similar sites that rate various services
- Amazon and other shopping sites
- eBay and other sites where you might be selling items and earning money

Three factors complicate planning for access to these sites. First, you might want to give access to different people depending on the circumstances and the type of account. For instance, you might want to give access to some accounts in the event of disability, others upon death, and still others (perhaps your online dating profiles, for instance) never.

Second, many online companies have their own rules about giving access to others, often severely limiting access even after you have passed away. On first impression, this seems contrary to law. After all, when you name an agent under your durable power of attorney or a personal representative in your will, they are supposed to stand in your shoes and have the same legal rights you do to act on your behalf. Yet Internet companies can restrict access because you checked off a box agreeing to those terms and conditions (that you probably didn't read) when you activated your access to the site. Those contractual rights can trump whatever legal rights your agent normally might have. These will have more of an effect on purely online businesses, such as Facebook and Google, than on other types of accounts that you merely use the Internet to access, such as those at banks and investments houses. Even if your agent is barred from online access to your bank accounts, she still can take her credentials to the institution and manage your accounts in person.

Third, while the terms and conditions you signed onto might govern the *legal* right to access, the reality is that anyone with your username and password has *actual* access. They might be cybercriminals intent on stealing from you, but they are more likely to be family members or other trusted individuals to whom you give your login information. This quickly becomes a gray area legally. You can't walk into your elderly mother's bank and withdraw money, but you can use her online login information to monitor her financial activity or to pay her bills. In doing so, you are acting as her authorized agent even if not doing so formally under her durable power of attorney. And you're not committing any crime, of course, since you're not stealing her money. But you are probably violating her agreement with the bank. Should you care? Probably not. But it is an interesting world we live in where huge formalities are required in one arena (physical access to your mother's account) and none are required in the other (online access).

While this can be complicated, there are a few steps you can take to make sure that your agents have access to your accounts when necessary.

1. Look at each of your online accounts to determine their rules. Some permit you to name a specific agent to act for you or to receive notice if you don't respond to their efforts to reach out to you. Take advantage these opportunities.

2. Keep a list of your usernames and passwords. Of course, writing them down means that they can be copied or stolen, but keep them in a safe place and let your agent know where to find them. There are many password management services that only require you (or your agent) to remember one master password in order to access passwords for all of your accounts. These include PasswordBox, LastPass, Dashlane, KeePass, and 1Password, among others. They are more secure than a paper list and are also easier to keep up-to-date with new accounts and

new passwords, but you will need to ensure your agent has access to the service if and when needed.

3. Some advisors suggest putting special provisions about digital assets in your durable power of attorney and will. This can't hurt, but shouldn't be necessary since your agent and personal representative should have access anyway to the extent permitted under the rules of each online provider.

4. In terms of the security of your online accounts, use strong passwords that include upper and lower case letters, numbers and symbols. Don't use the types of words or numbers that hackers can find, such as birthdates, family names or family names spelled backwards. It can be hard to remember these strong passwords, especially if internet providers force you to change them from time to time. But try to develop and remember three which you can use alternatively. This way if one doesn't work, you can try the others without exceeding the number of attempts to log in that most sites permit. And you can provide these three passwords to your agent or agents. If they save them in a way that is disconnected from you and your accounts, their knowledge of the passwords should not be a significant security risk.

PART 2

SPECIAL SITUATIONS IN ESTATE PLANNING

Our book so far has focused on the basic estate planning measures everyone should take to make certain that their affairs are handled smoothly in the event of their incapacity or death. While none of this is as simple as it should be, now it gets complicated. The following chapters focus on specialized issues that readers might consider due to their circumstances or goals, including estate and gift taxes, long-term care planning, planning for a child with special needs or for children from different marriages, and protecting assets from creditors. With the assistance of this book, and if you're not facing these specialized issues, you might well be able to create a plan using an online do-it-yourself program. However, if you are grappling with the issues that follow, I advise that you work with an estate planning attorney. But having read the relevant chapters, you will be better prepared to understand the discussion with your attorney, and better able to navigate the available planning options and guide the process to reach your goals.

CHAPTER 7

ESTATE AND GIFT TAXES

Since the Ryan-Trump tax bill raised the federal estate and gift tax exemption to $11.4 million (in 2019), you probably don't have to worry too much about federal estate taxes and gift taxes. With proper planning, spouses together can give away almost $23 million (in 2019) estate and gift tax free. Even before this latest change, the annual number of taxable estates had fallen under 5,000 a year by 2013 when the threshold was from more than 50,000 in 2000 when the exemption was $675,000. There were fewer than 2,000 taxable estates nationwide in 2018. Since this book is addressed to the other 99.9 percent, we won't spend a lot of time on steps those with larger estates can take to avoid or minimize their federal estate tax. If your estate is at risk of crossing the $11.8 million threshold because either (a) you're already there, (b) you might earn and save enough to put you over that level, or (c) you might inherit enough to put your net worth over that level, get thee to an estate planning attorney now and don't rely on the following advice.

A SHORT HISTORY OF THE FEDERAL ESTATE TAX

Up until the last century, the federal estate tax was imposed only during wartime to raise funds for the military and was disbanded when peace came. The first tax on inheritances was enacted in 1797 as part of the Stamp Act to raise funds for an undeclared war with France. It imposed duties on various papers and licenses, including licenses to practice law and receipts for inheritances. It was repealed in 1802 after the United States and France signed a peace treaty.

The next inheritance tax was enacted in 1862 to help finance the Civil War. It taxed inheritances exceeding $1,000 at rates ranging from 0.75 percent for property passing to issue to 5% for property passing to others. This was increased to a range of 1 to 6% in 1864 and then repealed in 1870. (The distinction between an estate tax and an inheritance tax is whether the tax is owed by the decedent's estate or by the people receiving an inheritance. Inheritance taxes generally impose different tax rates depending on the recipient's relationship to the person who died. A few states have inheritance taxes, but the current federal tax—and that of most states—are imposed on estates.)

The next inheritance tax was enacted in 1898 to finance the Spanish American War. It taxed estates worth more than $10,000 at rates ranging from .74% to 15% and was repealed in 1902. This tax came into existence during the Progressive Era and was in part motivated by a wish to prevent dynastic accumulations of wealth from passing from generation to generation. This goal has continued to influence debate on the estate tax.

An early form of our current estate tax was enacted a century ago in 1916 as the United States prepared to enter World War I. It taxed estates over $50,000 (about $1 million in today's dollars) at rates between 2% and 10%, the highest rate kicking in at $5 million (about $100 million in today's dollars). Congress quickly increased the rates in an effort to raise more funds, with the top rate reaching 25%. Since then, rates and exemption amounts have gone up and down depending on the need for revenue and the politics of using the tax as a wealth-leveling tool. The estate tax has never been a huge part of federal revenue, reaching a peak of 3.49% in 1922. Interestingly, given its history as a method of raising money during wartime, the most recent pullback of the estate tax (up until the Ryan-Trump doubling of the exemption) during George W. Bush's presidency took place during the Afghanistan and Iraq wars.

Inflation-adjusted, the current estate tax threshold is the highest it has ever been since the beginning of the current system in 1916. The 1916 threshold of $50,000 would be about $1 million in today's dollars, less than a tenth of the current threshold of $11.4 million. The amount went up and down over the years, reaching a high of about $1.4 million in 1930 and a low of about $366,000 in inflation-adjusted dollars in 1970. The $600,000 figure set in 1987 was a bit higher than $1 million in today's dollars and the figure stayed in that range until the increases that began in 2002 as a compromise of President Bush's efforts to repeal the tax completely.

Aside from these federal estate taxes that likely don't concern you (at their current levels), there are a few issues we do need to discuss: gifting and gift taxes, portability, income and capital gains taxation, and state estate tax planning (as separate from federal estate taxes, and at limits you're much more likely to exceed).

It's also important to understand the distinction between your probate and taxable estate. As we've discussed above, the probate court process for administering and distributing estates only applies to property and accounts *in your name alone*. Anything in joint names, in a trust you created, or with a named beneficiary passes outside of probate. However, your *taxable* estate includes all of these assets in addition to your probate property.

1. Gifting

Like many of our clients, you might be under the misconception that you are limited in making gifts to $15,000 per recipient per year. This is because $15,000 is the current gift tax exclusion figure—the amount that you may give away without having to file a gift tax return. (Many people also believe that the limit is $10,000 because that was the level of the exclusion for many years until it was indexed to the inflation rate.) In fact, this limit is irrelevant to almost everyone because of the combined estate and gift tax threshold (or "unified credit equivalent," if you want the technical term) of $11.4 million (in 2019).

Here's how it works: If you give away more than $15,000 to an individual in a year, you are supposed to report the excess. Every dollar uses up part of the $11.4 million you may give away tax free. So, for instance, if you give someone $115,000, you will have used up $100,000 of your $11.4 million credit, so you can give away *only* $11.3 million tax free at death. So, as you can see, the $15,000 exclusion is not really a limit for most people. It was much more significant when the federal estate tax thresholds, quite recently, were as low as $600,000 (1997) and $1 million (2003).

Even though the estate and gift tax system affects very few people, it is still on the books and everyone is required to report gifts in excess of $15,000 per individual per year. What happens if you don't report your gift of $15,000? Nothing. The penalty for not filing a gift tax return is a percentage of the gift tax owed. Since you won't owe any gift tax until you give away $11.4 million, it's quite unlikely that you'll ever pay a penalty for not filing a gift tax return. (That said, $15,000 may be a pretty good limit on how much anyone should give anyone else during a calendar year absent unusual need, assuming you don't want your children and grandchildren depending on your largess for their basic living expenses.)

A few more fun gift tax facts:

- There's no gift tax reporting requirement for gifts made to people you are obligated to support. So, there's no limit on what you give or spend for your children under age 18. In addition, gifts to your spouse during life or at death are exempt from both gift and estate taxes (unless they are not a U.S. citizen—a whole other issue discussed below).

- There's no limit or reporting requirement for payments for education or health care. You just need to make the payments directly to the education facility or health care provider. In addition, you can, in effect, prepay gifts into a 529 plan, putting in up to $75,000 at once for five years of gifts ($150,000 for a couple).

- While we'll discuss this more extensively in the next chapter, the gift tax exclusion has nothing to do with Medicaid planning. A gift of even as little as $15,000 must be reported on a Medicaid application if made within the prior five years and might cause a period of ineligibility for benefits.

- Gift taxes are payable by the giver. The recipient of a gift doesn't have to report it to the IRS and the gift is not taxable income.

- Both spouses can give up to $15,000 a year and a spouse can consent to the use of his or her exclusion. This means that either spouse may give up to $30,000 a year to a particular individual if the other spouse agrees.

While we've never had a client who has had to pay a gift tax, we did have one who received a taxable gift. Our client was a childhood friend of a man who became a very successful Hollywood star. He was also very generous and bought our client a condominium. Since the giver had already surpassed the gift tax threshold (which was much lower then), he also had to pay a substantial gift tax of 45 percent of the gift he made to our client. Unfortunately, in facilitating the arrangement we didn't get to talk with the star himself, just his tax accountants.

THE JORGENSONS

John and Joyce have been giving $10,000 a year to each of their children to help them out in the early working years when they're not earning very much. They thought this was all they were permitted to give each year. Though their attorney explained that the new limit is $15,000 a year, from each spouse, and that given their level of assets there would be no gift tax even if they gave more, they decided to stick to the $10,000 a year. They want to help their children to some extent, but also want their children to be able to support themselves. Further, they are concerned with not undermining their own financial security by giving away too much.

2. Portability

In 2012, Congress instituted portability—under which the surviving spouse may add the unused portion of a deceased spouse's unified credit to their own unified credit. Let's use hypothetical married couple Jack and Betty Sprat as an example of how it works: If Jack dies with an estate worth $4 million and bequeaths all of it to Betty, then she can elect portability to "port over" his entire $11.4 million estate tax allowance to herself, making her eligible to give away $24.8 million tax free at death. If, say, Jack gifts his entire estate to various other beneficiaries, then he still has $7.4 million of his unified credit remaining ($11.4 million - $4 million). In this case, if Betty elects portability, then her estate will be able to give away $18.8 million tax free ($11.4 million + $7.4 million). To elect portability, Betty must file a federal tax return for Jack (even though he owes no federal estate tax) within nine months of his death and make the portability election on the return.

Some estate tax professionals advise all of their clients to elect portability just in case. We had a client whose situation shows why this might be advisable. His wife died. Her estate and his together were well below the threshold in effect that year. However, he owned a substantial number of shares in a startup company. At the time of his wife's death, the prospects for the company were quite poor and he thought the stock was worthless. Fortunately, lightning struck and all of a sudden the stock was worth millions. Electing portability "just in case" enabled him to shield significantly more of his estate from taxes.

Portability was enacted in part to protect married taxpayers who had not done estate tax planning but it actually goes much further. In traditional planning, spouses separate their estates more or less in half and create trusts to shelter each half of their assets so that they will not be counted in the surviving spouse's estate. Let's assume, for example that Jack and Betty Sprat have $16 million between them that they separated into two $8 million shares. If Jack dies first (statistically, husbands usually do), his $8 million goes into trust for Betty's benefit. Usually these trusts provide that Betty will receive all of the income that the $8 million earns and additional distributions as needed for her health, education, maintenance and support in her customary standard of living, though there are a number of choices in how the trust is structured. The $8 million in Jack's trust will not be counted in Betty's taxable estate when she dies, even if it is invested and continues to grow in value. Without this planning, if Betty died with $16 million, her estate would be subject to taxes on the excess over $11.4 million, and a high rate of 40 percent.

Now, if Betty were to elect portability at Jack's death, there'd be no tax at her death because $16 million is well below $23 million, even without proper tax planning. As you can see, portability actually provides more tax protection than traditional estate tax planning, which would protect only the $8 million Jack left in trust. If we add this to Betty's $11.2 million unified credit, they could together shelter $19.2 million, a huge amount— but less than the $22 million available under portability. In addition, with portability Betty can totally control all her assets without having to deal with the formalities of a separate trust.

That said, there are other advantages to the traditional plan that Jack and Betty might want to consider, including creditor and incapacity protection. In addition, if Jack and Betty were previously married and had children from their prior unions, they may well want to protect those children through the use of a trust rather than leaving everything in the survivor's hands. If you have a potentially taxable estate, these are all issues to discuss with your estate tax professional.

3. Income and capital gains taxation

In addition to estate taxes, it's also possible that your estate will have to pay income taxes. In most cases, estates are relatively small, disbursed relatively quickly and kept under the decedent's social security number until disbursed, meaning that the estate does not have to file a separate income tax return. But in some situations, property or investment accounts have to be held for long enough that they need to be titled in the name of the estate and the estate must obtain a separate tax identification number and file an income tax return. In most cases, any income realized by the estate ultimately passes through to the beneficiaries. The estate files a 1041 income tax return and issues k-1s to the beneficiaries to report their share of the income. The beneficiaries then report this income on their tax returns, as they would any 1099 income. It's best that anyone needing to file an estate income tax return hire an accountant to prepare it.

The effect of death on taxation of capital gains might be the only silver lining in the passing of a loved one. When real estate and investments are sold, the owner pays taxes on the gain of up to 20 percent, depending on her other income. She might also have to pay state taxes. The gain is calculated as the difference between the basis and the money received on the property's sale. For most property, the basis is the purchase price. For instance, if a share of stock was purchased for $100 and is sold for $150, the gain will be $50. At a tax rate of 20 percent, the tax on the sale will be $10. Often it can be difficult to establish the purchase price of stock that has been held for a long time, meaning that the entire amount received might be treated as gain and subject to taxes.

The amount of gain can be substantial in the case of a large portfolio of stock or real estate that has been owned a long time. A house that was purchased for $50,000 several decades ago and sold today for $550,000 after the broker's commission and other expenses of sale, would realize a $500,000 gain and a $100,000 tax. With houses, however, there are some special rules. First, the basis might be increased by the cost of any improvements made to the house. Of course, you'll have to be able to prove those costs if you are ever audited, so keep good records. Second, if the property is the taxpayer's home and she has lived in it for at least two out of the prior five years (with some leniency on these rules under certain circumstances), she doesn't have to pay taxes on the first $250,000 of gain. If she's married, together she and her spouse can exclude $500,000 of gain.

If you give someone property during your life, he will receive it with the same basis as you. This is known as a "carry over" basis. If instead, you provide that the property will pass to him at death, the basis will be adjusted to the fair market value on your date of death. This is known as a "step-up" in basis. Here's how it works: If you purchased a Renoir years ago for $1 million and today it has a market value of $4 million, and you give it to your son, he will have the same $1 million basis as you. When he sells it, assuming the bottom hasn't dropped out of the art market and he gets $4 million, he'll have to pay taxes on $3 million. At 20 percent, he'll owe Uncle Sam $600,000 (plus something to the state). On the other hand, if you and he were more patient and he received the Renoir at your death, assuming no change in the art market between now and then, the basis would be stepped up to $4 million. If your son then sold it, he'd realize no gain and no tax, saving $600,000 (plus whatever the state would have received).

Another benefit of the rules surrounding this step-up in basis is that it cleans up some bookkeeping nightmares.

Heirs don't need to research the value when their parents and grandparents purchased stock or other property. They just need to establish the more recent date-of-death values.

While in office, President Obama proposed eliminating these step-up rules because they benefit wealthier families more than everyone else (because being subject to significant capital gain is a side effect of having more to begin with). While I appreciated and supported his effort to even the playing field, I disagreed with this proposal given the difficulty people often have in establishing the basis in property purchased decades in the past. It would have created significant bookkeeping difficulties for everyone inheriting any property. Instead, I favored lowering the threshold for estate taxation so that it applied to more than the top 0.1 percent of estates.

4. State estate and gift taxes

While it's unlikely that your estate will be subject to federal estate taxes, it might well have to pay state estate or inheritance taxes if you live in a state that applies them. Whereas *estate* taxes are based on the value of the entire estate, the *inheritance* tax is based on the relationship between the person inheriting and the deceased. Currently, 14 states have estate taxes, and six states along with the District of Columbia have an inheritance tax. Two—Maryland and New Jersey—have both. Rates and thresholds vary, with both subject to change by state legislatures. Here's where things stand as of this writing:

STATES WITH ESTATE TAXES	THRESHOLD	RATE
Connecticut	$2.6 mil	7.2-12%
DC	$11.4 mil	6.4-16%
Hawaii	$11.4 mil	10-15.7%
Illinois	$4 mil	0.8-16%
Maine	$11.4 mil	8-12%
Maryland	$4 mil	16% (phasing in a higher exemption amount to match the federal level by 2019)
Massachusetts	$1 mil	0.8-16%
Minnesota	$2.4 mil	13-16%
New York	$5.25 mil	3.06-16% (phasing in a higher exemption amount to match the federal level by 2019)
Oregon	$1 mil	10-16%
Rhode Island	$1.538 mil	0.8-16%
Vermont	$2.75 mil	16%
Washington	$2.193 mil	10-20%

INHERITANCE:

Nebraska	1-8%
Iowa	0-15%
Kentucky	0-16%
Pennsylvania	0-15%
New Jersey	0-16%
Maryland	0-10%

Every state has its own tax structure, but most are similar. They relate to the tax structure in existence before Congress increased the federal estate tax threshold beginning in 2004. Up until that time, many states had a so-called "sponge tax" based on the federal estate tax then in existence. The federal tax allowed a credit for state estate taxes up to set percentages depending on the size of the estate. For example, if the state estate tax was $100,000 and this fit within the federal credit limits, the estate could simply subtract this amount from the federal estate tax owed. If the federal tax was $500,000, the estate would pay $400,000 to the IRS and $100,000 to the state tax authorities, but if the state had no estate tax, the estate would pay the same total amount, $500,000, all to the IRS. Thus, many states simply said that they would charge the amount of the federal estate tax credit. That way the estate paid the same amount of tax, but a portion of it went to the state instead of to the IRS, in effect sponging up the state estate tax credit allowed on the federal return.

But this system was upended when Congress reformed the estate tax. In addition to raising the threshold for taxation from $600,000 to $5 million (at that time), it eliminated the state estate tax credit and, thus, the estate taxes of all of the states that tied their taxes to the credit. Since the states had not decided as a policy or budget matter to eliminate their estate tax systems, this came as a shock. Many states responded by reenacting their taxes to tie them to the federal system that was in place in 1999.

CASE STUDY
MASSACHUSETTS ESTATE TAXES

The way this works in Massachusetts, where I practice, is that for estates in excess of $1 million, we fill out the federal estate tax form in use in 1999 in order to determine the estate tax credit then in existence and the tax due today. Interestingly (at least to those who work in this field), unlike the federal estate tax, which only taxes the amount over the threshold for taxation, if a Massachusetts estate exceeds the $1 million threshold all of it is taxed, though at much lower rates than the federal estate tax. The gift tax structure is also different. Massachusetts has no gift tax. So, you can give any amount to anyone without reporting it to the state. However, these gifts, to the extent they exceed the $15,000 federal gift tax exclusion, must be added back into the estate to determine whether it exceeds the $1 million threshold. If it does, what's left will be taxed even if it is less than $1 million. Here's an example of how this works:

John Adams has $1.2 million. He gives $100,000 to each of his three children and then dies with an estate of $900,000. In preparing his estate tax return, the children must add back in their $300,000 in gifts to determine whether he has a taxable estate.

However, they need only pay taxes on the $900,000 remaining. So this saves some money in taxes, but not everything, reducing the tax from approximately $45,000 to approximately $28,000.

As described above in the discussion of portability, in traditional estate tax planning husbands and wives shelter the amount they can give away tax free through trusts that keep these funds out of the estate of the surviving spouse. Doing this in Massachusetts and other states with the same tax structure can shelter up to $1 million from being taxed when the surviving spouse passes away. Depending on the size of the estate, the marginal tax rate—since the estate tax is graduated—and whether it eliminates estate taxes entirely, this can save the estate of the surviving spouse anywhere from $60,000 to $160,000.

A final feature of the Massachusetts estate tax is that it taxes real estate in the state even if owned by people who died as residents of other states, but does so in proportion to their entire estate. Here's an example from a recent case in our office: The decedent died as a resident of New Hampshire, but she still owned a half interest in her former home in Massachusetts which was selling for $500,000 (rounding out the numbers). Her entire taxable estate totaled $2.1 million. The tax on this, if she had been a Massachusetts resident when she died would have been $107,000. However, this was reduced to $12,738, representing the portion of her estate in Massachusetts: ($250,000 ÷ $2,100,000) x $107,000 = $12,738.

We provide this detail about the Massachusetts estate tax system as an example. Since each state that has an estate or inheritance tax has its own structure, only a local estate planning attorney can advise on state estate tax planning or probate administration.

CHAPTER 8

LONG-TERM CARE

One of the biggest unknowns in estate planning—and planning one's life in general—is whether you will need long-term care and, if so, how much and for how long. While anyone may die in her sleep or from a sudden illness or accident, there is a strong possibility that the vast majority of us will need care from others at the end of life. This could involve shopping and housework, around-the-clock monitoring for dementia, or heavy-duty nursing care for myriad illnesses. It might last for a few weeks or several years. The older we get, having avoiding being felled by a shorter-term illness or event, the more likely we will need long-term care.

Most long-term care is still provided by family members, though as illness stretches on it is likely more care will be provided by non-family providers who are paid for their services. Often, seniors experience a continuum of increased care over time, whether in the home, or in an assisted living facility, nursing home, or smaller board and care home.

The trend in recent years is for care to move out of nursing homes and into assisted living or at home. This lowers costs and permits people to live in a less institutional environment. One result, however, is that those people who are in nursing homes are likely to be sicker than in the past and to need a higher level of care. Another factor in this changing marketplace is that long-term care costs, like other health care costs, have increased dramatically over the last two or three decades, far exceeding the inflation rate.

Costs for care can vary widely, from a few hundred dollars a week to pay for coverage when family members are at work to $300,000 or more a year for around-the-clock care or care in the most expensive nursing homes, perhaps with private aides hired on the side. Two clients I met with recently reflect two examples of care and costs. The first is an attorney in his 50s whose wife suffers from the after-effects of cancer treatment she had when she was young and cannot be left alone for more than an hour or two at a time. He spends $75,000 a year on care for her while he is at work as well as during the day on weekends so that he can get some respite and spend time with their young adult children. He's on duty the rest of the time. Fortunately, he earns a good income and the payments for his wife's care are tax deductible, but he's not able to put anything aside in savings. His wife's situation and care needs could go on indefinitely. They recently moved to a new house on one level, which was also an expensive transition.

The other client's husband was a prominent research scientist who worked well into his 70s, but now suffers from Parkinson's disease and Lewy body dementia. He recently moved to a posh nursing home at a cost of $23,000 a month ($276,000 a year). He has long-term care insurance, but it only pays $5,000 a month and the insurance company had been putting up roadblocks to paying the claim. (We resolved this for them.) Even with the insurance, the out-of-pocket cost is $216,000 a year. The couple has ample assets and can pay this for a while, but over time, the cost could seriously deplete their savings and undermine the financial security of the wife, who is substantially younger than her husband.

Both of these clients are affluent, which makes these high costs of care manageable even if difficult. Most Americans, however, don't have their resources and can be easily bankrupted by long-term care costs. Given that these costs are totally unpredictable, it's very difficult to plan ahead

—but not impossible. An understanding of the sources of payment for long-term care and planning options can help.

Long-term care costs, whether at home, in assisted living or in a nursing home, are paid for primarily from three sources: out-of-pocket, Medicaid, and long-term care insurance. Medicare, the health insurance for people over age 65, does not pay for long-term care. It was designed on a medical model. So it will pay for **up to** 100 days of skilled nursing facility care following a hospitalization, but only for so long as the patient is deemed to need skilled care. It will also pay for skilled care at home, in theory indefinitely, but this can take some advocacy. We'll talk briefly about each source of payment and a fourth, veterans' benefits, which covers fewer people but which can be very important for those who do qualify.

1. OUT-OF-POCKET

Simply paying for care out-of-pocket is the least complicated way to pay for care, but also (of course) the most expensive. In most cases, the cost can be mitigated to some extent because it is tax deductible as a medical expense. Health care costs can be deducted to the extent they exceed 7.5% of your adjusted gross income (AGI). Often, seniors are in very low tax brackets, meaning that the deduction provides little benefit, especially with the recent increase in the standard deduction to $12,000 for single taxpayers and $24,000 for those who are married, with an additional

$1,600 for single and $2,600 for married taxpayers over age 65. But if retirement plan funds are used to pay for care, the result can be that the withdrawals, which are usually taxable, in effect become non-taxable. In addition, if a child pays for a parent's care he can usually deduct these costs on his tax return, which may provide a larger benefit since the child will probably be in a higher tax bracket and more likely to be itemizing as the result of paying a mortgage. Of course, less of the payment may be tax deductible due to the 7.5% of AGI that is not deductible. For instance, for a senior earning $50,000 a year, the first $3,750 of the health care expenses will not be deductible. An adult child earning $200,000 will not be able to deduct the first $15,000 of health care expenses.

One of the issues for many families hiring in-home care is whether to do so above the table or below the table. Legally, any in-home worker is an employee and is entitled to all the rights of an employee, including FICA contributions, workers compensation, overtime and, in some states, personal and sick leave. Not only does this increase the cost of hiring care, but it's also very complicated. One service that helps with the process is HomePay from Care.com (www.care.com/homepay). Whatever a family decides to do, they should take into account the fact that payments made under the table are not tax deductible and those made above the table are almost always deductible.

2. VETERANS BENEFITS

Veterans benefits are very complicated and their full explanation would take up several books on their own. They can depend on several factors, including whether the veteran has a disability based on military service and where the care is provided.

The primary benefit for long-term care planning is an enhanced pension known as Aid & Attendance, which (in 2019) pays up to $2,230 a month for care for married veterans and up to $1,211 a month for care for widows of veterans. Single veterans can receive up to $1,881. The benefit can be used towards long-term care costs at home or in an assisted living facility, but is unavailable to pay for nursing home care. To be eligible, the veteran must have served during wartime, which includes World War II, the Korean War, the Vietnam War, both Iraq wars and the war in Afghanistan.

In addition, the veteran's assets, other than his home, may not exceed $126,420 (in 2019). For a married veteran, this limit, as well as the income limits discussed below, applies to both spouses' assets. As of October 18, 2018, the VA applies a period of ineligibility for transfers made within three years of the application for benefits, as opposed to the five-year "look back" period for Medicaid benefits (see below).

The purpose of the Aid & Attendance benefit is to bring the veteran's income up to the levels listed above after any medical and care costs. So, for instance, a veteran with an income of $3,000 a month, but care costs of $2,000 a month will be deemed to have an income of $1,000 a month for purposes of determining eligibility. So he'll be eligible, but $1,000 will be deducted from his Aid & Attendance benefit. If he's married, he'll receive $1,230 a month from the VA ($2,230 - ($3,000 - $2,000) = $1,230). In contrast, if he's paying $5,000 a month for assisted living care, he will have negative income and receive his full Aid & Attendance payment ($2,230 - ($3,000 - $5,000) = $4,230).

As more and more veterans have become aware of this benefit, the application process has taken longer and longer, with applicants waiting up to a year to get a response as of this writing. However, once their applications are approved they receive retroactive payments back to the date of application.

THE JORGENSONS

Ten years have passed since John and Joyce Jorgenson created their estate plan. They are now both 70 years old, retired, and, unfortunately, John has been diagnosed with Alzheimer's disease. John is a veteran.

Their financial picture now is as follows:

Income (annual)

John	$25,000
Joyce	$20,000

Savings and Investments

Checking	$15,000
Savings	$25,000
Investments	$135,000
John's IRA	$200,000
Joyce's IRA	$125,000
Total	$500,000

House	$400,000	fair market value, no mortgage

While John is okay on his own for now, Joyce knows that eventually she will have to begin hiring help or to move to an assisted living facility. She is heartened to learn that the VA might help pay for John's care, but not until they have spent down most of their assets and John's care expenses begin to exceed about $3,000 a month. To prepare ahead of time, she takes two steps. First, she transfers her savings to her children, who set it aside in a trust to be available for their parents when and if necessary. Second, she begins drawing down on her and John's IRAs. Doing so creates taxable income, but she'd rather stretch this out over several years than do it all at once, which would push her and John into a higher tax bracket.

3. MEDICAID FOR NURSING HOME CARE

Now things get really complicated. Medicaid, which at its root is a safety net program that provides health care for the poor, has become the primary source of payment for nursing home care and a growing source of coverage for home and assisted living care. The breakdown of sources of payment for all long-term care expenditures in 2010 was as follows:

Medicaid	62%
Out-of-pocket	22%
Other private	12%
Other public	4%

Compare those numbers to 1993:

	Nursing Home Care	Home Care
Medicaid	40%	18%
Out-of-pocket	48%	26%
Medicare	9%	46%
Other Public	2%	10%

Over the last two decades, Medicaid's role has increased by more than 50% and private insurance has become a much larger player in the field, though still relatively small. Medicare's role has become significantly smaller.

Medicaid's significance has grown as it has become the long-term care insurance of the middle class. And its rules have become increasingly complicated. Medicaid is a joint federal-state program. Each state has its own Medicaid system (renamed in some states: MediCal in California, MassHealth in Massachusetts, TennCare in Tennessee). In some other states it's referred to as Title 19, the section of the Social Security Act that governs Medicaid. But it's all the same thing, except to the extent it isn't. The federal government sets the framework and pays from half to 90% of the cost, depending on the state, but within that framework, each state has certain freedom or options to vary its program. Others simply interpret federal law differently. And California, in some instances, has simply refused to implement aspects of the federal program. The result is that while the generalities about Medicaid rules are the same around the country, the specifics are all different. So, what follows will have to be general and if you are considering doing either advance or crisis Medicaid planning, you will need to consult with an in-state elder law attorney. The best place to find one is at www.ElderLawAnswers.com. (Disclosure: I founded the site.)

With that introduction, here's how Medicaid coverage of nursing home care works. (We will not cover Medicaid coverage of assisted living or home care because the extent of coverage and the rules for eligibility are too different to summarize. Just as one example, MassHealth in Massachusetts has half a dozen different programs for assisted living and home care, each with its own eligibility rules and benefits.)

a. Qualifying

While two-thirds of nursing home residents are covered by Medicaid, at its root it is a health care program for the poor. The definition of "poor," however, has become quite complex in the area of nursing home coverage. In order to be eligible for Medicaid benefits, a nursing home resident may have no more than $2,000 (in most states) in "countable" assets. The spouse of the nursing home resident—called the "community spouse"—is limited to one half of the couple's joint assets up to $126,420 (in 2019) in countable assets. (In some states the community spouse may keep all of the couple's assets up to $126,420, not just half up to that amount.) This figure, called the community spouse resource allowance (CSRA), changes each year to reflect inflation. In addition, the community spouse may keep the first $25,284 (in 2019), even if that is more than half of the couple's assets. This figure is higher in some states, up to the full $126,420 as mentioned above.

All assets are counted against these limits unless the property falls within the short list of "noncountable" assets. These include:

1. Personal possessions, such as clothing, furniture, and jewelry.
2. One motor vehicle of any value as long as it is used for transportation.
3. The applicant's principal residence, provided it is in the same state in which the individual is applying for coverage. The home is not considered a countable asset for Medicaid eligibility purposes as long as the nursing home resident intends to return home to the extent the equity is less than $585,000 (in 2019), with the states having the option of raising this limit to $878,000 (in 2019). In all states, the house may be kept with no equity limit if the Medicaid applicant's spouse or another dependent relative lives there.
4. Prepaid funeral plans (many states limit the value), up to $1,500 set aside in a specified burial account, and a small amount of life insurance.
5. Assets that are considered "inaccessible" for one reason or another.
6. Business property that produces income essential for self support.

CASE STUDY
SPENDING DOWN

After her husband George moved to a nursing home, Alice comes with her daughter, Joyce, to consult with an elder law attorney. Alice had been caring for George for years at home as his Alzheimer's disease progressed. Eventually, she had to be hospitalized for minor surgery, and Joyce and her two siblings were able to convince Alice that it was time for George to move to a nursing home.

Alice and her daughter provide the attorney with the following financial information: Alice and her husband own their home, which has a fair market value of approximately $400,000 and an outstanding home equity loan of $25,000. They have $200,000 in savings and investments. George receives $1,500 a month in Social Security benefits and an additional pension of $500. Alice receives $750 a month from Social Security. The nursing home charges $10,000 a month.

The attorney advises Alice and her daughter that in their state Alice can keep half of the couple's combined savings—$100,000—and George can keep $2,000, for a combined total of $102,000. They have to spend down $98,000 before Medicaid begins to pick up the tab for George's nursing home care. He advises them that any spending is allowed—even encouraging Alice to take a much-needed vacation—but that giving away assets would be penalized by one month of ineligibility for every $8,000 transferred.

After much discussion (and overcoming Alice's aversion to spending large sums), Alice, Joyce and the attorney come up with the following plan to spend down $98,000:

$25,000	Pay off home equity loan
+10,000	One month of nursing home care
+23,000	Purchase an immediate annuity for Alice's benefit
+10,000	Trading in Alice's car for a new one
+15,000	Painting Alice and George's house
+15,000	Prepaying George and Alice's funerals
$98,000	

With this plan, Alice is able to preserve the bulk of the couple's savings by spending it in ways that preserve its value for her.

b. Treatment of Income

The basic Medicaid rule for nursing home residents is that they must pay all of their income, minus certain deductions, to the nursing home. Medicaid pays nursing home costs that exceed the resident's income. But in some states, known as "income cap" states, eligibility for Medicaid benefits is barred if the nursing home resident's income exceeds $2,313 a month (for 2019), unless the excess above this amount is paid into a "(d)(4)(B)" or "Miller" trust. If you live in an income cap state and require more information on such trusts, consult an elder law specialist in your state.

For Medicaid applicants who are married, the income of the community spouse is not counted in determining the Medicaid applicant's eligibility. Only income in the applicant's name is counted. Thus, even if the community spouse is still working and earning, say, $5,000 a month, she will not have to contribute to the cost of caring for her spouse in a nursing home if he is covered by Medicaid.

What if most of the couple's income is in the name of the institutionalized spouse, and the community spouse's income is not enough to live on? In such cases, the community spouse is entitled to some or all of the monthly income of the institutionalized spouse. How much the community spouse is entitled to depends on what the Medicaid agency determines to be a minimum income level for the community spouse. This figure, known as the minimum monthly maintenance needs allowance or MMMNA, is calculated for each community spouse according to a complicated formula based on his or her housing costs. The MMMNA may range from a low of

$2,057.50 to a high of $3,160.50 a month (for 2019). If the community spouse's own income falls below his or her MMMNA, the shortfall is made up from the nursing home spouse's income (but see a possible alternative under Increased Resource Allowance below).

CASE STUDY
PATIENT PAY AMOUNT

After Alice and George (see case study on page 149) spend down so that George qualifies for Medicaid coverage of his nursing home care, the state Medicaid agency calculates Alice's MMMNA to be $2,400 a month, based on her housing expenses and the utility costs in the state. Since her own monthly income is only $750 from Social Security, she has a shortfall of $1,650 a month. George is permitted to pay this amount from his own income over to Alice each month rather than pay all of his income to the nursing home. His "patient pay amount," the amount he has to pay the nursing home each month, is determined to be $790, calculated as follows:

$2,500	George's total monthly income
− $1,650	Income allowance to Alice
− 60	Personal needs allowance (income George may keep)
$ 790	Patient pay amount

---

c. Asset Transfers

Why not qualify for Medicaid coverage of nursing home care by simply transferring assets out of your name so your accounts total less than $2,000? Because Congress does not want you to move into a nursing home on Monday, give all your money away on Tuesday, and qualify for Medicaid on Wednesday. So it has imposed restrictions on transferring assets before applying for Medicaid coverage without receiving fair value in return.

The restrictions impose a penalty for asset transfers — a period of time during which the person transferring the assets (and his or her spouse) will be ineligible for Medicaid. The period of ineligibility is determined by dividing the amount transferred by what the state Medicaid agency determines to be the average private pay cost of a nursing home in your state. For example, if you live in a state where the average monthly cost of care has been determined to be $8,000, and you give away property worth $120,000, you will be ineligible for benefits for 15 months ($120,000 ÷ $8,000 = 15).

However, the key issue is when this transfer penalty begins and ends. When one applies for Medicaid coverage of nursing home care, she must report all transfers made during the prior five years and the penalty period will not begin until the applicant would *otherwise* be eligible for benefits. In our example, the 15-month penalty period will not begin until (1) the transferor has moved to a nursing home, (2) has spent down to the asset limit for Medicaid eligibility, and (3) has applied for Medicaid coverage.

For instance, if an individual in our example transfers $120,000 on April 1, 2018, moves to a nursing home on April 1, 2019, and spends down to Medicaid eligibility on April 1, 2020, that is when the 15-month penalty period will begin, and it will not end until July 1, 2021.

Transfers should be made carefully, with an understanding of all the consequences. People who make transfers must be careful not to apply for Medicaid before the five-year lookback period elapses without first consulting with an elder law attorney. This is because the penalty could ultimately extend even longer than five years.

Also, bear in mind that if you give money or other property to your children, it belongs to them and you should not rely on them to hold the money for your benefit. However well-intentioned they may be, your children could lose the funds due to bankruptcy, divorce or lawsuit. Any of these occurrences would jeopardize the savings you spent a lifetime accumulating. *Do not give away your savings unless you are ready for these risks.* In addition, transfers can affect grandchildren's eligibility for financial aid at college and have significant tax consequences for children receiving the funds.

Moreover, the transfer of appreciated property to your children during your life can mean that your children will not get a step-up in basis in the property by inheriting it from you at your death (as described above in the section on income and capital gains taxation). This is especially relevant with respect to real estate and stock, with potentially highly appreciated values that would be taxed if given as a gift prior to your death.

In any case, as a rule, never transfer assets for Medicaid planning unless you keep enough funds in your name to (1) pay for any care needs you may have during the resulting period of ineligibility for Medicaid, (2) feel comfortable making the gift and (3) have sufficient resources to maintain your present lifestyle.

Remember: You do not have to save your estate for your children. The bumper sticker wisdom, "I'm spending my children's inheritance," is a perfectly appropriate approach to estate and Medicaid planning.

d. Permitted Transfers

While most transfers are penalized with a period of Medicaid ineligibility, certain others are exempt from this sanction. Even after entering a nursing home, you may transfer any asset to the following individuals without having to wait out a period of Medicaid ineligibility:

- Your spouse (but this might not help you become eligible since the same asset limit on both spouses' assets will apply);
- Your child who is blind or permanently disabled; or
- Into trust for the sole benefit of anyone under age 65 and permanently disabled.

In addition, special exemptions apply to your home in addition to those listed above. You may also transfer your home to the following individuals:

- Your child who is under age 21 (rather unusual for nursing home residents);
- Your child who has lived in your home for at least two years prior to your moving to a nursing home and who provided you with care that allowed you to stay at home during that time (often referred to as the "caretaker" child); or
- A sibling who already has an equity interest in the house and who lived there for at least a year before you moved to a nursing home.

In a Massachusetts case, the state Medicaid agency attempted to make the argument that the second group of permitted transfers that apply only to the home meant that the broader group of exceptions did not apply to the home—in other words that one list of exceptions was for the nursing home resident's home and the other for all *other* assets not including the home, rather than the ones for the home being *in addition* to the broader exceptions. In the case, a woman had transferred her home into trust for the sole benefit of her disabled niece. The Massachusetts Medicaid agency made the argument that the transfer should be penalized because the niece was not the woman's child. The Massachusetts court ruled in the woman's favor that the transfer was not penalized because the broader exceptions applied no matter what was transferred into the trust for the niece. The court pointed out that it would be perverse to penalize a transfer of the house into the trust but not to transfer the proceeds of the sale of the home if it were sold first.

CASE STUDY
PERMITTED TRANSFERS

Emily and Ira go to visit an elder law attorney. They are quite concerned about their father, Frank, and their brother, Samuel. Samuel, now 54 years old, is mentally retarded and has lived with his parents his whole life. Since his mother's death seven years ago, Samuel had been living with only his father. Frank is 85 years old and recently had a stroke. He is receiving care in a rehabilitation facility, but it is unlikely that he will be able to come home. He certainly will not be able to care for Samuel any longer.

Since his father's stroke, Samuel has been staying

alternately with Emily and Ira. His presence, along with tending to Frank, has greatly disrupted their family and work lives. This fill-in arrangement is not working for anyone. But Emily and Ira do care a great deal about Samuel, showing his picture to the attorney, and explaining how his presence in the house had been at least as much a comfort for their parents as it was a burden.

Fortunately, they have located a group home that looks like a good setting for Samuel. Unfortunately, it costs $4,000 a month. Once Medicare coverage ends, Frank's nursing home expense will be $12,000 a month. Frank's estate, including the value of his house, which they plan to sell, is approximately $600,000. While Emily and Ira are not seeking an inheritance themselves, they see their parents' estate being depleted over the next several years and their having to support Samuel themselves, or find publicly funded care that might not be what they want for their brother.

They are much relieved when the elder law attorney advises them that Frank can create a trust to hold his estate for the sole benefit of Samuel, allowing Frank to immediately qualify for Medicaid coverage of his nursing home care. With the cost of care for both Frank and Samuel suddenly $4,000 rather than $16,000 a month, the trust fund will be able to pay for Samuel's care indefinitely, even footing the bill for extras that will enhance his life.

e. Trusts

The main problem with transferring assets to make sure that they don't have to be spent down on your care is that you have to give them away. You no longer control them, and even a trusted child or other relative may lose them, whether due to divorce, lawsuit or a premature death. A safer approach is to put them in an irrevocable trust.

Whether trust assets are counted against Medicaid's resource limits depends on the terms of the trust and who created it. Medicaid considers the principal of revocable trusts (that is, the funds held in the trust) to be assets that are countable in determining Medicaid eligibility. Thus, revocable trusts are of no use in Medicaid planning.

The funds in irrevocable trusts created by the applicant or his or her spouse are counted as available to the applicant for Medicaid purposes to the extent the trustee may distribute income or principal to the applicant or his or her spouse. On the other hand, the funds in most trusts created and funded by someone else are not considered available as long as distributions are subject to the trustee's discretion and are not mandatory.

However, some exceptions to these general rules can be used for planning. For instance, Medicaid does not count the *principal* of an "irrevocable, income-only" trust as a resource, even if created by the Medicaid applicant or his or her spouse, provided the trustee cannot pay principal to or for the benefit of the nursing home resident or his or her spouse. That is, only the *income* from the trust is payable. Unfortunately, while this seems like a simple rule, some state Medicaid agencies have begun ruling that these trusts are countable as well, coming up with some ingenious legal arguments. If you are considering transferring assets to an irrevocable trust for Medicaid planning purposes, you need to consult with a local elder law attorney who knows how the rules are applied by your state Medicaid agency.

f. Testamentary trusts

As explained in Chapter 4, testamentary trusts are trusts created under a will. The Medicaid rules provide a special "safe harbor" for testamentary trusts created by a deceased spouse for the benefit of a surviving spouse. Unlike a trust created during life for a spouse, the assets of these trusts are treated as available to the Medicaid applicant only to the extent that the trustee has an obligation to pay for the applicant's support. If payments are solely at the trustee's discretion, they are considered unavailable to the Medicaid applicant.

While totally illogical—if one spouse creates a trust during his life for his spouse, the funds will be considered available should she apply for Medicaid benefits, but if created in a properly written will, they won't be counted—this rule can be very useful for Medicaid planning for the surviving spouse. These trusts can allow a healthy spouse living in the community (a "community spouse") to leave funds for his surviving spouse that can be used to pay for services that are not covered by Medicaid should she need care. These may include extra therapy, a geriatric care manager, special equipment, evaluation by medical specialists or others, legal fees, visits by family members, or transfers to another nursing home if that becomes necessary. Any funds left over when the surviving spouse passes away will go to the couple's children or whoever they choose rather than be subject to claim by the state Medicaid agency (see below).

g. Safe harbor trusts

The Medicaid rules provide for three "safe harbor" trusts that are exceptions to the general trust rules.

The first, referred to as a "(d)(4)(A)" trust (a reference to the relevant statute) or "payback" trust (referring to one of its key features, explained below) may be created for the *sole* benefit of a disabled beneficiary under the age of

65. It may be created by the beneficiary or her parent, grandparent, guardian or a court and funded with the disabled individual's own funds. The trust property will not be considered available in determining the disabled individual's eligibility for Medicaid benefits as long as the trust provides that at the beneficiary's death the state will be reimbursed out of any remaining trust funds for Medicaid benefits paid on behalf of the beneficiary during his or her life. It's because of this last provision that these trusts are often referred to as "payback" trusts. They're also sometimes called "first-party" special needs trusts because they're funded with the beneficiary's own funds, rather than the funds of a third party, such as a parent or grandparent.

The second safe harbor trust, often referred to as a "(d)(4)(B)," "Miller" or "qualified income" trust, or simply a "QIT," permits nursing home residents in states with an "income cap" (described above) to shelter excess income and still qualify for Medicaid benefits.

The third safe harbor, often referred to as a "(d)(4)(C)" or "pooled" trust, is similar to a (d)(4)(A) payback trust with two main differences: (1) It must be administered by a not-for-profit corporation for the benefit of more than one beneficiary, though it can manage the funds in separate accounts for each beneficiary. (2) An alternative to reimbursing the state for Medicaid expenditures made on the beneficiary's behalf upon his or her death is to have the funds remain in the trust for the benefit of its other beneficiaries.

h. Estate recovery and liens

The rules described above limit who may receive Medicaid coverage of nursing home care. But they are not the whole story. Once someone receives Medicaid benefits, whether for nursing home care at any age or for any other health care costs after the age of 55, the state will seek reimbursement from his or her estate after death. However, no recovery can take place until the death of the recipient's spouse, or as long as there is a child of the deceased who is under 21 or who is blind or disabled. (How this deferral of estate recovery works in practice depends on the state in question.)

In most cases, Medicaid beneficiaries do not have any estate to speak of; otherwise they would not have been eligible for Medicaid in the first place. However, in many states, Medicaid beneficiaries can keep their homes. They also could inherit money unexpectedly (or through poor planning) or be the beneficiary of a personal injury claim, leading them to have money at the end of their life despite being impoverished before then.

In those cases, whether the state will successfully recover against the Medicaid beneficiary's estate depends on how the property is held, and on the particular state's laws. All states seek recovery against the probate estate of the deceased

Medicaid beneficiary. Some also seek recovery against non-probate property in which the deceased had an interest, such as jointly held real estate, life insurance and trust property (see Chapter 4 for a discussion of the difference between the probate and non-probate estate). With proper planning, most individuals can avoid recovery against their estates. In addition, states must waive estate recovery in the case of "hardship," which they are free to define.

Medicaid liens are often confused with estate recovery. While estate recovery only occurs at death, typically the state will place a lien on the Medicaid beneficiary's home, so that the state must be paid back if the house is sold while the beneficiary is alive. Exceptions to the lien exist, substantially paralleling the exceptions to the transfer penalty for giving away the home. Thus, no lien may be applied if a spouse, disabled or minor child, or caretaker child is living there. People often confuse these exceptions as protecting the house from estate recovery as well. They do not. To assume they will can be a costly error. While there is a deferral of estate recovery during the life of a surviving spouse or until a minor child reaches age 21, as described above, this only delays the estate recovery, not protecting against the ultimate payment to the state.

i. Advance Medicaid planning

Planning to become eligible for Medicaid to cover the cost of nursing home care generally takes place in one of two circumstances. In the first—advance planning—the individual or couple is planning ahead for the possibility that they might need long-term care in the future. In the second—crisis planning—a spouse, child or other family member is seeking to preserve as much of the assets as possible in the face of a costly nursing home placement that has occurred already or that is imminent.

While the crisis situation is the most difficult, the planning steps are often more clear-cut once the feared event has happened. In advance planning, one hopes the need for long-term care will never occur. And some of the steps one could take to plan ahead are difficult or even ill-advised, such as giving away assets.

Following is a discussion of the advance planning steps you might take while healthy, understanding that each involves a trade-off and only you can decide what makes the most sense for you in your situation.

GIVING ASSETS AWAY

An initial question is for whom are you protecting assets: yourself and your spouse, your children and grandchildren, someone else, or a combination of the above? If the reason you saved during your life was to provide for your old age and that of your spouse, then keep your savings and use them for the rainy day, when and if it arrives. If you would like to be sure to pass your savings on to your children, and you cannot afford long-term care insurance or are not insurable, the best way to be sure they get what you want them to inherit is to give it to them now.

Of course, there are a lot of problems with that, as outlined in the section above on Asset Transfers. If, despite these warnings, you still decide to begin transferring your estate to your children, remember that the transfer can cause you and your spouse to be ineligible for Medicaid benefits for up to 60 months. Make sure that you keep enough funds for your needs, whatever they might be, during that entire ineligibility period. Another alternative is to purchase long-term care insurance with the intention of holding it only for the five-year lookback period following the transfer, assuming that you can't afford the premiums on an ongoing basis.

All too often, we have clients who make gifts to children and grandchildren and then need Medicaid within five years. This creates difficult placement issues, especially when the children cannot return the transferred funds (which is usually the case). While nursing homes are not supposed to discriminate against people on Medicaid in terms of accepting them as residents, they have a perfect right to deny entrance to people who can't afford to pay for their care and who also don't have Medicaid coverage. No one should expect nursing homes to provide care for free.

INCOME-ONLY TRUSTS

It is possible to transfer assets out of your name for Medicaid purposes but still receive some benefit from them. This is done by putting them in an irrevocable trust if it is drafted to say that while the *income* is payable to you for life, the *principal* cannot be paid out to you or your spouse. At your death the principal is paid to your heirs. This way, the funds in the trust are protected and you can use the income for your living expenses. However, if you do move to a nursing home, the trust income will have to go to the nursing home.

You should be aware of the drawbacks to such an arrangement. First, it is very rigid, so you cannot gain access to the trust funds even if you need them for some other purpose. Think of it as the proverbial "lock box." Second, as noted above, the potential ineligibility period for transfers to trusts can be five years. For this reason, you should always leave an ample cushion of ready funds outside the trust.

This type of trust has three advantages over a direct transfer to children: First, you continue to receive the income. Second, the funds are not at risk, as they would be if placed in a child's name. Third, at your death, your children will receive the funds with a step-up in basis, as described above on page 128. A variation on this theme is to transfer assets to a trust without the right to receive the income. This protects the income from having to go to the nursing home and still benefits from a step-up in basis upon your death, so it can make sense for sheltering your home or highly appreciated stock.

You may also choose to place property in a trust that permits distributions to or for the benefit of your children, or others. These beneficiaries may, at their discretion, return the favor by using the property for your benefit if necessary. However, there is no legal requirement that they do so. And you shouldn't make a habit of doing this or the Medicaid agency may rightfully argue that the trust is a sham and that the funds are really being held for your benefit.

CASE STUDY
GIFTING AND REIMBURSEMENT CONSIDERATIONS

Lynne and Olive consult with an elder law attorney about Olive's mother, who is deteriorating. The family has hired some help for her, but they see nursing home care in her future. She has sold her house to move to an assisted living facility. Olive reports that her mother has about $500,000 in savings, of which $150,000 is in certificates of deposit and bank accounts and $350,000 is in highly appreciated stock.

Lynne and Olive discuss with the attorney the possibility of transferring half of this amount, with the result that Olive's mother could not apply for Medicaid coverage for the subsequent five years, but leaving her with enough funds to pay for her care during this time. The problem is which funds to transfer. If they transfer the stock, Olive and her siblings will receive it with their mother's basis, meaning that when and if they sell it they will have to pay a large tax on capital gains (which would not be the case if they inherited it from their mother, because the basis would be stepped up to its value on her date of death).

The attorney explains that an alternative would be to transfer the funds into an irrevocable trust drafted so that the children would receive a step-up in basis on their mother's death. Olive's mother would transfer $250,000 of her most appreciated stock into the trust and keep her remaining savings and investments in her own name, spending them down as needed over the next five years. She'll start with her cash. Once she runs through that, she will draw down her remaining stock, realizing capital gains as she cashes it out. However, she will be able to deduct her nursing home costs as a medical expense, offsetting some or all of the income realized on the sale of the stock.

An alternative approach would be for Olive's mother to transfer all of her money: the first $250,000 to the trust and the second $250,000 outright to Olive and her siblings. If one of them then uses the money to pay for her care, that child can then take a medical expense deduction for these payments on her own tax return to the extent they and her other health care costs exceed 7.5 percent of her adjusted gross income. The daughter can then reimburse her mother for the tax savings, helping the family to stretch their mother's money further. There will not be much benefit to this approach until Olive's mother's expenses get to be rather significant. In addition, choosing which child should pay the expenses and take the deduction depends on each child's income and other health care expenses. An example can show how this works:

If a child whose income is $50,000 pays his mother's health care costs (over and above the mother's own income) of $50,000, he will be able to deduct expenses over $5,000, or a total of $45,000. At a marginal federal tax rate of 22 percent, this will result in savings of $9,900 (plus any state income tax reduction). In comparison, a child whose income is $100,000 will only be able to deduct costs over $10,000, resulting in a deduction of $40,000. But at her marginal rate of 24 percent, this results in federal income tax savings of almost the same amount, $9,600. (If the children are married, the rates and the tax savings may be lower.)

As you can see, especially when you mix Medicaid and tax planning, matters can get quite complicated. Consulting with a qualified elder law attorney is an absolute necessity.

PROTECTING THE HOUSE FROM ESTATE RECOVERY

The principal asset for most people is their home, which often has sentimental as well as financial value. As is explained above, in most cases Medicaid recipients are permitted to keep their homes while they receive coverage but after a Medicaid recipient dies the state will seek to recoup from his or her estate whatever benefits it paid for the recipient's care. As I often quip to clients, if they don't get you coming, they'll get you (or your house) going. However, states that have not opted to broaden their estate recovery to include non-probate assets may not make a claim against the house if it is not in the Medicaid recipient's probate estate.

While you can protect your house by transferring it to your children outright now, this has the potential risks and adverse tax consequences we've discussed above. An additional risk is that your children decide that it's time for you to move to assisted living or to a nursing home before you feel you're ready to do so. If you don't own the house, you may have no legal leg to stand on in case of such a dispute. Instead, most clients protect their homes through a life estate or irrevocable trust.

Life Estate

For many people, setting up a "life estate" is the simplest and most appropriate alternative for protecting the home from estate recovery. It is created by the parent or parents deeding the house to the children, but on the deed reserving the right to live in the property for the rest of the parents' lives. It is, in essence, a form of joint ownership of property between two or more people where they have the right to possess the property for different periods of time. The person holding the life estate possesses the property currently and for the rest of his or her life. The other owner has a future or "remainder" interest in the property. He or she has a current ownership interest but cannot take possession until the end of the life estate, which occurs at the death of the life estate holder or holders.

In all but a few states, once the house passes to the person with the remainder interest, the state cannot recover against it for any Medicaid expenses the person holding the life estate may have incurred. Still, as with any transfer, putting the deed into a life estate within five years of an application for Medicaid can trigger an ineligibility period, so it's important if possible for the parents to keep enough savings to cover their care for the five years after creating the life estate.

The life estate has a few drawbacks. First, if the property is sold during the parent's life, the proceeds will be split between the parent and the children based on the parent's age and life expectancy at the time of the sale. If this occurs while she is in a nursing home, her share of the proceeds will have to be spent down on her care. Second, upon the sale, the parent will only be able to use the $250,000 capital gain exclusion for her share of the proceeds. The children will have to pay the taxes on the share of the capital gain going to them. Third, problems can occur if a child passes away before the parent or refuses to cooperate in the sale of the property.

Another potential application of the life estate concept (or joint ownership, which also passes automatically at death) is for parents to purchase a life estate in a child's home and then move in with the child. The purchase must be for the fair market value of the life interest. However, the purchase of a life estate within the five years prior to applying for Medicaid benefits will be considered a disqualifying transfer unless the Medicaid applicant lives in the property for at least a year.

Irrevocable Trust

These drawbacks can be avoided through another method of protecting the home from estate recovery, which is to transfer it to an irrevocable trust very similar to the income-only trust described above. Once the house is in the trust, it cannot be taken out again. Although it can be sold, the proceeds must remain in the trust. This can protect more of the value of the house if it is sold than might be the case with a life estate. The trust is more complicated and more expensive to set up than a life estate. Also, unlike a life estate, it cannot be reversed or "cured" if a parent needs nursing home care within the five years following the trust's creation. Where the parents have little funds other than the house or are already ill or showing signs of dementia, a life estate is generally preferable to a trust.

Beware that these standard planning devices might not work in states that have elected to seek estate recovery of non-probate as well as probate property. In any case, given state variations, changing state laws, and the circumstances of individual clients, it's important to consult with an experienced elder law attorney before taking any steps to shelter one's home or other assets.

THE JORGENSONS

John and Joyce Jorgenson are now both 75 years old and in good health. But they are concerned about what would happen if either should ever need long-term care. They want to make sure that there's enough money for the other spouse's needs and they also hope to leave something to their children, who are just making ends meet in today's economy.

John and Joyce's financial picture is as follows:

Income (annual)

John	$25,000
Joyce	$20,000

Savings and Investments

Checking	$15,000
Savings	$25,000
Investments	$135,000
John's IRA	$200,000
Joyce's IRA	$125,000
Total	$500,000

House	$400,000 fair market value, no mortgage

After meeting with an elder law attorney, John and Joyce decide to transfer their home to an irrevocable trust. They do not expect to need to apply for Medicaid benefits for at least five years (hopefully in more than 10 or 15 years, if ever). They expect to live in the home for as long as possible, but they understand that if they choose to sell it the trust could buy them another place to live. They are also comfortable not taking any steps to protect their savings, reasoning that they want that money available to pay for whatever they want to do during their retirement or for whatever care needs they might have. If they can be assured that they can pass on their house to their children, that makes them feel more comfortable.

CRISIS MEDICAID PLANNING

Whether or not you or a family member has taken any of the long-term care planning steps described above, generally there's more you can do to protect at least some of your savings, even at the last minute. The following strategies might be options, should you or a family member require nursing home care.

i. The "Half a Loaf" or "Rule of Halves" Strategy

One of the prime planning techniques used before a change in the law meant to bar it, often referred to as "half a loaf," was for the Medicaid applicant to give away approximately half of his or her assets. It worked this way: Before applying for Medicaid, the prospective applicant would transfer half of his or her resources, thus, creating a Medicaid penalty period. The applicant, who was often already in a nursing home, then used the other half of his or her resources to pay for care while waiting out the ensuing penalty period. After the penalty period had expired, the individual could apply for Medicaid coverage.

Congress attempted to bar this practice by delaying the start of the penalty period until the nursing home resident ran out of money. Nevertheless, the strategy still works in some states, but can be more complicated, often requiring one of three variations: First, the parent transfers all of her funds to her children and applies for Medicaid, receiving a long ineligibility period. Then the children return half the transferred funds, "curing" half of the ineligibility period and giving the nursing home resident the funds she needs to pay for her care. In the second variation, the parent gives half of his funds to his children and lends them the other half under a promissory note that meets certain requirements in the Medicaid law. The parent uses monthly repayments of the loan, along with his income, to pay his nursing home costs. In a third variation, rather than lending the money to the children, the nursing home resident buys an annuity that pays out enough funds to pay the nursing home during the ineligibility period. An elder law attorney can advise you on what, if any, strategy works in your state.

ii. Spending Down

While there's a penalty for giving savings away, there's no limit on how applicants for Medicaid and their spouses may spend their money. You may protect savings by spending them on any items or services that benefit you. These may include:

- paying off a mortgage or other loan;
- making repairs to a home;
- replacing an old automobile;
- updating home furnishings;
- paying for more care at home;
- buying a new home; or
- taking a vacation (although we have yet to see a community spouse spend down funds for this purpose).

In the case of married couples in states with a minimum community spouse resource allowance below $126,420 (in 2019), it can be important that any spend-down steps be taken only after the unhealthy spouse moves to a nursing home if this would affect the community spouse's resource allowance.

iii. Immediate Annuities

The purchase of immediate annuities can be an ideal planning tool for the spouses of nursing home residents. For single individuals, they are less useful. In its simplest form, an immediate annuity is a contract with an insurance company under which the consumer pays a sum of money to the company and the company sends the consumer a monthly check for the rest of his or her life or for a specific number of months. In most states the purchase of an annuity is not considered to be a transfer for purposes of eligibility for Medicaid as long as it satisfies certain requirements, but is instead the purchase of an investment. It transforms otherwise countable assets into a non-countable income stream for the community spouse. As long as the income is in the name of the community spouse, it's not a problem since there is no limit on the community spouse's income or a requirement that she contribute to the nursing home spouse's cost of care.

In order for the annuity purchase not to be considered a transfer, it must meet four basic requirements: (1) It must be irrevocable; you cannot have the right to take the funds out of the annuity except through the monthly payments. (2) You must receive back at least what you paid into the annuity during your actuarial life expectancy. For instance, if you have an actuarial life expectancy of 10 years, and you pay $60,000 for an annuity, you must receive annuity payments of at least $500 a month ($500 x 12 x 10 = $60,000). (3) If you purchase an annuity with a term certain (see below), it must be shorter than your actuarial life expectancy. And (4) the state must be named the remainder beneficiary up to the amount of Medicaid paid on the annuitant's behalf.

You can purchase an immediate annuity that will pay for as long as you live, whether that's one more month or three more decades, or one with a "term certain"—a guaranteed payment period, such as five years, no matter how long you live. With a term certain annuity, if you die before the end of the term, the future payments will be made to whomever you name as beneficiary.

Immediate annuities are a very powerful tool in the right circumstances, but of little or no use in others. They must also be distinguished from deferred annuities, which have no Medicaid planning purpose. The use of immediate annuities as a Medicaid planning tool is under attack in some states. Be sure to consult with a qualified elder law attorney in your state before pursuing this strategy.

THE JORGENSONS

John and Joyce Jorgenson are now both 80 years old. Unfortunately, John's Alzheimer's has progressed to a point Joyce can no longer care for him at home and makes the decision to move him to a nursing home. She is concerned about her own financial future and wants to qualify John for Medicaid coverage.

John and Joyce's financial picture is as follows:

Income (annual)
John	$25,000
Joyce	$20,000

Savings and Investments
Checking	$15,000
Savings	$25,000
Investments	$135,000
John's IRA	$200,000
Joyce's IRA	$125,000
Total	$500,000

House	$400,000 fair market value, no mortgage

In order for John to qualify for Medicaid coverage, they must spend down their $500,000 in countable assets to approximately $125,000. Joyce will be paying for the nursing home for a few months and will prepay both John's and her funerals. She'll also take care of some long-delayed repairs to the house and get a new car. But that will still leave her about $300,000 above the asset limit. So, she'll use $250,000 of those funds to purchase an immediate annuity for her own benefit. It will convert her excess savings into an income stream, and there is no limit on her income.

The balance of $50,000, unfortunately, will have to go to the IRS to cover the taxes on liquidating John's IRA. Fortunately, Joyce is philosophical about this, recognizing that these are taxes that will ultimately be paid in any case as the IRA is drawn down. And she will be able to keep all but $5,000 of her IRA in its tax-deferred status.

Joyce also uses John's durable power of attorney to transfer the house into her name. This way she will be free to move if she chooses to do so and after John's death the house won't be subject to Medicaid estate recovery for expenses paid on his behalf. Joyce also updates her estate plan to remove John as her agent on her documents and to create a testamentary trust for his benefit in the event she passes away before him.

iv. Spousal Refusal

Federal Medicaid law permits the community spouse to keep all of his or her assets by simply refusing to support the institutionalized spouse as long as the institutionalized spouse assigns his or her rights to spousal support to the state. This portion of the law, often referred to as "just say no" or "spousal refusal," is generally not used except in New York where the state elder law bar has adopted it as its principal crisis planning strategy for spouses of nursing home residents. In addition, in 2005 a federal appeals court upheld the right of the wife of a Connecticut nursing home resident to refuse to support her husband. The husband was able to qualify for Medicaid coverage, and assets that he had transferred to his wife were not counted in determining his eligibility.

Under spousal refusal, after awarding Medicaid benefits to the institutionalized spouse, the Medicaid agency then has the option of beginning a legal proceeding to force the community spouse to support the institutionalized spouse. However, this is rarely done, and when such cases do go to court, those in New York generally allow the community spouse to keep enough resources to maintain her former standard of living.

This spousal refusal strategy sometimes is used in other states in second-marriage situations where the healthy spouse truly refuses to support the nursing home spouse or where the spouses have separated but are not divorced—in other words, where the facts of the case seem to fit with the intent of the law. When it is used, it's often necessary to educate the Medicaid workers since they are likely not familiar with the applicable law and regulations.

v. Increased Resource Allowance

Under rules described earlier in this chapter, if the community spouse's income is below an amount determined by the state Medicaid agency to be the minimum he or she needs to live on, the community spouse can receive a share of the institutionalized spouse's income to bring his or her income up to this minimum level. For instance, if the state determines that the community spouse needs $2,500 a month to live on, and her own income is only $800 a month, she will be entitled to $1,700 of her husband's income each month to make up the difference. That amount will not have to be paid to the nursing home.

If the institutionalized spouse's income added to the community spouse's income is still not sufficient to reach the minimum income level, the community spouse may keep additional assets above the standard community spouse resource allowance (CSRA) (see "Qualifying for Medicaid" earlier in this chapter) to generate additional income. For instance, in the example above, if the husband's income is only $1,000, the wife would still have a shortfall of $700 a month ($2,500-($800 + $1,000) = $700). The difference may be made up by permitting the community spouse to keep additional savings and investments. The states differ on how this will be calculated, but with current low interest rates, this can turn into a large adjustment. With a rate of return of 1%, for instance, the community spouse would need to invest $840,000 to generate $700 a month of interest.

This increased CSRA cannot be granted at the time of the Medicaid application. Typically, the application for benefits is denied for excess assets and the community spouse must appeal it, seeking the increased CSRA at an administrative hearing. In some states, the practice is to seek a court order to obtain an increased CSRA.

vi. Increased Income Allowance

While the community spouse's income allowance is determined by a formula as is described above, where she has unusual medical expenses she can appeal this determination. As with the increased CSRA, the higher income allowance can only be awarded on appeal. It is only granted if a medical reason can be shown for the higher income need, such as when the community spouse needs home care herself or must live in assisted living. With the grant of an increased income allowance, community spouses often can qualify for a significantly higher CSRA as well.

k. The attorney's role in Medicaid planning

Do you need an attorney for even "simple" Medicaid planning? Yes. The description of the rules and planning techniques above can only provide a framework. It cannot explain how your state interprets the law, the latest developments in Medicaid agency practices, or the planning techniques that would work best in your situation. Only an experienced elder law attorney can do that.

If a family member is already in a nursing home, it may assign a social worker or other staff member to assist in preparing a Medicaid application. He may know a lot about the program, but maybe not the particular rule that applies in your case or the newest changes in the law. And he has something of a conflict of interest, since it might not be in the nursing home's interest that your family member qualifies sooner and stops paying at the facility's private rate. In addition, by the time you're applying for Medicaid, you might have missed out on significant planning opportunities.

The best bet is to consult with a qualified professional who can advise you on the entire situation. At the very least, the price of the consultation should purchase some peace of mind since you'll know that you haven't left any potential planning options on the table. More likely, what you learn can mean significant financial savings or better care for you or your loved one. As described above, this might involve the use of trusts, transfers of assets, or the purchase of annuities.

If you are going to consult with an elder law attorney, do so as soon as possible. If you wait, it might be too late to take some steps available to preserve your assets. You can find a qualified elder law attorney on the directory of the website www.ElderLawAnswers.com.

4. LONG-TERM CARE INSURANCE

a. Introduction

The best advance plan, unless you are so affluent that the cost of long-term care is not an issue, is long-term care insurance. Unfortunately, it's expensive. The biggest questions are whether you can afford it and whether you are insurable (meaning that the insurance company doesn't reject your application due to a preexisting condition).

The next question is when should you purchase a policy. More and more companies are offering long-term care insurance as an employee benefit, often at a more reasonable cost. If possible, take advantage of one of these offerings. If not, one rule of thumb is to buy long-term care insurance when you no longer need term life insurance—that is, when your children (if any) have completed their schooling so that you no longer need life insurance to support them if you pass away. Then you can begin using those premium dollars for long-term care insurance. (Of course, if you can afford both types of insurance at the same time, then don't wait.)

Given that the preferable outcome is that you'll never use the insurance, many potential customers balk at the high cost of the premiums. As a result, many insurance companies are now offering hybrid long-term care and life insurance policies, under which your family will still receive some benefit at death if you don't need the insurance for your long-term care costs. One type of this hybrid is a rider on a life insurance policy that permits you to draw down the death benefit to pay for long-term care costs. I have not seen an analysis as to whether these policies are more or less economical than purchasing separate long-term care and life insurance policies, but no doubt the insurance companies have done such analyses internally and it's unlikely that these hybrid policies provide any savings in premiums.

b. Policy structure and variables

One of the difficulties in shopping for long-term care insurance is that the different policies are almost impossible to compare. Typically, policies provide a daily benefit up to a specified dollar amount for a specified period of time. For instance, a policy may provide a daily benefit level of $150 for three years of coverage, for a total potential benefit of $165,000.

On this basis alone, it would seem relatively easy to compare two policies providing this benefit. But then the variations begin.

An important question is: What is the trigger for qualifying for coverage? Typically, policies base qualification on cognitive impairment or the need for assistance in two or three "activities of daily living," defined as the basic tasks of everyday life, such as dressing, toileting, eating, transferring, bathing and continence.

Another variable is whether the policy benefit will rise with inflation. While a daily insurance benefit of $150 (combined with income) might be sufficient to cover the cost of care today, the question arises as to what happens 10, 20 or 30 years from now. Buyers are given the option of purchasing an inflation rider with the policy, which typically provides that the daily benefit increases by 3 percent per year, either on a flat or compounded basis. This choice can significantly increase the annual premiums. Some advisors follow a rule of thumb that purchasers under age 70 should purchase an inflation rider and those over age 70 need not.

The next variable is the length of the elimination period, which is the period of time that must elapse before the insured will qualify for coverage and before the policy will kick in. This period is typically 20 or 100 days, but can be any length of time up to one year. The longer the elimination period, the lower the premium. I'm inclined to recommend a longer elimination period since most people who can afford to by LTCI can afford to pay for their care out-of-pocket for a significant period of time; it's the risk of needing care for many years for which they need insurance.

The most important variable in choosing among policies is the claims record for the company. Do they honor claims on their policies on a timely basis without too much hassle, or do they put up roadblocks every step of the way? Our bad experiences have been with companies that no longer offer the insurance; they seem to be trying to stem their losses by making it extremely difficult for the insured and their families to access benefits. While these companies are no longer selling new policies, we would recommend searching the Internet for information about the claims experience of customers before purchasing any company's LTCI.

All policies today must offer the option of naming a second person to receive notice of any late or missed premium payments. In the past, many policyholders stopped paying premiums due to the onset of cognitive impairment, resulting in a loss of the policies just when they were needed most. Now, at least, someone else can be given notice and the opportunity to step into the breach and save the policy.

One of the drawbacks of long-term care insurance is that, to date, companies have been unwilling to guarantee that the premiums will not rise over time. Life insurance with a long-term care rider offers a set fee. Another solution is an option offered by some companies known as "10-pay" policies. These policies only require ten annual premium payments and then the policies are paid up for life. Of course, the premiums are higher over these ten years than those of other policies, but when done the client's long-term care funding is complete.

Insurance companies offer a number of features that can be attractive to married couples if they both purchase LTCI. One is a simple discount on the premiums, usually 10 percent. Another permits both spouses to dip into the same pool. For instance, if they both purchase three years of coverage and one spouse's need for care exceeds that time limit, she can then start drawing on her spouse's policy. This will deplete the coverage available for the other spouse, but it's usually better to use the insurance to pay for a definite expense than to preserve it for a potential future need.

c. Who should purchase LTCI, and when?

Potential buyers of LTCI fall into one of three categories:

those wealthy enough to self-insure; those who cannot afford the premiums or who are uninsurable due to their health; and all of those in the middle who need to at least consider purchasing LTCI. While this formulation is straightforward, defining the lines among the three groups is not so clear.

Those who don't need LTCI because they can self-insure probably have annual income of at least $100,000 or liquid investments and savings of at least $1 million. The fact that this group can self-insure does not necessarily mean that they shouldn't purchase LTCI. First, they might consider LTCI a good investment. The second and more important reason has to do with human nature. Many people who can afford to pay their own long-term care costs avoid doing so, putting their own safety and health at risk and unduly stressing family caregivers. They might avoid paying for care because they are worried that they will run out of money, or they just can't stomach the high costs, or they don't want to deplete the inheritance that they will leave their children, or they would rather depend on family members (thus increasing the burden on them). On the other hand, if the costs are covered by insurance, many people feel more comfortable using this seemingly "free" money to pay for their necessary care.

Drawing the line between those who can afford the premiums and those who cannot is difficult. Ideally, a financial planner will project out the potential insurance buyer's likely future income and expenses to determine if the client can likely afford the premiums for the rest of his life. In doing so, she must make sure to include the possibility that the premiums will increase.

One rule of thumb is that the insurance premiums are "affordable" if they can be paid out of income you would otherwise be adding to savings. Another is to look at how much it would cost to purchase an annuity whose payout would cover the LTCI premiums and see whether you would feel comfortable committing this amount towards long-term care costs. Then you can either purchase the annuity or simply understand that you will be spending that amount of your savings to cover the LTCI premiums.

Of course, the impact of all of this analysis depends on the cost of the premiums, which reflects the wide range of variables discussed above.

Finally, at what age should you purchase LTCI? If you're a Baby Boomer, the answer is now. The younger your age when you buy the policy, the lower the premiums will be. But who in his 40s will want to purchase insurance that he is unlikely to need for 40 or more years? And given the changes in the long-term care marketplace and in LTCI itself over the past ten to 15 years, it is hard to imagine what the world will look like in 40 years.

But if you wait until your 70s, the premiums will be extremely high and you might be uninsurable for health reasons. On one company's online calculator, a policy offering a $150 per day long-term care benefit for four years, with no inflation rider costs a 55-year-old man $1,984 a year, while the same policy has an annual premium of $2,990 for a 65-year-old and $5,188 for a 70-year-old. The premiums for a woman of the same age would be $2,607, $4,519 and $7,424, respectively. Women are much more likely to need care because they live longer, meaning both that they could need care for more years and that they are more likely to be widowed when they need care without a spouse to step in to help out.

So, the ideal time to purchase is probably in your 50s or 60s. One approach is to see how the premiums fit into your life and other obligations. If you have children who have not yet graduated from college, they will be the major concern. You should carry enough life insurance to see them through. But after the children, if any, are on their own, it might be advisable to take the funds used to pay for life insurance premiums and use them to pay LTCI premiums.

d. How much LTCI should you buy?

A number of considerations go into determining how much insurance any consumer should buy. In many areas of the country, nursing homes cost as much as $400 a day and assisted living facilities can cost more than half that amount. Home care can be less or more expensive, depending on the amount and level of care required.

One easy way to calculate a daily benefit is to take the average cost of care where you live (or are likely to live when needing care) and subtract from that your daily income. If, for instance, nursing homes cost $300 a day where you live and your income is $3,000 a month, or $100 a day, then your daily benefit should be $200 a day.

The next consideration is what period of time the policy should cover. The shortest period of coverage available is two years. But policies can be purchased for longer periods of time or even for lifetime coverage. Of course, the longer the policy's coverage period, the higher the premium.

A standard length of time for coverage is five years. This is for two reasons. First, it is unusual for someone to need care for more than five years. Second, the Medicaid penalty for transferring assets is currently five years. This means that someone needing care could transfer most or all of her assets to her children or into trust, pay for her care with her insurance over five years and then, if her assets are spent down, qualify for Medicaid coverage.

A policy paying $200 a day for five years will be expensive, especially if it includes an inflation rider. For those who cannot afford such coverage, an alternative school of thought is to think of LTCI as "avoid nursing home" insurance. Under this approach, you may purchase sufficient insurance to pay for home care or assisted living care, which generally are not fully covered by Medicaid. Some seniors find themselves in the unfortunate situation of having to move to a nursing home because Medicaid will cover the cost of their nursing home care, but not assisted living or home care in the senior's home, which is where she would prefer to live. Having coverage for this purpose can prevent the financial pressure to move to a nursing home.

So, in our example above, if you purchased insurance with a daily benefit of $100 a day, together with your income you would have $6,000 a month to cover your living expenses plus home care or assisted living costs. Since the premium for this policy would be substantially less than one with a daily benefit of $200, it would be much more affordable.

An alternative approach that more financial advisors appear to be adopting is to cut the length of coverage rather than the daily benefit. This is because policyholders don't lose the benefit if they only use part of it. Instead, the policies can really be looked at as pools of funds for long-term care. So, for instance, a two-year policy paying a daily benefit of $200 is really a $146,000 long-term care fund (365 × 2 × 200). If the policyholder draws on the policy at the rate of $100 a day for one year, she will still have $109,500 ($146,000—$36,500) to pay for future long-term care costs, whether at home, in assisted living, or in a nursing home, no different than if she had a four-year policy paying $100 a day in benefits.

e. Tax benefits

"Qualified" LTCI policies receive special tax treatment. To be "qualified," policies must adhere to regulations passed by the National Association of Insurance Commissioners (NAIC). Virtually all policies sold today, if not all, adhere to the NAIC rules.

Premiums paid for qualified LTCI policies are treated as medical expenses and may be deducted as medical expenses along with other medical costs (including MediGap insurance premiums) to the extent that they exceed 7.5 percent of the taxpayer's adjusted gross income, limited to annual amounts based on the taxpayer's age. (The rules are more liberal if the taxpayer owns a business.)

Following are the deductibility limits for 2018 based on the taxpayer's age at the end of the year:

40 or under	$420
41–50	$780
51–60	$1,560
61–70	$4,160
71 and older	$5,200

It is unlikely that this tax benefit helps very many people or affects their decision on purchasing LTCI, especially for those who are still working, who are unlikely to have medical expenses exceeding 10 percent of their adjusted gross income. Those people who are retired, who have a combination of lower income and higher medical expenses, are more likely to save some taxes. This group, however, is also likely to be paying taxes at a lower rate and not able to afford LTCI in the first place.

f. Partnership programs

All states except Alaska, Massachusetts, Michigan, Mississippi, New Mexico and Utah now have so-called partnership programs linking Medicaid eligibility to the purchase of qualified long-term care insurance policies. In essence, the way these programs work is that the asset limit for Medicaid eligibility for long-term care coverage, which for most states is $2,000, will instead be the amount of LTCI coverage the applicant owns. For instance, if you have a policy providing three years of coverage at $150 a day, your Medicaid asset limit will be $165,000 instead of $2,000, meaning you can keep $165,000 and still gain Medicaid coverage of your nursing home care once you run through your LTCI coverage.

As with any government program, how this works differs from state to state. For instance, must the nursing home resident deplete the LTCI coverage before applying for

Medicaid? What if her income plus her LTCI benefit are insufficient to meet the cost of care? Must she pay the balance out of savings, potentially defeating the protection of assets the partnership program offers on its face?

Then what happens after she passes away? Will the savings that were protected during the nursing home resident's life be subject to claim for reimbursement by the state after her death? If so, the partnership's incentive to purchase LTCI might be limited. That doesn't mean the client shouldn't purchase a policy, just that she needs to understand the implications in her state.

g. Combining LTCI and Medicaid planning

While in large part people who purchase LTCI and those who plan to qualify for Medicaid coverage of long-term care costs fall into separate groups, this is not always the case. There are many seniors who have some LTCI coverage but not so much that it will pay for all of their care needs. Despite having LTCI, they might be advised to transfer assets to family members or to a trust, keeping enough funds so that along with their income and LTCI benefit they can pay for their care for the subsequent five years. After five years have passed, the Medicaid penalty for having transferred assets will have expired, permitting eligibility for Medicaid coverage if other assets have been spent down to the appropriate limit.

h. The future of LTCI and long-term care public policy

While, as discussed above, LTCI may well be a good solution for individuals to protect against the risk of high long-term care costs, it will not solve the public challenge of covering such costs for the millions of Americans who need care today and the tens of millions of baby boomers who will require care in the coming decades. The simple fact that most Americans cannot afford the premiums means that they will have to rely on government largesse for their care when needed.

To date, that largesse has been reluctantly provided more or less by default through the Medicaid program. While a more generous, planned program could provide better care in settings that better reflect the wishes of seniors, no one on the political stage is suggesting such an initiative. The result could well be a two-tiered system—luxury care at a high price for those who can afford it and good care covered by Medicaid for those who cannot afford private care. If this is our future, then it's even a stronger argument for individuals to purchase LTCI for themselves, if they can afford to do so.

THE JORGENSONS

John and Joyce Jorgenson are both 60 years old and in good health. They both continue to work and together earn $125,000 a year. Their savings total $500,000 and they own a mortgage-free house with a market value of about $400,000. Their income puts them at the very bottom of the top 20 percent of households in the country. Their wealth puts them in the top 10 percent of households, yet a long-term need for care could seriously deplete their assets, leaving the healthy spouse financially strapped and eroding what they could eventually leave to their children. Recognizing this, they look into purchasing LTCI.

According to one calculator, the cost of purchasing two policies paying $200 a day for four years each without inflation riders, would be approximately $5,000 a year. This is a small part of their overall income, but a very large part of their disposable income after paying all their taxes and household expenses. And it will be an even higher percentage once they retire and their income declines. The premiums over the next 20 years would total $100,000, also a large part of their $900,000 net worth. Yet, the potential coverage is almost $600,000. It's a very tough decision.

Ultimately, they decide to roll the dice and forego the insurance. They also resolve to meet with an elder law attorney to learn what steps they might take to protect their assets and to qualify for Medicaid coverage if that ever becomes necessary.

CHAPTER 9

SPECIAL NEEDS

There are two largely separate sides to special needs planning: parents planning for children with disabilities, and adults with disabilities planning to protect their savings or personal injury settlements. While many of the concepts overlap, we will discuss each separately.

1. PARENTS PLANNING FOR CHILDREN WITH SPECIAL NEEDS

All parents must plan to make sure that their minor children will be taken care of in the event of the parents' death or disability. But for parents of children with special needs, these concerns do not end when their children reach adulthood. Depending on the level of disability, their children will rely on their parents for financial and emotional support and guidance throughout the parents' lifetimes and beyond.

Due to advances in medical care, more families are dealing with these issues than ever before. More people with congenital disabilities or injuries are living longer; premature babies are surviving with ailments; and victims of accidents of all sorts are surviving. At the same time, health care has become more complex and more high-tech, and, thus, more expensive. It has become vital to maintain eligibility for Medicaid to cover health care costs, and to qualify for other public programs such as Supplemental Security Income (SSI) and subsidized housing. Additionally, Medicaid often provides crucial coverage of services not covered by traditional health insurance, such as personal care attendants for people with disabilities.

Financial planning, therefore, needs to cover not only the parents' retirement and long-term care needs, but ongoing support for any children with special needs. The challenges include:

- Making sure the funds you leave your child with a disability benefit her without causing her to lose important public benefits.

- Ensuring that the funds are well managed.

- Assuring that your other children are not

overburdened with caring for their disabled sibling, and that any burdens fall relatively evenly among the siblings.

- Trying to be fair in terms of distributing your estate between your disabled child and your other children.

- Making sure there's enough money to meet your disabled child's needs.

- Figuring out how much is "enough" in the first place.

Parents of children with special needs might try to resolve these issues by leaving their estates to their other children, and nothing to the disabled children. They have a number of reasons for this solution: The disabled child shouldn't receive anything because she can't manage money, and it would trigger loss of her benefits. She doesn't need any inheritance because she will be taken care of by the public benefits she receives. The other children will take care of their sister or brother.

We discourage this approach for a number of reasons. First, public benefits programs are usually inadequate. They need to be supplemented with other resources. Second, both public benefits programs and individual circumstances change over time. What's working today might not work tomorrow, and other resources need to be available just in case. Third, relying on one's other children to take care of their sibling could place an undue burden on them and strain relations between them. It makes it unclear whether inherited money belongs to the healthy child to spend as he pleases, or whether he must set it aside for his disabled sister. If one child sets money aside and the others don't, resentments can build that might split the family forever.

a. Special needs trusts

The better answer to many of these questions is the so-called "special needs trust" (or sometimes "supplemental needs trust"). Such trusts fulfill two primary functions: The first is to manage funds for someone who might not be able to do so himself due to disability. The second is to preserve the beneficiary's eligibility for public benefits, whether that be Medicaid, SSI, subsidized housing, or any other program. These trusts come into play in a multitude of situations, including parents or grandparents planning for a disabled child, a disabled individual coming into an inheritance or winning or settling a personal injury claim, or one spouse planning for a disabled spouse.

In essence, a special needs trust is a discretionary trust, permitting the trustee to use the trust funds as it deems appropriate for the beneficiary. The beneficiary has no right to demand payment of trust funds or to depend on it for support. It's this wording that assures that the trust funds will not be counted in determining the beneficiary's eligibility for public benefits. They are also not subject to claims, either by creditors of the beneficiary or by an ex-spouse in the event of a divorce. Depending on the source of the funds and whether the parents have particular tax or other planning goals, the exact terms of the trust will be tailored to meet those objectives.

All of this discussion assumes that the money, investments or real estate funding the trust are coming from the parents or grandparents. These are sometimes called "third-party" trusts because the donor and the beneficiary are not the same person. The rules of public benefits programs are much more strict if the applicant for coverage has a trust funded with his own money, sometimes referred to as "first-party" trusts. We will discuss these below under Personal Injury Settlements.

b. Choice of trustee

Often, choosing a trustee is the most difficult part of planning for a child with special needs. Since the individual with special needs will likely need the trust to last for her lifetime and will have no claim to the funds except as decided upon by the trustees, the selection of trustee or trustees is especially important.

Qualities of good trustees for a special needs trust include:

- the ability to make sound financial decisions and to invest and properly report trust transactions;
- an understanding of the rules around eligibility for

public benefits, or a willingness to learn and consult with appropriate experts;

- availability and the time to spend to perform the duties needed;
- honesty and integrity; and
- emotional attachment to the individual.

The trustee of a supplemental needs trust must be able to fulfill all of the normal functions of a trustee (such as accounting, managing investments, preparing tax returns and distributing funds) and also meet the needs of the special beneficiary. The latter can include an understanding of various public benefits programs, sensitivity to the beneficiary's particular style of communication, and knowledge of services that might be available. Often family members have the necessary emotional attachment, but don't have the experience, expertise or available time to handle the financial and legal aspects of serving as trustee. Professionals, such as lawyers and bank trustees, have the financial and legal experience necessary, but might not know the beneficiary well or be equipped to respond to the needs of a beneficiary who might be more demanding than their typical client.

There are a number of possible solutions available. Often parents choose to appoint co-trustees—a bank or law firm as a professional trustee along with another child as a family trustee. Working together, they can provide the necessary resources and experience to meet the needs of the child with special needs. Unfortunately, in many cases such a combination is not available. Professional trustees generally require a minimum amount of funds in the trust, usually at least $500,000. Otherwise their fees become unreasonable in relation to the size of the trust. In other situations, there is no appropriate family member to appoint as co-trustee.

Where the size of the trust is insufficient to justify hiring a professional trustee, two solutions are possible. The first is simply to have a family member trustee who would hire accountants, attorneys and investment advisors as needed to help with administering the trust. The second is to use a pooled trust managed by a nonprofit organization. These trusts generally provide the added benefit of the advocacy group providing information about the programs and benefits available in the community. (For a directory of pooled trusts nationwide, go to http://www.specialneedsanswers.com/resources/directory_of_pooled_trusts.asp.)

Where no appropriate family member is available to serve as co-trustee, the parent may direct the professional trustee to consult with named individuals who know and care for the child with special needs. These could be family members who are not appropriate trustees, but who can serve in an advisory role. Or they may be social workers or others who have both personal and professional knowledge of the beneficiary and the resources available for her care. This role may be formalized in the trust document as a "Care Committee."

c. Trust protectors

Often special needs trusts appoint one or more trust protectors who have the power to hire and fire trustees, appoint a successor trustee if the current trustee resigns or becomes incapacitated, review trust accounts and make limited amendments to the trust. This can be a good role for family members or friends who you trust, but who don't have the time available, live too far away, or are otherwise inappropriate to serve as trustee.

d. Funding the trust

A number of issues arise with respect to the question of how much to put into the trust. First, how much will the child with special needs require over her life? Second, should you leave the same portion of your estate to all of your children, no matter their need? Third, how will you assure that there's enough money to meet everyone's needs?

The first question is a difficult one. It depends on what assumptions you make about your child's needs and the availability of other resources to fulfill those needs. Financial planners who work in this field can help make projections to assist with this determination. But in all cases it's better to err on the side of more money rather than less. You can't be certain current programs will continue. And you have to factor in paying for services, such as case management, that the parents provide free-of-charge every day.

If these assumptions mean that the child with special needs will require a large percentage of your estate, how will his siblings feel if they receive less than their pro rata (proportional) share? After all, the estate might already be smaller than it would be otherwise due to the time and money spent providing for the child with special needs. And the other children might feel they have received less parental attention growing up than if they had not had a sibling with special needs.

One solution to the question of fairness and to the challenge of assuring that there are enough funds is life insurance. You can divide your estate equally among your children, but supplement the amount going to the special needs trust with life insurance. Unlike life insurance purchased to take care of minor children, which may be term insurance, insurance to fund a special needs trust should be permanent—whole or universal. It often makes sense to lower the premiums through a second-to-die policy that insures both parents but only pays a benefit upon the death of the second parent.

2. PERSONAL INJURY SETTLEMENTS AND OTHER INFLUXES OF FUNDS

People with disabilities can receive substantial funds whether due to settling a personal injury lawsuit or receiving an inheritance. And some people become disabled later in life after they have accumulated savings. In most cases, these individuals do not have enough funds to support themselves indefinitely and must depend on public benefits for their basic support. It's not unusual for newfound money to disrupt a carefully constructed system of support that depends on eligibility for various public benefits programs. Either way, preserving eligibility for benefits can be vital for the individual with a disability. In addition, if the disability is cognitive in nature, the beneficiary might not be able to handle the funds or might be vulnerable to financial abuse by others.

As with parents planning for their children, trusts can provide a solution. However, the trusts must be different. For the property and income in these so-called "self-settled" trusts not to be taken into account in determining the beneficiary's eligibility for benefits, they must meet some specific requirements set out in federal law at 42 USC § 1396p(d)(4)(A) and (d)(4)(C). As a result, these are often referred to as "(d)(4)(A)" and "(d)(4)(C)" trusts. The main difference between the two is that (d)(4)(A) trusts are individual trusts for each beneficiary and (d)(4)(C) trusts are managed for many beneficiaries by nonprofit organizations. But there are also some specific differences.

a. (d)(4)(A) trusts

Medicaid and SSI's treatment of trusts parallels the way that trust donors and beneficiaries are treated by creditors under traditional trust law. Under the common law, which goes back many centuries, a parent could create a so-called "spendthrift" trust for the benefit of a child and it would not be subject to claim by the child's creditors. But no one could escape her debts by transferring funds into trust for her own benefit. (As is discussed below in the chapter on Asset Protection, a number of states in recent years have begun to change the common law and to permit the creation of self-settled asset protection trusts.) Similarly, as we have discussed above, public benefits programs do not count trust funds as available to the applicant if the trust was created by a third party and the trustee has no obligation to make distributions to the beneficiary—in other words, if any distributions are entirely discretionary. On the other hand, if the trust was created and funded by the applicant for public benefits, the funds are considered available to the extent the trustee may distribute them to the applicant or spend them on her behalf.

Fortunately, Congress carved out two exceptions to this rule, in essence, saying that it would permit disabled individuals to shelter certain assets in trust under limited conditions, the primary one being that any funds left in the trust at the beneficiary's death be used to pay back the state for Medicaid costs (but not SSI benefits) paid out on the beneficiary's behalf during her life. This is why the trusts are sometimes called "payback" trusts.

Here are the requirements necessary for an individual (d)(4)(A) trust:

- **Sole benefit.** The trust must be for the sole benefit of the applicant for Medicaid or SSI. No one else can be named except as a potential remainder beneficiary to receive funds remaining after the state is reimbursed.

- **Disabled individual.** The beneficiary must be sufficiently disabled to qualify for SSI or SSDI benefits. Usually, the beneficiary is receiving these benefits already, so establishing disability is not an issue. But sometimes the individual has not applied for such benefits, in which case the state Medicaid agency should have its own procedure for establishing disability.

- **Under the age of 65.** The beneficiary must be under 65 when the trust is created and funded, but the trust still works after she is over that age.

- **Payback.** As is discussed above, the trust must provide that after the beneficiary's death, any remaining funds be used to reimburse the state (or states) for its Medicaid expenses paid out on the beneficiary's behalf.

- **Parent, grandparent, court, individual or guardian.** For unknown reasons, in enacting this safe harbor, Congress did not permit disabled beneficiaries to create these trusts for themselves. They had to be created by a parent, grandparent, court or guardian, which was often problematic. Fortunately, after a couple of decades of lobbying, Congress changed the law so disabled individuals can now create their own (d)(4)(A) trusts.

From my point of view, the payback requirement of (d)(4)(A) trusts is a very reasonable tradeoff. It permits individuals to receive public benefits but still retain funds to pay for the many things that meager SSI or SSDI payments won't cover. In most cases, little or nothing is left in these trusts when the beneficiary passes away, so the payback doesn't occur in any case. In addition, through planning even the small likelihood of payback can be reduced. For instance, if a disabled individual has both a (d)(4)(A) trust and a third-party special needs trust left by parents, the trustees would be advised to spend the funds in the (d)(4)(A) trust first and hold off on spending funds in the trust left by the parents because it should not include a payback provision. (We've seen payback provisions mistakenly included in third-party trusts. These should be avoided and fixed where they're found.) Once the funds in the (d)(4)(A) trust have been depleted, then the trustees can begin using the third-party special needs trust.

Often when teenagers with special needs approach age 18, their parents realize that funds they might have from family gifts or other sources will make them ineligible for SSI and Medicaid benefits, which they would otherwise be eligible for. These funds, if they can't be quickly spent down, can be sheltered in a (d)(4)(A) trust or ABLE account (described below).

b. (d)(4)(C) trusts

"Pooled disability" or (d)(4)(C) trusts are quite similar to (d)(4)(A) trusts, but also different in significant ways. They must be managed by a nonprofit organization for the benefit of many individuals with disabilities. Some actually pool the funds in a single investment account, similar to a mutual fund, while others maintain separate accounts for each of the beneficiaries. The Academy of Special Needs Planners provides a comprehensive directory of (d)(4)(C) trusts on its website at: http://specialneedsanswers.com/pooled-trust.

Here are some of the parallels and differences between (d)(4)(A) and (d)(4)(C) trusts:

- **Sole benefit.** This is the same. The trust must be for the sole benefit of the applicant for Medicaid or SSI.
- **Disabled individual.** Again, this is the same. The beneficiary must be disabled as required to qualify for SSI or SSDI benefits.

- **Age of 65.** This can get a bit complicated. As with (d)(4)(A) trusts, there's no age restriction on being a beneficiary of a (d)(4)(C) trust. However, due to an inconsistency in the Medicaid and SSI rules between their trust and their transfer rules, some states permit funding (d)(4)(C) trusts after age 65 and some do not. In states that permit post-65 transfers, such as Massachusetts where I practice, (d)(4)(C) trusts have become useful tools in long-term care planning.

- **Payback.** Pooled disability trusts have a payback requirement like (d)(4)(A) trusts, but they also have an exception that permits the nonprofit to retain some or all of the funds rather than pay them to the state. Pooled trusts vary greatly in how much they retain, from zero to 100%. Of course, the more they retain, the less will go to the state and less will be potentially available to remainder beneficiaries after the state is reimbursed. But it can be a way of supporting the functions of the nonprofit organization. Some states (in violation of federal law, in my opinion) have restricted the percentage that the nonprofit may keep.

- **Parent, grandparent, court, individual or guardian.** When it created the (d)(4)(C) trust safe harbor, Congress permitted individuals, as well as parents, grandparents, courts and guardians, to create their own accounts. Why they permitted individuals to create (d)(4)(C) trusts and not (d)(4)(A) trusts is a conundrum within an enigma, but now the rules are the same for both types of trust.

So, which should you use: a (d)(4)(A) or a (d)(4)(C) trust? Of course, it depends. It depends in large part on whether you have a reliable individual to serve as trustee or sufficient funds to shelter to justify retaining a professional trustee. It can also depend on the availability of a well-run (d)(4)(C) trust in your area. Pooled disability trusts in general provide the advantage of professional management as well as the added expertise about local programs for individuals with disabilities, an expertise which most individuals and professional trustees lack. The nonprofit trustees can be more or less rigid and bureaucratic in how they process and approve or disapprove of requests for distributions. And their costs can vary. They are usually higher than the standard 1% annual trustee's fee many professional trustees charge, in large part because they are usually managing smaller accounts and the public benefits rules require additional work. A local special needs planning attorney or financial planner can usually advise you on local experience with the various pooled trust options. (Go to http://specialneedsanswers.com/special-needs-planner to find one in your region.)

3. MEDICAID AND SSI INCOME RULES AND TRUST DISTRIBUTIONS

All of the discussion above involves planning to shelter assets (whether inherited, earned or won as a personal injury settlement or judgment), so they won't be counted in determining the beneficiary's eligibility for public benefits. Unfortunately, while this is sufficient for planning purposes, it is insufficient for purposes of trust administration. This is because public benefits programs also have income restrictions that can wreak havoc for both Medicaid and SSI purposes. I am not going to address the Medicaid rules for two reasons. First, for those people getting SSI, Medicaid is an automatic additional benefit. Second, the Medicaid rules are too complicated and too variable from state to state to cover here. Rules differ depending on whether the beneficiary is living in a nursing home or in the community and, if in the community, which of potentially up to six Medicaid programs the individual is seeking. They also can differ depending on the beneficiary's age. So, anyone seeking information on the Medicaid eligibility rules outside of SSI needs to seek local advice.

SSI is simpler in large part because it's a federal program and the same rules should apply nationwide. In some instances, however, local Social Security Administration (SSA) offices come up with different interpretations of the rules, but this is not the norm. In essence, under SSI every dollar of income above $20 a month paid directly to the SSI beneficiary is offset by a one dollar decrease in SSI benefits. So special needs trusts should never make distributions directly to beneficiaries receiving SSI. Payments made on behalf of the beneficiary are not counted, with two important exceptions: Payments for food or housing are considered to be in-kind income (thus, triggering an offset of one dollar of SSI for every dollar of value received). Fortunately, there's a cap on the offset of $277 a month (in 2019). So, even if a trust is paying rent of $1,500 a month for an SSI beneficiary, he will receive all but $277 of his monthly SSI benefit, a reasonable tradeoff to be able to live in a decent place.

This brings up a problem with the drafting of some special needs trusts that contain language restricting the trustee's ability to make distributions that might diminish eligibility for public benefits. Isn't it better to lose some benefits if the upside—in terms of lifestyle—far exceeds the value of the benefit foregone? In some instances, it might even be reasonable to give up SSI and its stringent restrictions altogether, especially in those states that permit Medicaid qualification separate from SSI eligibility.

These rules apply no matter where the income comes from, whether from a special needs trust or directly from parents or other relatives. The beneficiary has the obligation of reporting all income he receives.

Often paying for goods and services for SSI beneficiaries can be cumbersome. The trust may pay for haircuts and entertainment, but can't pay the funds directly to the beneficiary. In most instances, the trustee can't accompany the beneficiary to every appointment. One solution is to give the beneficiary a limited credit card that may be used up to a specified monthly dollar limit and cannot be used to pay for food items. A company called TrueLink (www.truelink.com) offers such a credit card with online monitoring and controls. The new ABLE accounts may be another good solution. (See the discussion below.)

Finally, every special needs trustee needs to know about the POMS. The Social Security Administration's Program Operations Manual System (https://secure.ssa.gov/poms. nsf/home!readform), which tells SSA workers in great detail how to decide various issues, including those around trust distributions.

4. SUBSIDIZED HOUSING

As if these rules weren't complicated enough, the Department of Housing and Urban Development (HUD) has its own trust rules for people living in subsidized housing under Section 8. Unlike SSI, which does not count trust distributions made on the beneficiary's behalf—rather than directly to the beneficiary—to be income (except for those made for housing and food), the HUD regulations deem all regular payments from trusts paid on the beneficiary's behalf to be income. As examples, this could include cable television charges, tuition payments, or health insurance premiums. These rules are interpreted differently by each local housing authority and at least one has gone so far as to deem fees paid to the trustee as income to the beneficiary. Under the HUD rules, the Section 8 subsidy is reduced by roughly one dollar for every three dollars of income.

Since the rules are interpreted differently by each housing authority, our practice is to call the local housing authority on behalf of our clients to determine what it treats as recurring income as opposed to intermittent payments that are not penalized. It's also important to make certain that the beneficiary is indeed receiving Section 8. Some subsidized housing programs are financed under state or city programs that have not adopted the same deeming rules.

An important recent case, *Decambre v. Brookline Housing Authority*, has both clarified and complicated the situation significantly. The ruling created a distinction between self-settled trusts, including (d)(4)(A) and (C) trusts, and third-party trusts funded by other people. Under *Decambre*, housing authorities are directed not to count distributions from self-settled trusts because essentially the funds already belong to the housing resident. This greatly frees up the ability to use these trusts on a regular basis for Section 8 beneficiaries.

It's complicated because now the rules for trusts with respect to Section 8 are almost the opposite of those for Medcaid and SSI, where trusts created by third parties are treated more liberally and those created and funded by the beneficiary are more restrictive.

5. ABLE ACCOUNTS

In 2014, Congress passed the much-anticipated Achieving a Better Life Experience (ABLE) Act to permit the creation of savings and investment accounts for people receiving public benefits, and to avoid the need for more restrictive special needs trusts as discussed above. In the process they gutted the bill, making the resulting accounts much less useful as a substitute for special needs trusts than was intended. One restriction is that they're only available to individuals who became disabled before age 26. However, the accounts can still be very useful for people who qualify by easing the $2,000 asset limit for SSI and Medicaid and by simplifying the administration of special needs trusts.

ABLE accounts were intended to be similar to 529 accounts through which parents and grandparents can set aside tax-preferred funds to pay for higher education for their children and grandchildren. The thought was to provide a similar benefit to children and grandchildren who will probably never go to college. But the following limitations restrict their use for this purpose:

- They may be funded with only $15,000 a year. This is the amount of the gift tax exclusion discussed above under estate taxes, but the gift tax rules permit anyone to receive $15,000 from any number of people every year. ABLE accounts may only receive this amount from all sources during a calendar year. And beneficiaries are limited to a single ABLE account.

- The accounts will only shelter up to $100,000. If the account holds more than $100,000, the Social Security Administration will disqualify the owner from SSI.

These two rules mean that no one can shelter more than $15,000 in an ABLE account in one year. So, no one can use these instead of a special needs trust as part of an estate plan unless they are only leaving their child $15,000. An individual who comes into money as the result of an inheritance or personal injury lawsuit cannot use these accounts unless they have received less than $15,000. A person turning 18 and wanting to qualify for benefits can only use an ABLE account if she has a small sum to shelter.

All of that said, ABLE accounts are very useful as a tool to loosen the rigid SSI limits on income and assets. SSI and many Medicaid programs limit beneficiaries' countable assets to $2,000. This figure has not been changed since 1989 and is extremely restrictive. ABLE accounts offer a safety hatch, permitting beneficiaries to have more than $2,000, even up to $100,000 if funded over time, that they can use as needed. Their use of the funds is not considered to be income since they already own the accounts. In addition, the SSA has ruled that contributions to ABLE accounts also will not be considered income for SSI eligibility purposes. This means that a trustee could deposit money into an ABLE account for a beneficiary, perhaps as much as $1,000 a month, that the beneficiary can then use freely for his support. This avoids burdensome work-arounds, such as paying off the beneficiary's credit card or creating accounts at each of the vendors the beneficiary is likely to use during a month.

Two organizations sponsor websites with information about ABLE accounts: the Academy of Special Needs Planners at www.specialneedsanswers.com/able-accounts and the ABLE National Resource Center at www.ablenrc.org.

6. GUARDIANSHIP AND CONSERVATORSHIP

When children with special needs reach age 18, their parents are no longer automatically their legal guardians and conservators. They might suddenly find that doctors and other health care professionals will no longer talk with them because doing so would violate the child's right to medical privacy. Or that school personnel will go around the parents to talk directly with the child about his educational plan, perhaps seeking to modify the plan and remove necessary supports. Parents then need to make a decision about whether to seek court appointment as guardian and conservator. We recommend that they pause to consider the pros and cons rather than automatically following the (often knee-jerk) advice to seek such appointments.

Guardianships and conservatorships not only give the parents the right to step in and make decisions for their child—they also take those legal rights away from the child. In most states, the courts will entertain a petition for a limited appointment that only takes away certain rights and permits the child to retain others, but this ability to tailor the appointment is in fact rarely used. In addition, these appointments, whether limited or comprehensive (often referred to as "plenary") can be costly and impose cumbersome reporting and preapproval requirements.

In order to get these appointments, parents have to establish their child's legal incapacity. In most states, guardianship and conservatorship have been separated. Guardianship is the court appointment of someone to make personal and health care decisions for another, such as what treatment to take and where the individual will live. Conservatorship involves the appointment of a fiduciary to make legal and financial decisions, such as how funds will be invested or spent and whether to sign contracts. (If the child has no money, in most instances a conservatorship is not necessary.) Each state has its own reporting requirements and rules on what decisions a conservator or guardian may make on her own and for which she must seek court approval. For instance, the state might or might not require approval prior to placing an individual under guardianship in a long-term care facility or prior to transferring the assets of a person under conservatorship into trust.

In some cases, the need for guardianship and conservatorship is obvious and the appointments are necessary to protect the child. In many others, it's not so clear. It might be more appropriate to ask the child to execute a durable power of attorney and health care proxy, or to seek just guardianship or just conservatorship, but not both. This allows the child to retain certain legal rights and a sense of autonomy while giving the parent the ability to step in and make crucial decisions as necessary. It doesn't have to be all one way or the other. Sometimes parents and their children with special needs can share these roles and responsibilities.

THE JORGENSONS

The Jorgensons learn that Jack's 7-year-old son, Austin, has been diagnosed as having moderate autism. Jack and his husband are doing everything they can to enhance Austin's functioning, but they fear that he will never be able to live independently. The Jorgensons ask how they can help out. Jack and his husband, Sam, explain that they have been advised to set up a special needs trust for Austin's benefit and to buy a significant life insurance policy to fund it. But at this stage in their careers they don't have any extra cash laying around to pay lawyers or insurance premiums. This is especially true because Sam has cut back to working part time due to the demands of caring for Austin.

The Jorgensons offer to pay the attorneys' fees to set up the special needs trust, along with the rest of Jack and Sam's estate plan, and to pay the premiums for their life insurance. They pay for two second-to-die policies, both a larger term policy and a smaller whole life one. The premiums for the term policy are actually quite reasonable, but they are fixed for just 20 years. The whole life premiums are quite a bit more expensive, but the policy will have a growing cash value and will be there for Austin whenever Jack and Sam both pass away.

Jack and Sam feel relieved that this necessary task and expense are no longer hanging over their heads and that Austin (and his sister) will be taken care of if anything happens to them. The insurance will also permit Jack and Sam to split their estate evenly between Austin and his sister, knowing that Austin's more extensive needs will be taken care of by the insurance. Similarly, the Jorgensons will keep their estate plan as it is, split evenly among their children, since they will have helped Austin with his special circumstances during their lives.

CHAPTER 10

SECOND MARRIAGES OR RELATIONSHIPS AND NON-TRADITIONAL FAMILIES

Life can get complicated, especially as people live longer and have more opportunities for relationships. Even if the Ozzie and Harriet model of a single happy marriage producing healthy children and lasting a lifetime was never as close to universal as advertised, it's even less prevalent today. Often referred to as "blended" families, today's relationships can include children from prior marriages or relationships on one or both sides. In these instances, planning becomes more important than ever since the rules of intestacy—the rules that apply when a decedent dies without an estate plan—assume a more traditional family structure. In addition, we have often seen unintended results when the person who dies hasn't updated beneficiary designations, with life insurance and retirement accounts passing to an ex-spouse or ex-lover.

EXAMPLE
HOW COMPLICATED CAN FAMILIES GET?

We met with a man to talk about planning for his mother who was beginning to show signs of dementia. Then we began talking about his own planning. Roger (not his real name) was 60 years old and never married, but more or less lived with his longtime girlfriend—who had another place as well. He had no children. He had one brother and three sisters, but one of his sisters passed away a few years earlier. He was closest with his brother who lived in one of the three apartments in Roger's triple-decker (a common type of housing in Boston with three floors, each of which is a separate apartment). One sister was married without children and lived in San Diego. The other lived close by, but they had a troubled relationship. She is a single mother of two sons who are about 20 years apart in age.

Roger's sister who passed away had adopted a young boy who she had befriended when he lived with his grandmother. When the grandmother died,

---

Roger's sister adopted him. After the sister died, Roger's brother adopted the child and at the time we met he lived in Roger's triple-decker. By the time he reached age 7 this young boy had lost his mother, his grandmother and his adopted mother. Roger wanted to provide for him but also for his other nephews whose lives were not so stable either. He also felt responsible for his mother, brother and girlfriend (who, after him, is the most financially stable member of the extended family).

At the end of this initial meeting, Roger mentioned his father, who had divorced his mother and remarried long ago, and had additional children with his second wife. Without an estate plan, these half sisters and brothers of Roger would have an equal claim on his estate as his full brother, sisters and nephews. Since this family complex may be difficult to picture, here's a diagram.

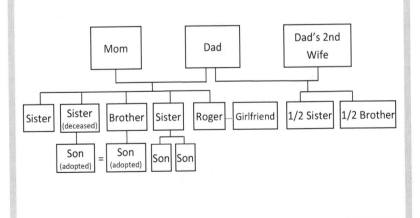

People do the craziest things. They:

- Get divorced.

- Get remarried after divorce (remarriage being the triumph of hope over experience?).

- Have children outside of marriage, with or without a committed partner.

- Have children with more than one partner.

- Remarry or enter committed relationships after the death of a spouse.

And they do all of these things in their 70s and 80s (except perhaps having children).

Fewer people of all ages are getting married. Between 2000 and 2010, while the U.S. population grew by almost 10 percent, the number of married households grew by less than 4 percent and the number of unmarried couple households by more than 40%. The percentage of the population getting married each year dropped from 0.82 percent in 2000 to 0.68 percent in 2012. While the law confers certain rights on spouses, and widows and widowers of deceased spouses, unmarried partners enjoy few of these rights. This means that estate planning is even more important for unmarried than for married couples, and with fewer marriages more people need to engage in such planning than ever before.

1. ISSUES TO CONSIDER

If any of these situations applies to you, then there's a good chance that plain vanilla estate planning documents and the rules of intestacy (see page 77) won't achieve the results you would desire. As careful estate planning becomes critical, here are some questions you need to consider, either with your partner or on your own. It's best that you ultimately answer them together so that you can work through any disagreements and avoid misunderstandings.

- If you have children from different relationships, do you want them all to be treated equally?

- If your current partner (here, this term applies to spouses as well as "significant others") has children who are not yours, do you want them to receive a portion of your estate? If so, how much?

- Do you want to support your partner if you pass away before her?

- Do you want to make sure that what you leave for your partner ultimately passes to your children? Or equally among her children and yours? Or do you want to leave it up to your partner to decide, if she survives you?

- Do you care if what you leave your partner subsequently goes to whomever she marries after you pass away?

Depending on how you answer these questions, you might want to use a trust in your estate plan and might want to enter into a prenuptial or other agreement with your partner. Through a trust you can set aside funds to support your partner during her life, but make sure that whatever is left when she passes away ultimately goes to the beneficiaries you choose. You will need to choose an impartial trustee and be clear about spending expectations. For instance, do you want to pay only for your partner's housing or for anything she might ultimately need? Do you want to give the trustee the option of helping your children and grandchildren during your partner's life or only after her death?

2. CREATING A PLAN

You should also consider a prenuptial, a postnuptial or, if you're not married, a partnership agreement. But first, make sure that you have a full discussion of expectations, both during life and after death. Who is going to pay for what? What support should either of you expect after the other passes away? Simply making assumptions or letting come what comes can lead to conflict and undesirable results. In almost all circumstances, one of you will die before the other. If you leave everything to your children, it could leave your partner high and dry, perhaps having to move at the same time she is grieving your loss. If you leave everything to your partner, even if she intends to share equally with your children at her death, this might not occur if she spends everything down paying for long-term care, loses contact with your children over time, or develops a stronger allegiance to her own children or to a new partner. She might change her plan. Or, if she does fall ill or become demented, her own children might step in to take care of her and take steps to protect her assets from the costs of long-term care, favoring themselves in the process.

In making any of these plans, the more transparency you have with your partner and your children the better.

CASE STUDY
LACK OF TRANSPARENCY
—WHAT CAN GO WRONG?

Our clients, "Paul" and "Georgina," were a committed couple in their early 60s who were not married, but planned to live together indefinitely. Each of them had two children from prior marriages. Both were still working full time. They executed trusts through which they would leave their own property in trust for the survivor of the two, with whatever was left in trust when the survivor died to be split equally among the four children. They were each co-trustees of each other's trust.

Tragically, Paul died soon after from a massive heart attack. Unfortunately, his children for some reason thought he was much wealthier than he was and that Georgina was holding out on them. Under their father's trust, they had the right to change trustees. We included that in the document to protect them in case the surviving partner began mismanaging the trust. In retrospect, this was a mistake. They removed Georgina and named an independent attorney as trustee. This worked terribly. This new trustee made no contact with Georgina and failed to take necessary steps regarding a retirement plan payable to the trust with adverse tax consequences. He also didn't make the required distributions of income from the trust to Georgina.

Once Paul's children became convinced that the money they thought Paul had didn't exist, they and their attorney simply stopped responding. Ultimately, we had to bring a lawsuit to remove the new trustee in order to bring everyone to the table and resolve the matter. While the new trustee had to pay some of the damages that occurred due to his lack of attention to his responsibilities, what he paid did not approach Georgina's out-of-pocket costs nor compensate her for the stress she went through. Not surprisingly, she ultimately changed her own estate plan so that her assets will ultimately go only to her children.

If Paul's children had had a better understanding of his estate and his plans, they might have been more likely to have accepted it. Could the plan have been different? Perhaps. Paul could have given his children something immediately to keep them happy, rather than having to wait for Georgina's death to get anything. Was it a mistake to give Paul's children the power to change trustees? In retrospect, yes. But what if Georgina failed to send them annual accounts over the years or began to raid the trust or became demented? Simply changing trustees could prevent an expensive and stressful action in court. In short, this plan did not achieve all of the results Paul and Georgina were seeking, but it did achieve a lot of them. After the litigation ended and Georgina paid off Paul's children with a small settlement, she had the financial security that Paul had intended. With no plan in place, his assets would have gone to his children who clearly would not have had Georgina's interests at heart.

3. WHAT ABOUT MARRIAGE?

There are legal and financial issues to consider in deciding whether to get married, in addition to religious, personal and social ones. Marriage confers legal rights to support and can affect eligibility for long-term care benefits under Medicaid and SSI. Most of these legal and financial rights can be waived in a prenuptial agreement, but the agreement can be challenged if there was not full financial disclosure between the prospective spouses. We would advise never getting married for a second time without consulting legal counsel to make sure that both of you are on the same page and you and your families are protected. But we also do not advise avoiding marriage just because you're worried about the legal and financial consequences. Through careful planning you can protect your own interests as well as those of your partner and your respective children, regardless of whether you ultimately decide to tie the knot.

THE JORGENSONS

Unfortunately, after 30 rocky years of marriage, the Jorgensons decide that it's time to go their separate ways. Of course, two separately can't live as cheaply as two together. After they split their assets more or less equally, they are as follows:

	JOHN	JOYCE
Income (annual)		
	$75,000	$50,000

Savings and Investments

	JOHN	JOYCE
Checking	$10,000	$5,000
Savings	$15,000	$20,000
Investments	$35,000	$100,000
IRA	$200,000	$125,000
Total	$260,000	$250,000
Condominium	$200,000	$200,000

John agrees to pay Joyce alimony of $1,000 a month for 10 years. They both drop their life insurance policies and let Jack and Sam know that they can no longer continue to pay the premiums for the life insurance they had purchased to fund Austin's special needs trust. Both John and Joyce expect to keep working for at least another 10 years, until they're both 70 and can get their full Social Security retirement benefits.

Not too long after the divorce is finalized both John and Joyce meet new partners and eventually move in with them. John's new partner, Martha, has three children of her own and has financial resources more or less equivalent to John's. Joyce's new partner, Georgina, has no children and far greater resources than Joyce. (Children are expensive.) But she is close to various nieces and nephews.

John and Martha decide not to get married and to keep their finances separate, sharing a single checking account to cover living and housing expenses. They have moved into a new, larger condominium that is in joint names, which means that it will pass to the survivor of the two of them. So they also update their wills to direct that when the second passes away, it will be sold and the proceeds split among all six of their children. Their lawyer advises them that this is risky since the surviving partner could always change his or her will or sell the condo and commingle the proceeds with his or her other funds so that they pass exclusively to his or her children. He recommends that instead they put the condominium into a trust that would make sure that the proceeds ultimately will be split six ways. John and Martha, however, reject this option, being put off by the complexity of the trust and the higher legal fees a trust involves. They trust one another and prefer to take their chances.

Joyce and Georgina, on the other hand, do get married. But they enter into a prenuptial agreement that provides that in the event of divorce they will each leave with what they brought into the marriage and they keep their finances separate. Joyce's estate plan continues to give her assets to her children. Georgina's leaves her assets in trust for Joyce with the remainder at her death split between Joyce's children and Georgina's nieces and nephews. They both purchase long-term care insurance.

CHAPTER 11

RETIREMENT PLANS

The rules around retirement plans are much too complicated. Back in the day, your parents or grandparents might have worked for the same company and upon retirement received a pension payable until they and their spouse had both passed away. Few, other than most public employees, have this benefit today. Instead, you probably have a 401(k) or 403(b) plan, which upon retirement you may convert to an individual retirement plan (IRA). While your employer (or employers over the years) may contribute to your plan, it's mostly up to you how much you save, how you invest your savings and how much and when you withdraw your nest egg. Unlike a pension, which will last you the rest of your life no matter how long you live, your decisions around your retirement plan can be crucial. You could be left high and dry if, for example, you run out of funds at age 85 but live to 95.

This chapter will not cover financial planning and will provide no advice about how much to invest, how to invest it or when to retire. Instead, it will describe the rules around beneficiary designations, the options you have, and how you can maximize the benefit of your retirement plans for your heirs.

Fortunately, the rules for the most part are the same for 401(k) and 403(b) accounts and IRAs, so we do not have to distinguish between them. They are somewhat different for Roth IRAs. To give you my two-cents worth, while Roth IRAs can be advantageous for some taxpayers, they should never have been created. They further complicate the financial life of taxpayers. Few people use them, though many feel they need to consider them. And some wealthy people have used them to avoid taxes on huge investment gains in a way that is unavailable to the average taxpayer. So, since you probably don't have much money in Roth IRAs, we are not going to clutter up this book with a discussion of how they work.

1. THE BASIC RULES

There are two main benefits to retirement plans: First, that you are not taxed on earnings you divert to the retirement plan, but instead are taxed as you withdraw the funds, presumably in retirement. Second, while the funds are invested they grow free of capital gains and income taxes. Presumably, when you withdraw funds during retirement you will be in a lower tax bracket than when you were working and saving up. In addition, over time your retirement investments should grow faster than your other investments since you have the opportunity to reinvest all of your investment earnings. Here's how that works: If your IRA earns $1,000 in interest and dividends this year, you can reinvest all of it for further earnings next year. In contrast, if your non-retirement plan account earns $1,000 this year, you'll have to pay taxes on those earnings. If, for instance, your combined marginal federal and state income tax rate is 33%, you'll only have $667 to invest next year. Over decades this can add up significantly.

Since the idea of retirement plans is that you will use the funds to finance your retirement, the rules penalize you both for early withdrawal (before retirement) and for not withdrawing funds during retirement. With some exceptions, if you withdraw retirement plan funds before age 59 ½, you must pay a 10% excise tax on the amount withdrawn in addition to the withdrawal being treated as taxable income. On the other end, you must begin taking withdrawals by April 1st of the year following the calendar year in which you turn 70 ½. The amount you must withdraw is figured by dividing the total of all of your retirement accounts on December 31st of the prior year by your life expectancy (as provided on the IRS table reprinted below). If, for instance, you were still 70 years old as of the end of the prior year, the divisor is 17. If you had $350,000 in your retirement accounts as of December 31st, your minimum distribution would be $20,588 ($350,000 ÷ 17 = $20,588). The divisor goes down with your life expectancy each year which means that the percentage you must withdraw goes up. For instance, if you were 85 years old at the end of the prior year, your divisor would be 7.6, meaning that if you still had $350,000 in retirement funds you would have to take out a minimum distribution of at least $46,053 ($350,000 ÷ 7.6 = $46,053).

Don't miss your required minimum distribution! The penalty is a whopping 50% of what you should have withdrawn. It's possible to ask the IRS for a waiver if this occurred due to a "reasonable error," but don't put yourself in a position of having to ask for forgiveness. Make the calculation and make the withdrawal. Of course, you can always take out more, but then you would lose the tax benefits of continuing to invest the funds tax free and may be at risk of running out funds before you run out of life.

TABLE I
(SINGLE LIFE EXPECTANCY)
(FOR USE BY BENEFICIARIES)

AGE	LIFE EXPECTANCY	AGE	LIFE EXPECTANCY
56	28.7	84	8.1
57	27.9	85	7.6
58	27.0	86	7.1
59	26.1	87	6.7
60	25.2	88	6.3
61	24.4	89	5.9
62	23.5	90	5.5
63	22.7	91	5.2
64	21.8	92	4.9
65	21.0	93	4.6
66	20.2	94	4.3
67	19.4	95	4.1
68	18.6	96	3.8
69	17.8	97	3.6
70	17.0	98	3.4
71	16.3	99	3.1
72	15.5	100	2.9
73	14.8	101	2.7
74	14.1	102	2.5
75	13.4	103	2.3
76	12.7	104	2.1
77	12.1	105	1.9
78	11.4	106	1.7

79	10.8	107	1.5
80	10.2	108	1.4
81	9.7	109	1.2
82	9.1	110	1.1
83	8.6	111 and over	1.0

The same table applies to everyone, no matter their gender or medical condition, with one exception. If you are married and your spouse is more than 10 years younger than you, and you name him as your beneficiary, you can use the IRS Joint Life and Last Survivor table that takes into account both spouse's ages. As an example of how this works, if at the end of last year you were 70 years old and your spouse was 59, the divisor for this year would be 28.1, for a required distribution much lower than 17 under the standard table. If you had $350,000 in retirement funds, your required distribution would be just $12,456 instead of $20,588. Over time, the effect of this difference can be dramatic. You can find the Joint Life and Last Survivor Table in the IRS Publication 590-B at www.irs.gov/publications/p590b/index.html#en US 2014 publink1000231236.

Remember, these are required minimum distributions (often referred to as RMDs); they are not maximum distributions. After age 59 ½ you can withdraw as much as you want without penalty, other than paying taxes on the amount withdrawn.

2. TREATMENT OF INHERITED IRAS

The rules above govern the treatment of retirement plans during your life. After you pass away, the rules on required distributions depend on whether you named one or more beneficiaries and whether you were married to the beneficiary. With some variations, here are the varying outcomes:

a. No designated beneficiary

If you have not named a beneficiary, your retirement plans will pass to your estate and be distributed according to the terms of your will, if you have one. Absent a will, the funds will pass under your state's intestacy rules to your closest surviving relatives. They must withdraw the funds by December 31st of the fifth year after your death. If, for instance, you were to pass away anytime during 2020, your heirs would have to complete the retirement plan withdrawals by December 31, 2025. They would not have the opportunity to defer the withdrawals throughout their lifetimes, simply taking the minimum distributions each year. And depending on the size of the retirement plan, if they waited to take the withdrawals until the fifth year, the lump sum withdrawal might push them into a higher tax bracket.

In addition, your retirement plan might be the only asset that requires that your estate be probated, creating an expense and hassle for your heirs. Financial institutions also can present roadblocks when there's no designated beneficiary. For instance, they might make it complicated to set up separate accounts for each of your heirs. This means that your different heirs would not be able to determine the withdrawal rates separately from one another and your estate might have to remain open for five years adding to the cost of administration and the workload for your personal representative. For all of these reasons, all financial advisors and estate planners strongly recommend that clients designate beneficiaries to all of their retirement plans. If you have any question about whether you have done so, check now.

b. Spouse

If you inherit a retirement plan from your spouse, you may convert it into your own IRA and it will be treated as if you had funded the account yourself. So you would then use your own life expectancy in determining minimum withdrawals. If your spouse was older than 70 ½ and had already begun taking required minimum distributions, but you're younger than 70 ½, you can stop taking distributions until you reach the required age. Don't forget to name beneficiaries to your new IRA.

c. Non-spouse beneficiary

Designated beneficiaries who are not surviving spouses of the decedent have the option of converting their share of the retirement plan to an inherited IRA. Unlike with their own retirement plan, the beneficiary of an inherited IRA must begin withdrawals by December 31st of the year after the year in which the original owner passed away. For instance, if you passed away in 2020, your beneficiaries would have to begin withdrawals by December 31, 2021. They would each take minimum distributions based on their own individual life expectancies using the table above on page 247. This explains why the table begins before age 70 ½, the earliest age by when you must take a minimum distribution from your own retirement plans. Above, we only printed the table beginning at age 56, but here's the rest of the table from age 0 to 55. (Yes, even babies have minimum distribution requirements if they inherit a retirement plan.)

TABLE I
(SINGLE LIFE EXPECTANCY)

(FOR USE BY BENEFICIARIES)

AGE	LIFE EXPECTANCY	AGE	LIFE EXPECTANCY
0	82.4	28	55.3
1	81.6	29	54.3
2	80.6	30	53.3
3	79.7	31	52.4
4	78.7	32	51.4
5	77.7	33	50.4
6	76.7	34	49.4
7	75.8	35	48.5

8	74.8	36	47.5
9	73.8	37	46.5
10	72.8	38	45.6
11	71.8	39	44.6
12	70.8	40	43.6
13	69.9	41	42.7
14	68.9	42	41.7
15	67.9	43	40.7
16	66.9	44	39.8
17	66.0	45	38.8
18	65.0	46	37.9
19	64.0	47	37.0
20	63.0	48	36.0
21	62.1	49	35.1
22	61.1	50	34.2
23	60.1	51	33.3
24	59.1	52	32.3
25	58.2	53	31.4
26	57.2	54	30.5
27	56.2	55	29.6

So, for instance, if 30-year-old "Beth" inherits a $350,000 retirement plan, she will only be required to withdraw $6,567 in the first year ($350,000 ÷ 53.3 = $6,567). However, she can withdraw as much as she wants even before age 59 ½ without paying a penalty (just paying income taxes). Beth can and should name beneficiaries to her inherited IRA, but if she passes away before withdrawing everything, they can't then stretch the IRA even longer but instead must continue making withdrawals based on Beth's hypothetical age if she were still alive. So, if Beth passes away at 55 and Ben, who then is 30 years old, inherits the IRA, Ben will have to withdraw 1/29.6 of the IRA before the end of the following year rather than 1/53.3 of it as Beth did when she originally inherited the account.

In short, inherited IRAs still allow significant deferral of taxes but not as much as your own retirement plans.

d. Charity

Advisors and charities often recommend that donors gift retirement plan assets, whether during life or at death, because charities have tax exempt status and as a result can get full value for a retirement plan gift. (This is also an argument for giving highly appreciated stock or real estate to nonprofits.) An example can help explain how this might work:

> John has a $1 million estate consisting of a house worth $500,000, investments and savings of $300,000 and an IRA worth $200,000. He wants to divide his estate equally among his four children and a local college where he will fund an annual scholarship in his wife's memory. If each asset is divided in fifths, each child will receive a $40,000 share of the IRA, which will be subject to income

tax when they liquidate it, whether immediately or over their lifetimes. If, instead, he gave the IRA to the college and divided the rest of his estate four ways among his children, they would have no tax costs in using their $200,000 inheritances and the college would still get its full $200,000. (Remember, John's house and stock holdings will get a step-up in basis at his death so there would be no capital gain upon their sale. See page 129 for an explanation of this concept.)

Of course, while the concept is straightforward, in practice this can get complicated. The simplest way to have the IRA to go to charity would be for John to name the college as the beneficiary and to divide the rest of his estate among his four children. But what if the IRA and the other assets fluctuate in value so that ultimately the IRA makes up substantially more or less than one fifth of his estate—will John care? It's more likely that the IRA will drop in value as John takes his minimum distributions than that it will increase, but there's certainly no guarantee. It's easier to provide for the IRA constituting less than a fifth of John's estate; John's will or trust could say that if necessary the college would receive enough funds to make up the difference between the value of the IRA and a fifth of the estate. If, for instance, at John's death his estate still totaled $1 million, but the IRA was only $150,000, his estate could give the college $50,000 before dividing the remaining $800,000 among his four children. (He might be obliged to give $200,000 in order to underwrite the scholarship in his wife's memory.)

But if the IRA made up $250,000 of his $1 million estate it would be much more difficult to make the adjustment because it's difficult to create complex beneficiary designations. The forms most financial institutions provide, whether paper forms or online, are rather limited and a complicated formula won't fit their parameters. At least in theory, John could provide his own beneficiary designation that said that to the extent the IRA exceeds a fifth of his entire estate the balance above one fifth would be distributed equally among his four children. But he might have a hard time getting any financial institution to accept this and he would probably be paying a lawyer for more time drafting the document and convincing the financial institution (or institutions, if he has more than one account) to accept it. Better to worry just about the downside—if the IRA drops in value to the extent that he can no longer fund the scholarship. He can keep the IRA beneficiary designation simple, having it go entirely to the college, and simply have his will or trust make up the difference if necessary, whether a specific dollar amount or a percentage of his estate.

A related issue is whether you can name both individuals and charities as beneficiaries of the same IRA. The issue here is that you will want your individual beneficiaries to be able to take their distributions out during their lifetimes, but in order to do so they must be "designated" beneficiaries, which charities cannot be. There are post-death fixes available to preserve the "stretch" benefits of delayed withdrawal for the individuals even with charities named on the same IRA, but it gets complicated. The much better practice is not to mix charities and individuals as beneficiaries of the same IRA.

3. Using Trusts

You might want some or all of your retirement plan assets to go into trust for the benefit of your heirs. Here are some possible reasons to use a trust:

- For estate tax planning.
- In the case of a second (or subsequent) relationship, to provide for your current partner or spouse but to make sure that upon his death the remaining funds go to your children.
- To protect inherited IRAs from creditors (the Supreme Court has ruled that inherited IRAs do not have the same creditor protection that your own retirement plans have).
- In case your children inherit your retirement plan while they're too young to manage it.
- To make sure your heirs don't spend the money too quickly and lose the benefit of deferred taxation.
- If your child or another beneficiary has special needs.

Unfortunately, what's already too complicated gets even more complicated when a trust becomes involved. To understand this, you will need to learn about three concepts: designated beneficiary, conduit trust, and accumulation trust.

a. Designated beneficiary

Up until now, I've been playing a bit fast and loose with the term "designated beneficiary," but it has significant implications with respect to retirement plans. For a beneficiary to receive the benefits of an inherited IRA or a spousal IRA as is discussed above, she must qualify as a "designated" beneficiary. This is not at all difficult when individuals are named; they are automatically designated beneficiaries. A charity cannot be a designated beneficiary and must withdraw all funds within five years of the donor's death, but this is not a problem since the charity will not be taxed on these withdrawals.

Matters get a bit more complicated when a trust is involved. In order to qualify as a designated beneficiary, the trust must meet the following requirements:

- It must be valid under state law.
- It must be irrevocable or become irrevocable at the grantor's death, which is the case with revocable trusts.

- The ultimate beneficiaries of the trust must be identifiable. This is the most difficult requirement. You can say "my children," since anyone should be able to figure out who they are, but you cannot say "it's up to my trustee," since then we can't know who the trustee will choose.

- None of the ultimate beneficiaries can be a charity (or other non-person), since a charity cannot be a "designated" beneficiary.

- The trust documentation must be provided to the IRA custodian (the financial institution) by October 31st of the year following the owner's death. Trust documentation includes the trust instrument (simply meaning the actual document that creates the trust), a list of the current and contingent beneficiaries and a certification by the trustee that all of the above requirements have been met.

These requirements do not seem so hard to satisfy. But keep reading—determining the ultimate beneficiaries of the trust can be difficult. To understand why determining the ultimate beneficiaries is important we have to go back to the RMD charts above. Remember that the required minimum distributions are based on the age of the IRA beneficiary. But if there is more than one beneficiary, whose age do we use for determining the RMD? If we can't figure that out, the trust doesn't qualify and the IRA must be withdrawn within five years of the death of the owner, with the taxes paid on the withdrawals at that time. Two types of trusts, "conduit" and "accumulation" trusts, permit the identification of the designated beneficiary.

b. Conduit or "see through" trust

A conduit trust requires that any RMDs being withdrawn from the IRA are also disbursed to the beneficiaries in the same year. Thus, the trust acts merely as a "conduit" for funneling the funds to beneficiaries (as opposed to holding the income, as accumulation trusts do).

If the conduit trust provides that the annual RMDs must be paid out to a single person, such as a surviving spouse, then they will be based on her life expectancy. If it provides that they must be distributed to a number of different beneficiaries, then the RMDs will be based on the age of the oldest beneficiary. For instance, if the trust provides that the RMDs will go equally to the owners' four children, then the oldest child's age will be used to determine the annual RMDs. (But don't include a charity as an income beneficiary, since a charity is not a designated beneficiary and that will disqualify the trust entirely.)

With the one caveat of not including a charity, this works well as long as the trust provides that all the RMD income be distributed each year to known beneficiaries. The IRS does not look past the current income of beneficiaries in determining whether everyone qualifies as a designated beneficiary. In other words, in our example of the four children, a provision that a child's share goes to her children if she dies before her siblings does not affect the RMDs.

c. Accumulation trust

But what if you don't want all of the income to be distributed? For instance, you might want the trust to grow in value for estate tax reasons. You might not want one or more beneficiaries to have control over the funds because you don't think they will spend them wisely. Or, in the case of someone receiving public benefits, the distributions would make him ineligible with drastic consequences. You might be concerned about creditor protection. For all of these reasons you may opt for an accumulation trust, which can hold the RMDs, rather than a conduit trust, that must disburse them.

An accumulation trust does not require the annual distribution of RMDs *to the beneficiaries*. Instead, the RMDs are distributed from the IRA *to the trust*, and the trustee has discretion over whether, when and how much of the RMD to distribute out to beneficiaries.

With such trusts, the IRS will look to those beneficiaries named to receive the ultimate trust distribution, determining if they qualify as designated (if they are identifiable individuals) and using the age of the oldest individual to establish the RMDs. So, if your trust says that it will continue for the life of your spouse and that the remainder will go to your children, the IRS will look to make sure that each child is identifiable. Presumably your spouse (except in some second marriages) will be older than your children and RMDs will be based on her life expectancy. If the trust says that it will continue until all of your children have passed away and that then everything will be distributed to your grandchildren, this is okay so long as at least one grandchild is living at your death. In this instance the oldest grandchild will be identifiable, so it works.

But don't permit your children unfettered discretion to permit who will receive their shares of the IRA if they were to die before its complete distribution, since that would make it impossible to determine the ultimate beneficiaries and as a result the entire retirement plan would have to be liquidated and income taxes paid within five years of your death. Often trusts give beneficiaries the right to direct who will receive their interest in a trust after they die. This is known as a "power of appointment." If the power of appointment permits a distribution to anyone who might be older than the beneficiary, such as a spouse, it's impossible to determine ahead of time which spouse is older (remember, people can remarry), so it's impossible to determine the oldest beneficiary for purposes of determining the annual RMD.

In addition, if a charity is a potential beneficiary, that could also disqualify the trust, requiring all retirement plans to be liquidated within five years of death. In short, it's much easier to use a conduit trust, but you might need to use an accumulation trust in situations where you do not want the mandatory minimum distributions paid outright to the beneficiary. This can be the case under the following circumstances:

i.   In a second marriage where you do not want all of the RMD funds to go to the surviving spouse, but you do want them available to him if needed.

ii. For tax reasons where you do not want the RMD funds in the surviving spouse's or your children's taxable estates. (This applies to very few people.)

iii. Where the beneficiaries are minors or too young to responsibly handle the funds.

iv. Where you would like to protect the RMDs as well as the principal from the reach of the beneficiaries' creditors.

v.   For special needs trusts where, either for financial management purposes or to maintain eligibility for public benefits (or both), the RMDs should not be distributed directly to the beneficiary.

Given the complications of accumulation trusts and the potential that they could be disqualified by mistake, in planning we often try to avoid their use. For instance, if parents have one child with special needs and two who do not need the same protection, we may discuss having the retirement plans go to the two who do not need a trust with only non-retirement funds going into the special needs trust. Of course, this can make it more difficult to ensure everyone's share of the estate is equal, especially if the retirement plans constitute a large portion of the parents' estate. In such cases, we will draft special needs trusts designed as accumulation trusts. (Then, we often have the problem of explaining the somewhat arcane provisions in the trusts as well as our higher fees creating such a complicated plan, but we do the best we can.)

THE JORGENSONS

For the Jorgensons, their retirement plan picture is relatively simple. They name each other as beneficiaries of their IRAs and their children as alternate beneficiaries after they both pass away. They will delay withdrawals until the year after they reach 70½ and then begin taking their required minimum draws. After the first of them passes away, the survivor will consolidate both IRAs and continue taking the RMDs. Whatever is left after they have both passed away will pass to their three children.

Each will then have a survivorship IRA and will have to begin taking RMDs based on his or her own age. They will not be able to consolidate these IRAs with their other retirement plans. That option is only available to surviving spouses.

CHAPTER 12

ASSET PROTECTION

Any discussion of asset protection has to start with two questions: What are the risks you're concerned about? And what assets do you want to protect?

Unfortunately, our world abounds with financial risk, including investment risk, risk of lawsuit, divorce, poor spending decisions, long-term care costs, inability to work, crime, drug addiction, death at a relatively young age, and natural disaster. These unfortunate events might happen to you or to your loved ones. Insurance of all forms—homeowners, disability, life, long-term care—provides protection against many of these risks. And all of the planning discussed earlier in this book can help as well.

In addition to considering the risks, any plan depends on what you want to protect. This may include your own savings and investments, your home, retirement plans, your inheritance, or what you plan to leave your children and grandchildren. Depending on what you hope to protect and what risk you're concerned about—for instance, whether it's risk of lawsuit by tenants of rental property you own or by your patients if you're a physician, or a risk (or hope) that your daughter will finally divorce your good-for-nothing son-in-law—different solutions are available, each with its own tradeoffs.

There are also generally three types of asset protection:

1. Protection from someone's bad decisions—perhaps a child's or grandchild's.

2. Protecting assets from having to be spent down to be eligible for public benefits.

3. Protection from a lawsuit, whether you are sued for a personal injury, failure to pay a debt, on a contractual claim, or for divorce.

The first risk, protection from bad decisions, primarily involves holding funds in trust, discussed later in this chapter's section on third-party trusts. The second risk has been covered in the earlier chapters on long-term care and special needs planning. In terms of the third risk, protection from lawsuit, the level of risk is variable depending on the type of asset involved and how it is held. This often plays itself out in bankruptcy court, since you can avoid paying many of your debts by declaring bankruptcy if your debts exceed your assets. The federal and state bankruptcy laws provide certain exemptions, typically for homes and retirement accounts, which are discussed below. The other legal framework that often comes into play involves laws against fraudulent conveyance. Many debtors and potential debtors attempt to protect their assets by transferring them out of their names, often to spouses, other family members or certain trusts. The law bars them from doing so to avoid current or anticipated debts and creditors can use the fraudulent conveyance laws to claw back transferred assets.

Since the potential risks, protective steps and tradeoffs are so varied, this chapter can only provide an introduction and framework to consider these issues. If you wish to take any substantial asset-protection steps, you will need to study further or consult with a qualified attorney (or both). We will discuss protection of your home, savings and investments, retirement plans, and business property through the use of trusts, homestead exemptions and limited liability entities.

1. YOUR HOME

Because a home is often worth so much more than its monetary value—taking into account the memories and the inconvenience of moving, among many other things

—it is frequently one of the most important assets for a client to shield.

Most states provide a homestead exemption that protects some or all of the equity in your home from claim in the event of bankruptcy. (Causing some confusion, many states also use the term "homestead exemption" to refer to a property tax reduction for owner-occupied property.) Most, but not all states, put a limit on the amount of equity protected, limiting it either by dollar value or a specific number of acres, sometimes having different acreage limits for urban and rural areas of the state. Depending on the state, the protection might be automatic or might require the recording of a declaration of homestead at the registry of deeds or elsewhere. In my state of Massachusetts, for instance, all homeowners have automatic protection of $125,000. They can protect an additional $375,000 ($500,000 in total) by filing a declaration of homestead at the appropriate registry of deeds. In most cases, these limits apply to both spouses. But if both spouses are disabled or are over age 62, they can each protect up to $500,000 of equity for a total protection of $1 million.

Note that homestead protections do not supersede mortgages or other liens. In addition, there's no homestead protection for non-owner occupied property and you will lose the homestead protection if you move out of your home. The exception in some states is for multi-unit buildings.

Some states permit protection of the entire structure if you live in one of the units.

Once the property is sold, you will have cash that is not protected—though your state might permit a grace period while you are investing the money in a new home. Finally, when you pass away, the homestead protection disappears, though there might be some protection extended to a surviving spouse and, if your heirs live in the house, they can establish their own homestead protection.

Florida has no limit on the equity protected by its homestead exemption and, as a result, has become the refuge of some notorious debtors, the most famous being Bowie Kuhn and O.J. Simpson. Bowie Kuhn, a former commissioner of baseball, fled to Florida after the bankruptcy of the Myerson & Kuhn law firm in 1989, avoiding a $3.1 million claim from a bank that had lent money to the firm. O.J. Simpson won his murder trial, but lost a $33.5 million civil suit brought by Ron Goldman and Nicole Brown's families. He moved to Miami to shelter money through this provision, but eventually lost the house to the mortgage holder after he was jailed in Nevada.

2. RETIREMENT PLANS

As part of the bankruptcy law overhaul in 2005, Congress exempted retirement plans and pensions, meaning that even if you have to declare bankruptcy, you will not have to forfeit your 401(k) and IRA plans to your creditors—one more reason to sock away as much money as possible into your retirement plans. There is no limit on the amount in your employment-related retirement plans you can protect or in such plans rolled over into IRAs. However, the creditor protection for your own IRAs or Roth IRAs is limited to $1,283,025. Beware rolling over an employment-related retirement plan into your personal IRA because then it will fall under this limitation (assuming that you have enough set aside so that the limitation is relevant).

While your own retirement plans qualify for this protection, the U.S. Supreme Court in 2014 in *Clark v. Rameker* ruled that these protections do not apply to inherited IRAs. So, if you inherited an IRA from your mother, it will not be protected in your bankruptcy proceeding. If, on the other hand, you inherited it from your wife, then you can protect it by converting it to your own IRA (up to the limit cited above). If you think that one of your heirs may run into bankruptcy issues, consider naming a trust as beneficiary rather than him personally. For more information on this issue, see Chapter 11 on retirement plans and Section 4 below on third-party trusts.

3. SELF-SETTLED TRUSTS

The rule under traditional, or "common-law," trust law is that you cannot be a beneficiary of a trust you create yourself and protect the property from your creditors. You can, however, create a trust for someone else—often called a "third-party" trust—and write it in such a way that it will be protected from her creditors.

There are three ways around this rule about self-settled trusts. The first is to create an irrevocable trust that restricts your access. For instance, you can create a trust that pays out the income (interest and dividends) to you but which completely restricts your access to principal. These trusts are often used in the context of planning for Medicaid coverage of nursing home care. You might also title real estate in such a trust preserving only the right to use and occupy the property. In any of these trusts, beware of the tax consequences and the differing state rules on Medicaid-qualifying trusts.

The second option is to create a trust for the benefit of a third party, such as a spouse or child who you want to provide for or who will share the trust benefit with you, though they're not legally required to do so. This is a third-party trust (other benefits of which are described below), but one which carries out a goal or goals towards which you might normally spend funds. This might be easier with a spouse, since if the trust, for instance, pays all housing costs and you happen to live in the house as well, you will still reap a benefit. If, on the other hand, a child funnels trust distributions back to you, the trust might be treated as a sham since you might be deemed as the true beneficiary. So, if you're transferring your own funds into a trust for asset-protection purposes be sure that you're ready to give up access to such property. Hybrids of the first two approaches might also be available. For instance, you may create a trust that permits distributions of income to you and principal to your children and grandchildren.

The third option is to take advantage of the laws in those states that have recently overturned the common law and permitted the creation of self-settled asset protection trusts. Led by Delaware, Alaska, Nevada and South Dakota, 15 states (Alaska, Delaware, Hawaii, Mississippi, Missouri, Nevada, New Hampshire, Ohio, Rhode Island, South Dakota, Tennessee, Utah, Virginia, West Virginia and Wyoming) now permit such trusts. Each state has its own rules, but typically they require that the trust property be held in a financial institution in its state and that at least one trustee—whether institutional or individual—be from the state. While you cannot serve as trustee, you can appoint someone you trust—perhaps your lawyer or accountant or a close family member—to serve as "trust protector" to have certain rights, such as the ability to change trustees, amend the trust as needed to comply with changes in the law, or even to change beneficiaries.

So far, there have been few cases actually testing these trusts and statutes. Their proponents argue that even if the trusts were to be challenged, the prospect of litigating the issue would serve as a hurdle to recovery, making a favorable settlement of a claim much more likely. At best, the trusts totally protect the assets they hold from creditors. Since these trusts are somewhat expensive to set up and administer (and potentially to defend in court), they are generally used by people of high net worth in potentially risky businesses—such as medical professionals who may be sued for malpractice. If you would be interested in pursuing an out-of-state asset protection trust, you will need to consult with a specialist in the field.

Note that you may not serve as your own trustee of your self-settled asset protection and trusts, and that your other rights—such as the ability to change the trustee or beneficiaries—depend on state law. And remember that the fraudulent conveyance rules apply to these trusts. You cannot use them to protect assets from claims that already exist, only potential future ones. (How that's defined depends on each state's laws.)

4. THIRD-PARTY TRUSTS

As we mentioned above, the common law has always permitted donors to create trusts for others (thus, "third-party" trusts) that would not be subject to the beneficiary's creditors. These are often called "spendthrift" trusts because they are designed to protect beneficiaries from their own bad decisions and bad luck, as well as to keep funds in the family. To work, the trust must be discretionary, meaning that the trustee has full authority to determine when, whether and how to make distributions to beneficiaries or on their behalf. It must also contain language barring beneficiaries from pledging or conveying their interest in the trust to someone else. With those provisions, the trusts are protected from the beneficiaries' creditors. But, as a result, they can be very restrictive. There's an apocryphal story about how restrictive they can be:

> A young Harvard student crosses the Charles River into the Boston business district to meet with the gray-haired trustee of his trust to ask for money to buy a new suit. This, of course, was back in the days when Harvard students wore suits. The trustee responds: "When I was at Harvard, I had one suit that lasted me all four years." Before continuing, he pauses to pick some lint off of his sleeve. "In fact, it's still standing up pretty well today."

The moral of the story is that when choosing your trustee, it's important to choose people or institutions who share your values, or to provide them guidance as to how you would like the trust funds to be spent. Perhaps the young Harvard student's grandparents would have been happy for him to get a new suit every year. And while a trust as described above will protect the funds left for the benefit of our Harvard student, if it is used to provide his basic support, it still might be subject to claim in divorce. Judges can be a law unto themselves.

In our practice, we often prepare for our clients what we call "family protection" trusts (borrowing the name from my colleague Michael Gilfix of Gilfix & Associates in Palo Alto, California). In an attempt to balance protection with practicality, we typically design the trusts as follows:

a. We create a separate trust for each beneficiary.

b. The beneficiary (usually a child) may serve as trustee and even as the only trustee.

c. But while he may manage and invest the trust funds as he sees fit, he may only distribute *income* to himself.

d. If he needs access to *principal*, he must appoint an independent trustee who would have discretion to distribute principal for his benefit or refuse to do so.

This trust design is meant to provide protection while responding to the reluctance of many clients (and their children) to give up control. It will work as long as the child actually follows the rules of the trust. Its great Achilles heel is that the beneficiary has access to the trust property and could easily drain the trust even though doing so would violate the terms of the trust and make him liable to a claim by the remainder beneficiaries. But they are likely to be his children or siblings and would be unlikely to sue him. In addition, if he's the type of person who would drain the trust he also might be likely to spend the trust assets and not have other assets available to pay the resulting judgment. Even if the beneficiary trustee does not completely drain the trust, but merely starts spending some of the principal, he will undermine its protection. By failing to follow the rules of the trust, he undermines the protections those rules are meant to provide. This means that the trustee needs careful instruction when the family protection trust is funded. Appointing an independent, professional trustee from the outset is definitely more secure. Unfortunately, many clients sacrifice safety in the interest of avoiding payment of professional trustee fees.

So, in determining whether to create a family protection trust and whether to name a family member or an independent trustee, you will need to balance your children and grandchildren's need for protection and their likely level of responsibility. While bad things, financial and otherwise, can happen to anyone, those most likely to need protection may also be more likely to need an independent trustee.

In addition to creditor and divorce protection, family protection trusts also offer tax protection. Because distribution of the principal funds in the trust are not in the beneficiary's control, they will not be included in the child's taxable estate. For this reason, they are sometimes referred to as "generation skipping" trusts, since the ultimate distribution goes to the grandchildren, skipping the children. Because a lot of rich families were using these trusts to avoid taxation at the passing of each generation, allowing accumulated wealth to continue potentially for centuries, Congress enacted a generation skipping tax. This gets very complicated, but the bottom line is that it limits how much can pass tax free from generation to generation. Also, under the new federal estate tax thresholds these tax issues are relevant to very few people today.

Yet for the less wealthy, family protection trusts can still serve an important purpose: They keep assets in the family in the event of the premature death of a child. If a child directly inherits funds and then passes away, they will likely pass to her spouse. The spouse may get remarried, have additional children, and even become estranged from the children of his first marriage (we have seen this happen). Those children may then receive none of the property that came from their grandparents. If, instead, the grandparents had left the funds in a family protection trust, at the death of the parent they would remain in trust for the benefit of her children.

5. LIMITED-LIABILITY ENTITIES

The legal structures of limited liability entities make them another important tool for shielding personal assets from creditors and lawsuits.

Corporations date back to Renaissance Holland as a structure for investors to share the rewards and risks of business ventures without risking anything beyond their actual investment. One salient benefit corporations offer is limitation of liability: claims against the corporation for debts and any injuries do not flow back to the shareholders. Only the corporate holdings are at risk, not the other property of its owners. This is distinguished from a sole proprietorship. If, for instance, you own a rental property in your own name, fail to shovel the walk after a snowstorm and someone falls and hurts himself, he can sue you personally for his injuries and seek recovery against all of your assets, not just the rental property. If, however, the property was held in a corporation the injured party could only seek recovery against the corporate assets, presumably just the building itself and a bank account maintained for operating expenses.

Since corporations are formal entities and somewhat cumbersome and expensive to manage, recent decades have seen a proliferation of other limited liability business forms, each with its own acronym and features, including limited liability partnerships (LLPs), professional corporations (PCs), and limited liability corporations (LLCs). While each entity is a bit different (and they differ from state-to-state), all of these corporate forms have the following in common:

a. They permit multiple owners.

b. One or more owners may be named to manage the business.

c. Liability for corporate actions extends only to the entity's assets, not those of its owners.

To determine which form of business best fits your needs you will need to consult with a local corporate attorney.

Often landlords who own multiple buildings have them each owned by a separate corporation or partnership. That way if anyone sues due to an injury occurring at one building, the other properties will not be at risk. This strategy can also be used for other types of business property, such as ships.

When I was in law school, I spent a summer working at a large New York City law firm specializing in bankruptcy. I was assigned to work on the bankruptcy of a shipping company that owned several old freighters that sailed up and down the east coasts of North and South America. It turned out that each ship was owned by a separate corporate entity, meaning that we had to prepare separate filings for each ship. (Unfortunately, in terms of our workload, this was before the days of word processing, so we couldn't simply copy and paste.)

One of the biggest immediate problems for the company was that one ship full of ripe bananas was just off the port of Galveston. The company couldn't afford to pay the dock fees and was also concerned that if they did come into port, that ship would be seized by its creditors. As the week went on, the bananas began to rot. In addition, there was concern that it and other ships would run out of fuel to run their bilge pumps, potentially resulting in their sinking. As part of the bankruptcy process, the company was permitted to use its cash on hand to keep the ships afloat rather than pay it to creditors. (Of course, they were also permitted to pay their attorneys.)

One caveat to be aware of if you choose to use any of these corporate forms for purposes of limiting liability: You will need to follow all the formalities required by law, whether that includes annual filings with the state, notices to shareholders, or annual meetings. Otherwise, you could lose the benefit of the protections provided by the limited liability structure. If you do not follow these rules and your corporate entity is sued, the plaintiff may seek to "pierce the corporate veil" by showing that despite the incorporation you treated the business as if it were a sole proprietorship. If the plaintiff is successful, all of your property could be at risk despite having tried to avail yourself of the liability protection of the corporate entity. As an example, if you were to place rental property in a corporation or partnership, make sure that the tenants make their checks out to the company, not to you personally. And make sure that you deposit the checks into an account in the corporation or partnership's name, not your own bank account. Run all the expenses through the business account and file a separate income tax return for the business each year.

6. CONCLUSION

As you can see, there are many ways to limit or avoid liability from lawsuit and to protect property from the effects of bad decisions and bad luck. Which, if any, makes sense in your situation depends on a lot of factors, including the level and sources of risk you foresee and the nature and value of the property you wish to protect.

THE JORGENSONS

The last few years have been financially advantageous for the Jorgensons. Joyce's uncle died. He had never married and left Joyce a sizeable inheritance. John's business (finally) went public making his stock options valuable. Their financial picture now looks like this:

Savings and Investments

Checking	$45,000
Savings	$125,000
Investments	$935,000
John's IRA	$400,000
Joyce's IRA	$225,000
Total	$1,730,000

House	$500,000 fair market value, no mortgage

Life Insurance

John	$250,000
Joyce	$125,000

Both are term policies with no cash value.

At the same time, Jack and Sarah's marriage has become strained, in part by the stresses of raising Austin. It looks like divorce is on the horizon. And Jennifer has proved herself to be something of a spendthrift. John and Joyce have had to bail her out of credit card debt a number of times, and they don't know if she will ever grow out of her spending ways.

As a result of these developments, John and Joyce feel they have more to protect and more reason to be concerned about what will happen to their funds once they pass to their children. While each child's financial and personal situation is different, they want to treat them all the same. They decide to revise their estate plan to leave everything in trust for the children. Each child will have a separate trust so that they can each go their separate ways and have privacy about what they do. John and Joyce have chosen a local bank to serve as trustee for the trusts, but the trust document gives each child the right to change his or her trustee—just requiring that there always be a professional trustee. John and Joyce rest more easily once the papers are signed.

CHAPTER 13

VACATION HOMES

A family vacation house can be the boon or bane of a family's life together: a place where generations gather to relax and recharge, or the focus of disputes over use, costs and maintenance. In *The Big House*, George Howe Colt describes the large house his industrialist great-grandfather built on Cape Cod in 1903. For a century it served as the locus where his sprawling family reconvened every summer, central to their identity. But, by the end of the last century, the family was so scattered and the upkeep of the old house so expensive, that the family could no longer maintain it. Fortunately, one of their number had done quite well financially and was able to buy out the rest of the family— keeping the house in at least one branch of the extended

Colt family. It could have turned out much worse, with litigation and the property falling into disrepair. A client recently told me that he and his brother are no longer on speaking terms because the brother is so upset that the client was not able to find a way to preserve their family house on the Cape and was forced to sell it.

If you have a vacation house, what is your vision for it? Will it continue as a family retreat? Will it be sold after you can no longer use it, whether upon your death or earlier? Is the whole family on the same page? Are all your children interested in keeping it, or have some moved across the country and can no longer make use of the place on the Maine coast? Or on the other hand, is it the family living a continent away that most values the family reunions? Can all your children equally afford the upkeep? Who will decide on its use, or manage renting out the place to cover costs? Should you leave these decisions to your children or make them yourself so that your heirs don't end up fighting about them? How well do the vision and the reality of finances and people's lives mesh?

As time passes, the impact of these properties can be quite positive, or—in the absence of intentional planning— quite negative. An attorney who used to work in my firm goes back to a lake on the Indiana-Michigan border every summer where she, her parents and her brother all have neighboring houses. It helped keep her own sons well grounded while growing up in a wealthy Boston suburb. And now that they're out of the house, it ensures that the family is all together for at least a few days every year. Fortunately, houses on this lake are inexpensive and there's no dispute about what will happen when the parents pass on. On the other hand, I had clients who never executed their estate plan in part because they could not achieve all of their goals. They owned a vacation house in Maine that one son cared about more than their other children. Unfortunately, the father had expensive care costs due to a disability. The parents did not have sufficient resources to (1) give the vacation house to their son, (2) pay for their own care needs, and (3) be sure to give an equal amount to their other two children. Additionally, the son couldn't afford to simply buy out his parents or, down the road, his siblings. The result, unfortunately, was a stalemate.

If you own a vacation house, don't make plans in a vacuum; get input. Talk to your children about what they want and what interest they have in keeping the house in the family. Depending on family dynamics this may be done through a series of individual discussions or may take place in one or more family meetings. But, ultimately, make the decision yourself so that there's finality and the family can move on knowing how the house will be owned and managed.

Then, consider using a trust. The trust can provide a structure for managing the property. It can prevent a stalemate by ensuring that the trustees are in charge; they don't need to get approval for their actions from all family members (unless you want them to do so and put that requirement in the trust). At the same time, the trustees will have a fiduciary duty to all the beneficiaries, meaning that they need to be as fair as possible in their decision making. In creating the trust, you will have to answer the following questions (and perhaps some others):

1. WHO SHOULD BE IN CHARGE?

Who should manage the vacation home, decide on its use and maintenance, determine whether to rent it out, and set any charges to pay for upkeep or use? Depending on the number of children you have, you might name them all to manage the property together or you may name one or two who you think can act most fairly and have the time and interest to take this on. In any case, the trust should provide for majority rule, rather than requiring that all trustees agree on all decisions. Otherwise, one person could easily hold up the whole family.

2. WHO CAN CHANGE TRUSTEES OR APPOINT SUCCESSORS?

In addition to choosing the original trustees, you will need to determine whether there should be a mechanism to remove them for any reason, and who should serve as successor trustees when any of the original trustees stops serving for any reason (removal, incapacity or death).

Should all of your children together be able to remove any trustee? Should the vote be unanimous (by everyone but the trustee) or simply a majority? Should the grandchildren be included as voting members for this purpose? Or should the vote be by family, so if a child trustee is no longer living and competent, her children together could have a single vote. Do you want to name particular individuals to serve as successor in the event anyone stops serving, or have a similar mechanism to choose successors? You could, for instance, permit each family to choose a trustee or limit the trustees to the next generation until none can continue to serve and then permit the appointment of grandchildren.

As you can see, there are many options available and none is right for all families and all situations. It's more important that you have a mechanism in place than which particular mechanism you choose.

3. HOW WILL THE FINANCES WORK?

Every house costs money for taxes, maintenance, insurance and repairs. There are a number of ways to pay for these including your leaving money in trust in addition to the real estate, charging family members for use, renting out the property, and family members sharing the costs equally. What's fair is often in the eye of the beholder, along with how much money needs to be held in reserve. If the house is on Cape Cod and the child living in Massachusetts uses it most, should she pay more of the costs? But what if she contributes sweat equity by taking care of maintenance and renting out the property to cover at least some costs? What if she was also the person who enabled the parents to use the house for as long as possible by driving them to the Cape and disrupting her life to provide care and transportation to doctors' visits while they were down there?

What's fair and reasonable for year-to-year maintenance might not work when a large expense is required to replace a boiler or a roof. It's possible that not everyone will be able to afford to pitch in at the same level. If they don't, what adjustments should be made? Even if you deposit a large sum into the trust to cover costs, this may be seen as unfair by children who don't use the house. Not only would a part of their inheritance be tied up in the house, but some cash would be as well.

As with the other questions, there's no one-size-fits-all answer here. But unlike the other issues, it may be impossible to provide a mechanism in the trust itself because it could be too rigid, not responsive to circumstances as they change and develop over time. Again, it makes sense to discuss this with the family to get some idea of what seems fair. You might develop a system with the trustees and write it down as a separate document from the trust. That way there can be a common understanding without the rigidity of having the system embodied in the trust itself.

4. WHAT IF ONE CHILD WANTS TO OPT OUT?

What happens if one or more of your children are no longer interested in the vacation house? Do you give them the option of opting out, and what form does opting out take? One point of view is that the vacation house is a family benefit that family members can take advantage of or not, but that it will remain available to the family either indefinitely or until a future date (perhaps when all your children have passed away). An opposite perspective is that it would be great if the vacation house were to continue for family use, but that you don't want to bind anyone to it and to foregoing a part of his inheritance. In that case, it's possible to put a trigger in the trust which permits each child to elect to be bought out by the other children. The trigger we put into such trusts generally has the following elements:

a. The child gives notice to his siblings that he wants to opt out.

b. The other children or the trustees have a certain amount of time, perhaps 60 days, to elect to buy out that child.

c. If they do so, they are permitted to make the purchase at a set discount from fair market value. The discount has three purposes. First, it recognizes the fact that no brokerage commission will have to be paid. Second, it makes it easier to keep the home within the family. And, third, it provides a disincentive to opting out.

d. If the other children elect to buy out the opting out sibling, they have a certain amount of time, perhaps 90 days, to close the transaction.

e. If the other children or trustees do not elect to buy out the sibling or fail to do so after the close of 90 days, the trustees will be obligated to put the property on the market, sell it, and distribute the proceeds to the trust beneficiaries.

If you decide to include this or a similar provision in your trust, the biggest decision is what the purchase discount should be. We've seen this range from 10% to 25%.

5. WHO CAN FORCE A SALE?

As you can see, if you include the mechanism described above in your vacation home trust it could lead to an outright sale of the property if the remaining siblings choose not to—or cannot—buy out the opting out sibling. Instead of, or in conjunction with, the opting out provision you may want to permit or require the trustees to sell the property under certain circumstances.

If you permit the trustees to sell the property, you can leave this decision entirely to their discretion or include standards, such as permitting the sale when the trustees determine that the family is no longer using the property or when it is no longer economical to maintain it.

If you give the children the power to direct the trustees to sell, you need to decide whether to require unanimity, a simple majority, or another percentage of children. If you choose a simple majority and, for instance, you have four children, this will require three to sell, meaning that one hold out could not prevent the sale. If you have three children, it would mean two could elect to sell. But if you have two children, then they would both have to agree. Further, while we all hope and expect that our children will outlive us, they won't live forever. Even if you have four children today, eventually three, two and then one will be surviving. The question is whether a single surviving (and elderly) family member should be able to control the vacation home for the entire extended family. This relates back to the provisions for trustee removal and succession related above as well as to the decision as to whether it's time to sell the property. Perhaps the answer to this question is yes, keep control centralized. Or, if the trustees have the power to sell under set circumstances, we don't have to be too concerned about a single surviving member of the next generation refusing to sell property that might be unused and falling into disrepair. Typically, we do see trusts that permit a simple majority of the children to direct a sale of the property, but this is combined with a trustee power to sell under certain circumstances and provisions for a broader group to "hire and fire" trustees.

6. FOR HOW MANY GENERATIONS SHOULD THE TRUST CONTINUE?

The issue of the rights and responsibilities of future generations past the children of the grantors has already come up in the context of their rights to use the property and the appointment and removal of trustees. Often, the determination of the use of the property and the obligation to contribute to its costs are left in the hands of trustees, but you may choose to include grandchildren and great-grandchildren in the group that may use the property and participate in trustee selection decisions. However, if the property is sold, distribution of the proceeds usually goes to children, with the children of any deceased child taking his share. But should the trust direct that the property be sold at a particular time—perhaps at the death of the last surviving child? If the property is not sold, can the trust continue indefinitely? If not, when does it end and what happens to the property when it does end?

Under the common law, a doctrine known as the "rule against perpetuities" prevents trusts from continuing indefinitely. Long a challenge to first-year law students, the rule essentially says that trusts will end automatically 21 years after the death of the last surviving beneficiary who was mentioned in the trust and alive when the trust was created. So, if in 2020 you create a trust that includes your six-year-old granddaughter as a beneficiary and she lives to age 106 (given modern medicine), then the trust must end by 2141 (21 years after her death in 2120), after a good long run of 121 years. Even though this is more than enough time for most people, in recent years several states have overturned the rule against perpetuities completely or extended it, in some cases to 1,000 years.

When the trust ends, the trust property must then be distributed outright to the trust beneficiaries. This can be problematic if by then there are dozens of potential beneficiaries. And the difficulties can be compounded if the property to be distributed is real estate since by then dozens of people would have an interest in the property, creating significant title problems. For instance, you would need all the great-grandchildren to sign a deed to convey it. If even one beneficiary cannot be located, is legally incompetent, or refuses to participate in the sale, the deed might not be able to be conveyed. For these reasons, the trust should provide that the property be sold by the trustees before the trust ends, perhaps upon the death of the last surviving child or grandchild. The trust might also limit the beneficiaries to grandchildren and not include great-grandchildren. But this could also depend on the size of your family. If there are two children at each generation, you will have eight great-grandchildren (2 children x 2 grandchildren x 2 great-grandchildren = 8 great-grandchildren), perhaps a small enough number to keep track of. But if your family has four children at each generation, the number gets exponentially larger with the potential of 64 people to track down (4 children x 4 grandchildren x 4 great-grandchildren = 64 great-grandchildren). In addition, with these greater numbers, each one's share of the house proceeds would be rather small—making the additional effort and legal cost of tracking them down less worth the expense.

7. ARE LONG-TERM CARE COSTS A CONCERN?

Are you concerned about how you will pay for your long-term care, if needed? If so, you should make sure that the equity in your vacation home is either available to pay for your needs as they arise, or protected so that you can qualify for Medicaid if you run through your other assets. If your care needs are the higher priority, then your vacation home should be put in a revocable trust so that you can access it if necessary. If, on the other hand, you would like to shelter it from any such costs, you will need to use an irrevocable trust that forecloses your access to the equity in the property.

Similarly, if you are at all concerned about the care needs of any of your beneficiaries or, for that matter, their potential need for public benefits, the possibility of divorce, or the chances that they might be subject to bankruptcy or lawsuit, you should consider keeping the property in trust during their lives.

8. TRUST VS. LLC

These questions can be used to begin a family discussion about the disposition of the vacation house, whether you ultimately use a trust or not. Some advisors recommend using a limited liability partnership or corporation rather than a trust. This can be useful in terms of clearly dividing governance (general partners) from owners (limited partners). It also can facilitate transfers of ownership over time since limited partnership shares can be relatively easily transferred. It can also help resolve the challenges of many owners with different ownership interests that can be tracked more easily with partnership shares than fractional shares that often result in trusts.

There can also be tax implications to how the house ownership is structured, about which an estate planning attorney can advise. The trust or LLC can be structured to limit both estate and capital gains taxes. Finally, another advantage of a trust or LLC—if the property is in a different state from where you live—is that they can be used to avoid a second (or "ancillary") probate in the second state.

THE JORGENSONS

In addition to their other assets, John and Joyce own a cottage on a lake in the state north of where they live. It's unheated, so they use it only in the summer. It was a great place to go for weekends and extended vacations when they were raising their children and now that grandchildren are coming along the family is beginning to meet up there more and more. The problem is that it can be a bit tight when everyone shows up, so they've had to rent out other cottages on the lake. They're thinking about expanding their cottage, adding a smaller cottage next door, or subdividing their land so each of their children can build their own places. One problem is that each of their kids has a different interest in coming to the lake and a different level of financial resources to be able to build their own place.

The Jorgensons decide that they will not subdivide their land now, but will build a smaller guesthouse so that they can accommodate everyone who wants to come. It will still be tight quarters, but it's unlikely that all of their children and their families will be there together for more than a week or two a year. But what to do with their estate plan? They want the cottage (or cottages) to be available to their family members, but realize that it could either be a godsend—allowing successive generations to spend time together every summer—or a point of contention if there are fights about its use and costs of maintenance. If a child moves far away and never comes to the lake, he or she may resent the fact that part of his or her inheritance is tied up in the house. (Fortunately, the house is not in the Hamptons, so its market value is not so high that anyone is going to be much deprived.)

The Jorgensons decide to put the lake house into trust with all three children as trustees after they pass away. The trust says that the cottage will be managed for the benefit of all the children and grandchildren and that the trustees together will determine both access to the property and assessments for its upkeep. The trust says that the assessments should be based at least partially on use. It also says that if there's a disagreement about anything, that two out of three trustees can make decisions for the trust. And it provides that if any of the children wants to opt out, the trust will buy out his or her share at 90 percent of the fair market value as determined by an independent appraiser. If the remaining children (or child) cannot come up with the money to buy out the sibling who wants out, then the house will be sold. The trust also provides that the house will be sold when the last of the children passes away, since it will be harder for the grandchildren to manage together. But when it's sold in either circumstance, the trustees must first offer it to the grandchildren who individually or together may purchase it, also for 90% of the fair market value.

The Jorgensons hope through this arrangement to balance their interests in preserving the cottage for the family, being fair to all of their children and grandchildren, and not controlling the property from the grave for an overly long time.

CHAPTER 14

NON-U.S. CITIZENS

First: the good news! If you, your spouse or anyone you want to include in your estate plan is not a United States citizen, for the most part that won't change your plan. The probate laws of the various states do not distinguish between citizens and noncitizens, or even between legal and undocumented immigrants. In short, property rights are blind as to nationality as well as to the location of the owner. So, you can also include residents of other countries (whether or not they are U.S. citizens) in your estate plan. Of course, as a practical matter, locating and communicating with them may prove difficult and costly for your personal representative or trustee.

CASE STUDY
TRUST DISTRIBUTION

We once had clients who had come from Colombia and who have one son with significant disabilities. We drafted a special needs trust for his benefit, but when we got to the question of who would receive the trust funds after his death, we ran into a problem. After a charitable gift to an agency that had been of great assistance to their son, the parents wanted any remaining funds to go half to the mother's closest relatives and half to the father's. The mother had five brothers and sisters and the father 11.

We explained that this could be an administrative nightmare for the trustee, especially since many of their son's aunts and uncles may not be alive upon his death. That raised a question as to whether their shares would pass to their son's cousins or only to his surviving aunts and uncles. In either case, we explained, the trust funds would be divided into so many shares that each of the shares would be quite small. They countered that even a little bit of money goes a long way in Colombia and would be very important to their relatives.

Our solution: Our clients agreed to name one beneficiary for each side of the family to receive half of the remaining trust funds with the request that he or she share it with the rest of the family.

> For each family, we named a succession of possible beneficiaries since, as mentioned above, many of the aunts and uncles might not survive their son.

Now the bad news. While probate and property laws do not distinguish between citizens and noncitizens or between residents and nonresidents, the federal estate tax laws do and they are much tougher on non-citizens. The first major difference is that the unlimited marital deduction does not apply to transfers to a noncitizen spouse, whether at death or as a gift during life.

As a quick reminder of gifting (covered in detail in Chapter 7 on estate taxation), if you make gifts above $15,000 to an individual other than your spouse during a calendar year, you are supposed to file a gift tax return reporting the gift. The excess over $15,000 is then deducted from the $11.4 million (in 2019) that you can give away tax free, reducing that amount. So, if you gave someone $1.4 million this year, you could only give away $10 million estate tax free at death. If you gave away more than $11.4 million of cumulative excess gifts, you would have to pay a gift tax. Since few people have more than $11.4 million (or $22.8 million for a couple) to give away either during life or at death, this affects very few people.

For American citizens, there's no reporting requirement for gifts of any amount between spouses. However, this is not true of gifts to noncitizen spouses living in the United States. They must report gifts to one another in excess of $155,000 (in 2019) in any calendar year. So, if your spouse is not a U.S. citizen, you can avoid the reporting requirement by keeping spousal transfers below this threshold each year. If you exceed it, you'll have to file a return. But, again, you're unlikely to have to pay a tax since you can still give away up to $11.4 million tax free during life and at death.

Matters can also get a bit more complicated at your death if your surviving spouse is a non-citizen since the marital deduction does not apply here either. Gifts to your spouse will be taxable just like gifts to anyone else. Again, unless your estate is more than $11.4 million, this should be of little concern. If, however, you want to make sure that what you leave your spouse does not end up in his taxable estate, potentially putting it over $11.4 million, you can shelter it through a special trust, known as a qualified domestic trust (or QDOT). When determining whether this makes sense for you, be aware that even noncitizens are taxed on their worldwide assets if they are domiciled in the United States when they pass away. So, consider your non-U.S. property as well as your U.S. holdings. Also, be aware that all of these rules only apply if the recipient of the gift or inheritance is a noncitizen. If you are not a U.S. citizen, but your spouse is, he will qualify for the marital deduction like all other U.S. citizens.

In addition to the QDOT, there are three other potential ways to avoid the effect of no marital deduction available to noncitizen surviving spouses. The first is for the surviving spouse to become a U.S. citizen, which he must do before the estate tax return is due, nine months after the death of his spouse.

The second strategy would be to take advantage of portability (also described in more detail in Chapter 7), which Congress enacted in 2013 to permit surviving spouses, in effect, to inherit the unused estate exemption of the first spouse to pass away. As an example, if you were to pass away with an $8 million estate, your spouse could add your unused $3.4 million exemption to her $11.4 million exemption to give away $14.8 million tax free at death. To take advantage of this option, she would have to file an estate tax return at your death even though your estate would not be taxable and otherwise no return would have to be filed. The good news is that portability is available to U.S. residents whether or not the decedent or the surviving spouse is a U.S. citizen. But to complicate things a bit further, portability is generally not available if a QDOT is used.

The third planning option would be for the surviving spouse to move out of the United States. This won't help if the estate of the first spouse to die is more than $11.4 million when she passes away, but could if the couple's combined estates exceed this limit. However, the change of residence and severing of ties with the United States have to be very clear. The IRS has a lot of rules about how domicile is defined for tax purposes.

Further, if you or your spouse or both are considering moving out of the United States, you need to be aware of the nonresident estate tax rules. Yes, even nonresident, noncitizens (known as "aliens" to the IRS) may be subject to the U.S. estate tax, but only on their U.S. property. If you have property—including real estate, tangible personal property such as artwork, and stock in U.S. corporations—situated in the United States that's worth more than $60,000, your estate will have to file an estate tax return at your death. To compound this problem, the estate tax threshold is $60,000 rather than $11.4 million. This can be avoided through planning, often using offshore trusts or other entities to hold title to the property. In addition, many countries have tax treaties with the United States that provide offsets. So, if your estate would also be paying a tax in your home country on your U.S. residence, the U.S. tax might be reduced or eliminated. These include Australia, Austria, Canada, Denmark, Finland, France, Germany,

Greece, Ireland, Italy, Japan, the Netherlands, Norway, South Africa, Switzerland and the United Kingdom.

The bottom line is that all of this is very complicated. You are best advised to consult with a U.S. tax attorney or accountant if either of two situations apply to you: First, if you are a nonresident alien with property in the United States. Second, if you are a U.S. resident, but you or your spouse (or both) is not a U.S. citizen and either of you or both of you together have more than $11.4 million (or could at some point in the future). If you're not at risk of having that much money, then simply make sure you don't give each other more than $155,000 each year.

CHAPTER 15

PROPERTY IN OTHER COUNTRIES

Whether or not you are a U.S. citizen, you may own real estate in another country—either that vacation condo you bought in Aruba or the family property you inherited in Italy. What happens to that in terms of estate taxes and passing on ownership?

1. ESTATE TAXATION

For federal estate tax purposes, the answer is simple: If you are a U.S. citizen, the value of your overseas property will be included in your estate and taxed like any other property, if your estate exceeds $11.4 million (in 2019).

However, there might be offset if you must pay estate taxes in the other country, which would depend on tax treaties between the two nations. The United States has such tax treaties with Australia, Austria, Denmark, Finland, France, Germany, Greece, Ireland, Italy, Japan, the Netherlands, Norway, South Africa, Switzerland, and the United Kingdom. Pursuant to these treaties, these countries may tax the estates of U.S. decedents for property in those countries and the United States will permit such estates to apply a credit for such taxes on their U.S. estate tax returns, thus, avoiding double taxation.

The states with estate taxes of their own, on the other hand, should not tax out-of-state or out-of-country property because doing so violates provisions of the U.S. Constitution. On the other hand, they may apply an estate tax on property in the state even if the owner died as a resident of another state or another country.

2. INHERITANCE

But what about ownership of overseas property? Will the other country honor your U.S. will and trust? The answer is a definite maybe. Unlike the United States, where each state must honor a will that's valid in the state in which it is executed, foreign nations are under no such obligation. So, the other country may look to see if the will is valid under its laws. For instance, if your will was witnessed by two people and the foreign nation requires three witnesses, your will may not be honored there. In addition, if your property is located in a non-English-speaking country your estate might incur extra costs in having the will translated and certified. Even if your will is considered valid and will be honored in the other country, many countries have forced heirship statutes that could supersede the terms of your estate plan. In essence, these require that a certain percentage of your property stay within the family and pass to your children, so you can't give everything to your second or third spouse. Finally, not all countries recognize trusts as they do in the United States or, if they do, they might subject them to additional taxation.

Belgium, Bosnia-Herzegovina, Canada, Cyprus, Ecuador, France, Italy, Libya, Niger, Portugal, and Slovenia have enacted the Uniform International Wills Act, often referred to as the Washington Convention. The Holy See, Iran, Laos, the Russian Federation, Sierra Leone, the United Kingdom, and the United States have signed a related treaty. By doing so, they have all agreed to honor wills that meet certain requirements, including two witnesses, a notary's seal, the testator's signature on every page, and an attestation by a notary or other authorized person. Since in the United States probate laws fall under state rather than federal jurisdiction, the Washington Convention must also be adopted by the individual states. So far, the following 23 states and the District of Columbia have taken this step: Alaska, Arizona, California, Colorado, Connecticut,

Delaware, District of Columbia, Florida, Hawaii, Idaho, Illinois, Maine, Michigan, Minnesota, Montana, Nebraska, New Hampshire, New Mexico, North Dakota, Oregon, Pennsylvania, Utah, Virginia, Vermont.

So, what should you do if you own property overseas? The answer is to consult with an estate planning attorney in that country to understand what, if any, other steps you should take there. Then, if you do execute an estate plan in the other country, be certain that it does not contradict or interfere with your U.S. estate plan. For instance, it could be problematic if your new Greek will revoked your U.S. will or if your Italian will gives your property there to your cousin while your U.S. plan gives everything to your spouse. In short, your U.S. and non-U.S. attorneys need to consult and coordinate their efforts.

Of course, you might still decide it's not worth the trouble of doing anything. We've had clients who have legal rights to family land in the country from which a parent or grandparent emigrated, but the legal difficulty of establishing those rights, combined with the social difficulty of dealing with distant relatives who might be acting as if they are sole owners of the property, dissuades them from taking any steps to confirm their ownership. Who knows how title would be established if the property were ever sold? But the clients often decide that that's not their problem.

THE JORGENSONS

It turns out that the Jorgensons' lake cottage is not in the next state north of them, but in Canada. They are concerned about whether they can create the trust they had anticipated to hold the house for their family and whether there are any taxes they should be aware of in Canada. According to a quick Google search, they learn that a trust may be used in Canada just as in the United States, but that transferring the property into a trust could trigger a tax on capital gain. In addition, this tax may be incurred every 21 years if the property continues in trust. They consult with their local estate planning attorney who recommends that they meet with her counterpart in Canada the next time they are there on vacation.

CHAPTER 16

PETS

No doubt, your pet or pets are significant parts of your family. (Does it sometimes seem like your dog is the only one happy to see you come home after work?) Yet most people do not include them in their estate plans, either assuming that their pets will pass away long before they do or that family and friends will simply step in to take care of them. And this is usually the case.

But if you do not have family or friends who are likely to step in, would like to compensate whoever does step up to the plate, or have exotic pets that require special care or have long lifespans, you might want to make provisions for them in your plan. We once had clients who owned rare parrots and made arrangements for them to go to a particular sanctuary if the parrots outlived them.

The first thing to know about planning for pets is that they are treated like property so that through your will you can give them to whomever you choose just like any other property. But first talk to the planned recipient to make sure that they are ready to take on this responsibility.

The second factor to consider is that you cannot leave money directly to a pet. So, if you want to compensate the person taking care of your pet or pets or provide a fund to pay for expenses, such as for veterinarians, dog walkers, or people to care for the pets when the primary caregiver is traveling or otherwise unavailable, this can be done in one of two ways, or both. You can simply leave money to the caregiver with the understanding, whether explicit in your will or trust or through conversations with the caregiver, as to why you are making the gift. Or you can create a trust for the benefit of your pet.

1. PET TRUSTS

All states now permit pet trusts (with Minnesota being the last to pass authorizing legislation), which was not the case as recently as 15 years ago. There are several advantages to a pet trust. It makes certain sufficient money is available for whatever your pet's needs might be in the future, and in case circumstances change so that your designated caregiver can no longer take care of your pet. It also permits you to leave specific instructions, such as providing for a romp in the dog park every day or a visit to the veterinarian at least twice a year. The disadvantage is simply that a trust, as opposed to a less formal arrangement, creates another level of planning and administrative cost. However, those pet owners who do not have a natural care system in place—friends and family— generally find these costs to be more than justified by the reassurance that their pet will be cared for appropriately. A further advantage of a pet trust is that it can go into effect during your life in the event of incapacity; the protections it provides do not have to wait until you pass away. Of course, you still need to find the right people to take your pet and serve as trustee.

Some states also have statutory pet trusts—laws containing all the trust provisions—which make these easier to set up and mean that pet owners have fewer decisions to make about the trust terms. If they like their provisions, pet owners can also use them without hiring a lawyer to prepare the trust. Of course, for some people the cost of setting up a tailored trust is not an undue burden.

CASE STUDY
LEONA HELMSLEY

In probably the most famous pet trust case, hotel heiress Leona Helmsley, who died in 2007, left $12 million for the benefit of her white Maltese, Trouble, and nothing to two of her four grandchildren. The court later reduced this amount to $2 million, determining that the extra $10 million was unnecessary. According to an article in *The New York Times* when Trouble died in 2012, her annual expenses were about $190,000, the bulk of which—$100,000—went for security costs. Her guardian, the general manager of the Helmsley Sandcastle Hotel in Sarasota, Florida, received $60,000, and the balance of the expenses went for grooming, food and veterinary costs.

2. OTHER PET PROTECTION DOCUMENTS

In addition to creating a pet trust, other steps you can take to protect your pet in the event of your incapacity or death include the following:

Animal Card. You can prepare a card that you keep in your wallet or purse that tells whoever reads it about your pet or pets, their care needs, their veterinarian and who should be called in case of emergency. Here's a sample wallet card and form to post at home (see below): http://2ndchance4pets. org/idcards.pdf

Animal Document. This can be more expansive than the animal card, and kept on your refrigerator or wherever you store your pet's food or other pet care items. You might also give your estate planning attorney a copy to keep with your estate planning documents. Here's a sample document: http://hautedogmagazine.com/wp-content/uploads/2009/11/Information-for-Emergency-Care-Givers-of-My-Pet-Document2.pdf

Door Sign. This will alert emergency workers in case of fire, illness or accident that there are pets inside. Here are places where you can purchases pet stickers at very reasonable cost: http://www.zazzle.com/pet_alert_emergency_square_sticker-217558093161097127 and http://www.safetysign.com/products/p88128/please-rescue-our-cat-sticker and http://www.petrescuestickers.com/PRS/Rescue-Stickers-Breed.aspx.

Durable Power of Attorney. You might also add a provision to your durable power of attorney specifically authorizing your agent to care for your pet and to spend money on its behalf.

Without taking these steps, people who step in to take care of you in the event of incapacity might not know what to do and the pet could easily be sent to the pound rather than put in the hands of the person or people you want to care for it. Remember, your pet can't speak for itself.

THE JORGENSONS

John and Joyce have two dogs and one cat, but they make no plans for their care. They reason that they'll probably outlive the animals and if by chance they don't, their children will take care of them.

Joyce's sister Beatrice, on the other hand, is older, unmarried and has no children. She is extremely devoted to her Corgi, Sam. She approaches Joyce to ask if she would take care of the dog if it's still alive when Bea passes away. Joyce assures her that she would and Bea executes a new will giving Sam to Joyce along with $25,000 to cover costs. Bea also writes a memorandum describing Sam's medical treatment, likes and dislikes, and contact information for his veterinarian and dog walker. Bea rests easier having taken these steps. Joyce gets a bit impatient, since Bea continues to bring this up every time they get together.

CHAPTER 17

CHARITABLE GIVING

When we ask our clients if they would like to include charitable gifts in their estate plans, there's a split between those who feel that they give sufficiently during life and those who want to make a larger gift at death when they are no longer concerned about whether they'll need the money themselves. Our clients without children are much more likely to make substantial charitable gifts at death, sometimes giving their entire estates away. Others are more likely to include charities in their "disaster" provisions—directions as to where the estate will go if no relatives survive them, an unlikely occurrence for most of us.

If you want to consider charitable gifts as part of your planning, here are some issues to consider:

1. TAX BENEFITS

The tax benefits of charitable giving accrue to most of us for gifts made during life rather than those at death. This is because lifetime gifts may be deducted from your income for tax purposes (up to a limit of 50% of your adjusted gross income, with a 30% limitation for some specific types of charities). So, for instance, if you are in the 33% federal tax bracket, a third of whatever you give away will be made up by lower taxes. If you give away $1,000, you will reduce your federal income tax by $330, reducing the after-tax cost of the gift to $770. The tax savings will be even greater if you live in a state with its own income tax, since you will also receive a state income tax deduction.

Of course, as with all tax deductions, the higher your income, the higher your tax bracket, and the bigger your charitable deduction. In addition, to take advantage of the charitable deduction at all, you have to itemize your deductions. This has become more of an issue under the 2017 tax reform law which raised the standard deduction from $6,350 for individuals and $12,700 for married couples to $12,000 and $24,000, respectively. It only makes sense to itemize if the total of all of your deductions exceeds these amounts. Hitting this number is more likely if you are paying a mortgage (and. deducting mortgage interest). Taxpayers who wouldn't normally be able to take advantage of their charitable deductions under the new tax structure are using two tactics to retain some benefit. The first is to bunch their donations, giving a large amount in one year and little or nothing in others. The second approach is a variation on this: Taxpayers can make a large contribution to a donor advised fund (more on this below) and then dole out the funds to charities in subsequent years.

If you have a federally taxable estate (more than $11.4 million in 2019, twice that for a married couple), the benefit of the deduction might be even greater, since you will get two tax benefits from the gift: the income tax deduction plus lower estate taxes (since the value of your estate will be that much lower). The latter can be significant since the federal estate tax rate starts at 40%. For a simplified example, let's assume your estate totals $15 million and you want to give $1 million to a charity (perhaps your alma mater will name a professorship in your memory). Assuming that you are in the 35% income tax bracket, if you give this money during life, you will save $350,000 on your income taxes (assuming that you're also earning more than $1 million a year), bringing the after-tax cost of the gift down to $650,000. (You'll have to give the money over several years in order to take full advantage of the deduction if you're not making $1 million a year.) At your death, your estate will be $650,000 smaller, reducing your estate tax by $260,000 (40% x $650,000), resulting in $610,000 of combined income and estate tax savings. If you simply made the gift at death, your estate would save $400,000 in estate taxes (40% x $1 million), a loss of more than $200,000 in potential tax savings.

Of course, this calculation is irrelevant to most people who don't have federally taxable estates. While the deduction will also be available if you live in a state with its own estate tax, which kicks in at a lower threshold, the state estate tax rate is likely to be substantially lower than the federal tax rate, reducing the benefit of this deduction.

In short, tax-driven charitable giving through estate planning is the domain of the very wealthy who have federally taxable estates. They should consult their tax advisors in making charitable giving plans. For everyone else who itemizes their deductions, there's a tax incentive to make donations during life rather than at death. But that needs to be balanced with the need to maintain financial security. Taxes can also be an issue in determining which assets to give, which will be discussed below in the section on retirement plans and appreciated stock.

2. SPECIFIC VS. GENERAL GIFTS

Most people who make charitable bequests are very specific about their beneficiaries and the amount of money they will give them. For instance, a will or trust might say:

I give:

    a. $10,000 to my alma mater, Wonderful College, of Bucolic Town, Vermont;

    b. $15,000 to the Old Codgers Soccer League of Retirement City, Utah; and

    c. $50,000 to the Old Soccer Players Orthopedic Hospital of Retirement City, Utah, for getting me back in the game.

If making larger gifts, donors may limit their bequests to a fixed percentage of their estate, so if their estate ends up significantly smaller over time, the charitable gifts do not end up constituting too large a portion. For instance, an individual with a $1 million estate may give $100,000 to her alma mater, but if her estate dwindles to $500,000 due to health care expenses, bad investment returns, and other unanticipated expenses, she might not want so much to go to the university instead of to her family. She can plan for such a change in circumstance by limiting the gift to 10 percent of her estate. If she does so, however, she must be clear about her definition of estate for this purpose. Is she talking about her gross estate before any taxes or expenses, or the final distributable estate after everything has been paid?

Gifts may be given to charities' general funds or for specific purposes—for instance to support a scholarship or to create a memorial in the name of the decedent or of someone else. If you are interested in funding anything along these lines, it is important that you consult with the charity in advance to make sure this is something it can manage. If you do not restrict the donation in your gift, the charity will be able to use the money for its own purposes, whether to spend or to add to its endowment. Sometimes wills and trusts are drafted to say specifically that the recipient can use the funds "for its general purposes," but this language is not necessary. In general, charities prefer unrestricted funds because they are easier to manage. They do not have to account for them separately and can deploy the funds as needs and goals develop.

It's also important to contact the charities or look at their websites to make sure that you identify them appropriately in your estate planning documents. You don't want to create any confusion if two similarly named groups have a claim on your gift. In addition, many national organizations have local chapters. So, for instance, if you are making a donation to the Alzheimer's Association, you need to be clear about whether the money should go to the national organization or your local office.

The alternative to making specific bequests is to leave the decision to your personal representative or trustee. In that case, your will or trust might read as follows:

> I leave $100,000 to be distributed by my personal representative as she in her sole discretion determines appropriate to colleges and universities providing low-cost, high-quality education.

This can be a useful approach if you are unable to decide what charitable organizations should receive your gift and don't want to hold up executing your plan while you figure this out. Or you might be aware that the organizations furthering the cause or causes you want to support change over time. In the example above, you might not want to support a particular school today that tomorrow might be seeking to raise its U.S. News & World Report ranking rather than continue to support low-income or minority students. By simply stating a purpose and permitting your personal representative or trustee to make the ultimate decision, you create flexibility. However, you also create more work and responsibility for that personal representative or trustee who needs to research the various organizations that purport to carry out the work you want to support. So, if you can choose the recipients of your largesse, it's usually better to name them. But if you can't, a general provision stating your goals will work.

THE JORGENSONS

John Jorgenson is very committed to his alma mater, which he feels was instrumental in launching him on his life and career. He gives money every year and participates in interviewing prospective students and other alumni activities. He'd like to make a larger gift that has more impact, especially helping students who can't afford to pay today's high tuition. He has discussed setting up a scholarship in his and Joyce's memory with the school's development office and has been told that that would take a minimum contribution of $100,000. That's much more than they can afford today, but less than 10 percent of their estate. John and Joyce decide to make the pledge, but to limit their bequest to the lesser of $100,000 and 10 percent of their estate. They don't want to significantly limit what goes to their children and grandchildren if there's a substantial drop in the value of their estate. This approach balances their two goals, to help their family and to assist lower-income students. If, ultimately, their bequest drops below $100,000, they won't get their names on the scholarship, but their contribution will still go to providing more financial aid to less wealthy students.

3. RETIREMENT PLANS AND APPRECIATED STOCK

Charities often encourage donors to make gifts of retirement plans or appreciated stock (or other assets, such as real estate) due to the tax benefits of doing so. Retirement plans, of course, are taxed when the funds are withdrawn. But nonprofit organizations don't pay taxes on their income. As a result, if you leave an IRA or other retirement plan to a charity, it will get full advantage of your generosity without paying taxes on the funds, unlike what you leave to your children or other individual heirs. So, if you plan to make a charitable bequest, you might want to name the charity as a beneficiary of your retirement plan, leaving non-taxable funds to your other heirs. However, if you are using a trust, beware splitting any of your retirement accounts with your individual beneficiaries because they might then lose their opportunity to stretch their distributions throughout their lifetimes (as discussed in Chapter 11 on retirement plans). Instead, designate any retirement funds going to charities directly to them and have other plans payable to your trust for your family or other beneficiaries.

The IRS also permits taxpayers over age 70½ to give up to $100,000 of retirement funds annually directly to charities without realizing any income on the transfer. This provision helps people who don't itemize their deductions. If you do itemize, withdrawing money for a charitable contribution will bring an offsetting deduction for the income you received on your IRA withdrawal. But if you don't itemize, you will have to pay tax on the withdrawal without the benefit of the offsetting charitable deduction. In either case, one advantage of transferring retirement funds to charities directly is that they are not then counted as part of your adjusted gross income. The level of your AGI can sometimes push you into a higher bracket in terms of Medicare premiums and increasing the amount of your Social Security income that is taxable.

Two items to be aware of when making a charitable rollover: First, you can only use this method with an IRA or Roth IRA, not with a 401(k) or 403(b) plan. Second, make sure you coordinate this with the financial institution where you hold your IRA and the charity to which you're making the contribution. Otherwise, there's the risk that something falls through the cracks and you don't benefit from the rollover.

The advice to give away appreciated assets has to do with capital gains taxes. If you purchased shares of stock for $200 and sold them for $1,000 to raise money for a charitable gift, the gain would be $800 and the tax (depending on your tax bracket and state tax rates) would be in the range of $200—costing you about $1,200 to make a gift of $1,000. Your tax savings (via a deduction for charitable gifts) might or might not offset the extra $200 (also depending on whether you itemize and the tax variables mentioned above). For purposes of this example, let's assume that your marginal tax rate (federal and state combined) is 20% so that the capital gains tax and the savings from the charitable deduction offset one another exactly. If, instead of selling the stock and making a gift of the proceeds, you had given the charity the stock itself without selling it first, you would still have a $1,000 deduction without having to pay any tax on capital gains. With your $200 in tax savings, the net cost of the gift to you would be $800 instead of $1,000. For clarity, here are those numbers laid out:

	GIFT OF STOCK PROCEEDS	GIFT OF STOCK
Stock Value Tax on Capital Gains Cost to Taxpayer	$1,000 + 200 $1,200	$1,000 + 0 $1,000
Charitable Tax Deduction After Tax Cost	- 200 $1,000	- 200 $ 800

These calculations assume that the taxpayer itemizes. If he doesn't, the benefit of the tax deduction doesn't apply and the out-of-pocket cost is $200 higher under both approaches.

This benefit—through the avoidance of paying a tax on capital gains on the liquidation of appreciated assets—does not exist for bequests at death because capital gains disappear at death through an adjustment of basis (see Chapter 7). With no one paying taxes on capital gains, there's no benefit to charities' non-taxpaying status. So, charitable bequests should simply be made in dollar or percentage amounts, rather than giving specific appreciated property.

4. PRIVATE FOUNDATIONS VS. DONOR-ADVISED FUNDS

You might want to give money away during life or at death for tax or other reasons, but not want it to be distributed out to charitable beneficiaries immediately. This might be because you're not sure who should receive the funds, you want them to be distributed over time to make sure that your donations are well used, or you want to set up a structure so that other family members—children and grandchildren probably—will participate in making the distributions. With passage of the new tax law, an additional reason might be that normally your charitable gifts and other tax deductions do not exceed the new standard deduction of $6,500 for individuals and $9,550 for heads of households in 2018, but if you were to combine several years' worth of contributions together, you would benefit from the charitable deduction. You accomplish these goals in two ways: either through a private foundation or a donor-advised fund.

A private foundation involves obtaining IRS approval, many formalities, and annual returns filed with the IRS. If you are not planning to set aside at least $500,000 for this purpose, it's probably not worth the cost and effort, given that there's a good alternative. If, however, you are interested in pursuing the creation of a private foundation, we recommend consulting with a tax or estate planning attorney with experience in this field.

Donor-advised funds permit you to set aside money now, take a current charitable deduction, and decide later which charities will receive distributions. They are created and managed by local community foundations, such as The Boston Foundation, and large investment companies, such as Fidelity, Charles Schwab and Vanguard. These funds can be created as easily as setting up an investment account and distributions can be made by entering the necessary information online. Family members can be made part of the decision-making process. Costs are relatively low—0.6% a year, for example, for the Fidelity Charitable Fund (plus whatever they charge for their investment fees, which can range considerably depending on the investment chosen). Taxpayers can contribute during their higher income and tax rate years and make distributions later or budget a certain amount each year for charitable contributions, deciding at the end of the year which charities to support. They can do this with smaller or larger amounts, all without the administrative burdens and costs of creating a private foundation. Donor-advised funds can also provide guidance to donors on which charities to support. This is especially the case for community-based foundations if donors wish to support nonprofits in their own cities and states.

While donor-advised funds make a lot of sense for taxpayers, some have questioned their benefit for charities since all of the money sitting in these funds, more than $110 billion by last count, is money that did not go to charities despite the grantors having received a tax deduction. (At a cost of 0.6% a year, the foundations and investment companies holding and investing these funds are earning in excess of $600 million a year.) In 2017, for example, donors contributed $29.2 billion to donor-advised funds while those same funds gave only $19.1 billion to charities. The question, which may be impossible to answer, is whether these same donors would have given more or less than $12.5 billion absent the ability to use donor-advised funds.

5. CHARITABLE GIFT ANNUITIES

Charitable gift annuities are a way to have your cake and eat it too, at least to some extent. Assume, for instance, that you want to give your alma mater $100,000, but you don't want to give up the income you earn on it (which these days might not be that much in any case). The answer might be a form of annuity. By way of background, commercial annuities are contracts with insurance companies through which you pay them a fixed sum in exchange for a monthly income, either for a term of years or for the rest of your life (or for the rest of your life with a guaranteed minimum number of payments to your family in the event you die prematurely). A charitable annuity is similar, except that your deal is with a charity instead of an insurance company and you will receive less than you would in the case of a commercial annuity—the difference being your charitable gift. Based on the value of your retained income stream, you will be able to take a deduction for your gift. The final difference is that nothing goes to your children or other beneficiaries in the event of your death before the end of a guaranteed term. The older you are and the lower the monthly payments, the lower the value of your income stream and the higher the amount of deduction you may take.

If, for instance, you were 65 years old when you made your $100,000 gift to your alma mater, it might pay you $7,300 a year for life. If your spouse was the same age and you wanted payments to continue for both of your lives, you would receive a bit less, or $6,800 a year. At these levels of payment, in fact you might not receive a charitable deduction. If you both were 85 years of age and received $9,700 a year, you would be entitled to a charitable deduction of approximately $30,000. Another alternative that would increase both your monthly payments and your charitable deduction would be making your contribution today but postponing your income. Deferring your income—for instance contributing at age 65 but beginning payments at age 80—will increase both your income when it begins and your charitable deduction when you pay in, since you'll be foregoing 15 years of income and presumably the funds will be invested and grow in value. These numbers are just examples, and will vary according to institution.

Donors often make use of charitable gift annuities when they have highly appreciated assets. If, for instance, you had $100,000 in highly appreciated stock, you might have a tax on capital gains of as much as $20,000 on their sale, reducing the amount you could use to purchase a commercial annuity (to $80,000). If, instead, you contributed the stock directly to your alma mater or other charitable organization, it could liquidate the stock at no tax cost and your annuity payments would be based on the entire $100,000 value. While this might still be less than what you could receive in payments on an $80,000 commercial annuity, the differential will be less and you will be making a significant gift to your charity of choice. And if you pass away before receiving back the full value of your donation, it's the institution you value—rather than the commercial insurance company—which gets the windfall of only paying you for just a few years.

6. CHARITABLE REMAINDER TRUSTS

Another tool for charitable planning are charitable remainder trusts, which permit more flexibility and control than charitable annuities. The architecture of these trusts is as follows: the trust grantor transfers funds into an irrevocable trust but continues to receive distributions of a specific dollar amount (similar to an annuity), or a set percentage of the trust assets each year, for instance 10%. The latter is often referred to as a charitable remainder unitrust, or CRUT. The grantor will receive a charitable deduction based on the annual payout and her age: the higher the payout, the lower the deduction and the higher her age, the higher the deduction. Charitable remainder trusts usually last for the grantor's lifetime, but can also pay out for a specific number of years. In addition, they can pay to the grantor's children or others.

If highly appreciated property, whether real estate or stock, is transferred to the trust, the capital gains tax on its sale can be amortized over the projected life of the trust rather than having to be paid immediately.

While a charitable remainder trust is more complex and expensive to create or administer than a charitable annuity, it leaves the grantor with more control. The grantor can select and change the trustee and even serve in that role herself. She or the trustee she selects can also change the ultimate charitable beneficiary or beneficiaries if she changes her mind over time.

THE JORGENSONS

John Jorgenson owns a commercial building that has appreciated in value during his life, especially in recent years with a hot real estate market and the growing popularity of the neighborhood where the building is located. John is getting older and no longer wants to manage the building, but he also doesn't want to pay the substantial taxes on capital gains that will be due upon sale of the building. He doesn't need the capital—after all, it was always tied up in the building—but could still use some income from the investment. His solution is to transfer the building to a charitable remainder unitrust that will pay him 5 percent of the trust investments each year. The trust sells the building for $1 million, which is then invested in a diversified stock and bond portfolio. The trust pays John $50,000 a year (or a bit more or less depending on how the investments do). Some of this is taxable as capital gain. At John's death the remaining funds will be paid to John's alma mater, unless he changes his mind, which he has the right to do as long as he directs the proceeds to another charity.

CHAPTER 18

INTERGENERATIONAL LIVING

Multiple generations have lived together since homo sapiens started walking the earth. But that changed in recent centuries as the world industrialized and people started living longer. In 1900, the life expectancy in the United States at birth was 47 and now it's 79. (Of course, the major impact in this increase has to do with children surviving to adulthood, and in recent years it has been declining as a result of the opioid crisis.) While not nearly as dramatic, life expectancy at age 65 has also increased, from 14 years on average in 1950 to 19 years in 2010. But the changes, along with a lower birth rate in industrialized nations such as the United States, mean that there are a lot more people in different generations living at the same time. And while the trend has been for the adult generations to live separately as younger adults make their way in the world, many families still prefer to live together or are forced to do so by circumstances, whether driven by financial, health or child-raising concerns.

In most cases, these arrangements work very well. Often, they're temporary or relatively short-term and the family members can work out how they'll live together in a relatively informal way. But matters can get complicated when living arrangements become permanent, when conditions change, and especially when a parent needs care. Misunderstandings often arise both among the family members living together and those living elsewhere who might feel that a sibling is taking advantage of the situation. What happens when a grandmother who helped raise her grandchildren now develops dementia and needs around-the-clock attention? Should a daughter who gives up her job to move in with and take care of her father be compensated? If so, how much? Does it matter whether she was ready to give up the job in any case or was struggling to make ends meet living on her own? Or what if the other adult children feel that their father would be better off if the house were sold and he moved to assisted living, perhaps closer to where they live?

Unfortunately, these issues often are not discussed in advance and situations develop as circumstances change.

The parent who today simply needs someone else living in the house, tomorrow can't be left alone, and ultimately needs hands-on care with showering and changing his Depends. The child who first moves in out of love and devotion, ultimately may feel put upon and unappreciated and seek financial recompense. He might do this under the table with small transfers of funds at first, with the amounts growing along with his resentment. While he might see this as just payment, siblings and other outsiders might view it as theft. Of course, in other families the siblings might be relieved that their brother has stepped into the breach and not care about the financial implications.

In our practice, we've seen the whole spectrum of solutions and responses. What we've learned is that the most important step for the family to take is to talk. More communication results in fewer suspicions and a better understanding of the circumstances as they develop. If family members cannot agree on how to move forward, they should seek mediation rather than look for legal solutions. When families do talk, here are some of the issues they might want to discuss:

1. Financial arrangements: Will whoever is moving in, whether a child with parents or a parent with a child, pay rent? Will they contribute to the cost of utilities and food?

2. Large expenses: What happens if the homeowner needs to add an in-law apartment or make other

alterations to the house, or if everyone needs to move to a larger house? Who pays the additional cost? If a parent moves in with children and pays to make this possible, what happens if the living arrangement doesn't work out, whether because his care needs increase, living together proves too stressful for all concerned, or he passes away relatively soon? Should the parent receive an ownership interest in the house? Or should the payment be a loan to the child and her spouse, to be forgiven over time assuming the co-living arrangement works as planned? What about equalizing the "gift" with other children?

3. Care costs: If a parent who needs assistance is living with a child, should the child be compensated for the care he provides? What about hiring home health aides? Who should make the decision as to what is an appropriate expense?

4. Decisionmaking in general: While everyone is competent, they should be able to make their own decisions. But if a parent can no longer make decisions for himself, who should decide about his care and finances? The child he's living with will know best what he needs, but might also have a conflict of interest. Where there's a disagreement among family members, geriatric care managers can often be very useful, providing a reality check about the appropriate care for the parent and the likely

progression of his needs.

5. Estate planning: It's important that health care proxies and durable powers of attorney are in place. If a caretaker child is going to receive a larger share of a parent's estate in recognition of the care provided, this needs to be set out in the parent's will or trust. Sometimes even when the parent does not need any assistance, she might want to give a house to the child who has lived there for many years so as not to disrupt her life and because, unlike her siblings, she might not have another house. This might or might not create intrafamily resentments, but if it's what the parent wants she needs to be clear and needs to meet with the attorney on her own so there's no question of undue influence about the gift.

In addition, to talking about these issues, family members need to write down the results of their discussions in order to avoid misunderstandings. This is best done in a family agreement that all family members sign. The purpose of the agreement is not so much to create a binding contract, since hopefully no one is going to sue anyone else for any breach, but to make sure everyone is on the same page. The act of attempting to summarize the discussions on paper will, by itself, raise more issues that need to be discussed. It will reveal any differences of opinion about what was agreed upon. And it will help avoid different memories about what was agreed.

Families can certainly develop these agreements on their own, but consulting with an attorney can be useful. Lawyers who have worked with families in the past might raise issues the family members don't anticipate, can answer legal questions about tax implications and other issues, and might be able to suggest win-win solutions that the family members didn't see or know about.

CASE STUDY
INTERGENERATIONAL HOMEOWNERSHIP

Some years ago, we had a terrible case in our office. An older, childless woman agreed to a proposal from her niece that she help the niece and her husband purchase a house where the aunt could live with them for the rest of her life. The aunt put most of her savings into the purchase. Unfortunately, living together did not work out as well as they hoped, and after about a year, the niece and her husband kicked the aunt out. She moved to a small apartment in subsidized senior housing in their town.

The aunt eventually found her way to our office and we sued the niece and her husband on her behalf for the return of her money, which would require the sale of the house. We ran into some legal roadblocks but eventually got them removed and were moving towards a trial on the merits of the case with confidence that we would win. In the meantime, however, the niece's mother— our client's sister—pressured the aunt to drop the lawsuit. She told her that her success would mean that her niece would lose her home, that this would be disruptive for the niece's children who would have to change schools. We argued against dropping the suit, explaining that there were many other options. The niece could take out a mortgage or could pay our client over time, or the aunt could accept less than everything she was owed. There was a big difference between nothing and the full value of the house.

But our client was isolated and it was clear that if she pursued the case, she would be penalized by losing all contact with her sister and the rest of her family. It looked like blackmail to us, but she dropped the case.

Finally, any family agreement should be reviewed on an annual basis. Circumstances change. The reality of living together or providing care often is quite different from what everyone imagines ahead of time. While family agreements are vital for all of the reasons stated above, they should not be set in stone but should be modified as necessary.

THE JORGENSONS

It's 20 years later and the Jorgensons are now 80 years old and John's health is beginning to fail him. Joyce is having trouble caring for John and maintaining the house. They have a family meeting with all three children and decide that the best solution is for John and Joyce to sell their home and move in with Jennifer and her husband, Hank (Jennifer has gotten married since we first met the family, but she and Hank have no children). But they also want to live in a separate "in-law" apartment, so they're debating whether to add one to Jennifer's house or for Hank and Jennifer to sell their house as well so that they can move into a new house that already has the additional unit.

John and Joyce's financial picture has changed: Their IRAs have been drawn down to some extent and in retirement their income is lower, limited to their Social Security and a small pension. Their house has appreciated in value. So their financial picture now appears as follows:

Income (annual)
John $35,000
Joyce $25,000

Savings and Investments

Checking	$15,000
Savings	$55,000
Investments	$235,000
John's IRA	$150,000
Joyce's IRA	$75,000
Total	$530,000

House	$500,000 fair market value, no mortgage

The family agrees that it makes sense for John and Joyce to pay whatever Jennifer and Hank's costs will be to house them, whether for an addition to their current home or the additional cost to purchase a new larger home. While this will increase the value of Jennifer and Hank's home, that's a small price to pay for the security and assistance they will provide to John and Joyce. Of course, they're assuming that this plan will work and John and Joyce won't be moving out after just a short period of time.

John and Joyce will have a lot more cash after they sell their home to pay for whatever care needs they might have in the future. And they have agreed with Jennifer and Hank that they will pay for half of the utilities, taxes and maintenance on the house, but will not contribute towards the mortgage. They put all of this in writing so that there won't be any questions or disagreements in the future about what everyone agreed to.

CHAPTER 19

FINANCIAL PLANNING

Consumers are often confused about the difference between estate and financial planning, and for good reason. Even professionals in these fields may use these terms interchangeably, or financial planners and investment companies will purport to do estate planning. Strictly speaking, financial planning concerns your money—savings, investments, spending, insurance—and estate planning involves your legal rights—appointment of agents, creation of trusts, direction as to who ultimately will receive your property.

A financial planner should help you determine how much money you will need to retire and how you will get from here to there in terms of maximizing savings, limiting spending and investing appropriately. He will advise on the types of insurance—life, disability, long-term care, umbrella—that can protect you and your family. He should be able to help you make decisions about when you can comfortably retire (partially or fully) and when you should begin taking your Social Security benefits. Your estate planning attorney may advise on these issues as well, but more likely based simply on past experience rather than actually crunching the numbers as the financial planner should do.

Financial planners are compensated in one or more of three methods, each with their pros and cons:

1. FEE ONLY

Some financial planners, like some lawyers, simply charge for their time: by the hour or a flat fee for various projects. This is often the least expensive approach, though it might not feel like it since you're writing a check or passing over your credit card. It avoids potential conflicts of interest inherent in other approaches. However, problems can arise if you're reluctant to contact the planner with questions because you're concerned about the cost, or the planner is unaware of developments because you're not in as close touch as you might be with other approaches.

2. MONEY UNDER MANAGEMENT

Many planners take responsibility for all of your financial life and charge a fee based on the size of the estate, often 1% per year. So, if your investable assets totaled $1 million the annual fee would be $10,000. There are several advantages to this approach. The financial planner has responsibility to stay on top of your financial life and can monitor changes in investments or spending habits. This can be very important for older clients who might stop paying bills or become the victims of financial fraud. This approach also means that there's no additional charge for calling the planner and asking questions, so you're more likely to develop a closer relationship with your planner. Having the fee relate to your level of assets aligns your interests with that of the financial planner at least to some extent since her fee will increase along with your level of assets.

3. COMMISSION

The third way financial planners get compensated is through commissions for selling insurance and brokerage products, such as life insurance, long-term care insurance, annuities and some mutual funds. This might feel like the least expensive approach because you don't have to write a check, but it can end up being the most expensive if you end up spending money on products you don't need or that don't produce the same investment results as less expensive products. With the broker's compensation only coming if you purchase an insurance or investment product, the incentives can cause them to push sales that are not always in your best interest.

I don't mean to cast aspersions on all insurance brokers here. Insurance and the right annuities are hedges against various risk that can be important parts of virtually every financial plan. There's nothing wrong with your financial planner receiving a commission on helping you choose the right insurance product for you and your situation. And if the insurance company is willing to pay the broker rather than you, that's great. I'm just concerned that the incentive structure leads to poor results for many consumers. The best protection against this occurring is to make sure that you always get a second opinion before purchasing any insurance or investment product.

Some financial planners adopt a combination of the above compensation systems, charging a flat fee for the initial plan and then either charging a percentage fee if you hire them to manage your finances or collecting a commission if the plan entails purchasing insurance.

Most financial planners encourage their clients to complete their estate plans and often play an instrumental role in aligning the investments with the plan, making sure that the beneficiary designations on life insurance policies and retirement plans are properly stated and helping title investments in trusts, if necessary.

A last word with respect to the fees financial planners charge: they are well earned. Financial planners help their clients navigate our increasingly complicated financial world, much of which seems designed to fleece consumers of their hard-earned dollars. It's not difficult for good financial planners to save their clients multiples of what they charge, whether it's 1% per year or an hourly fee. This has nothing to do with investment results. The common wisdom these days is that no one can time the market or pick the right stocks. Your investment portfolio should be diversified and invested primarily in low-cost index funds or ETFs. A financial planner can help you set up and monitor your portfolio, often at a lower cost than the fees imbedded (concealed) in higher-cost investment products.

CHAPTER 20

LIFE INSURANCE

Life insurance can be an important tool in financial and estate planning to ensure that your loved ones have an inheritance if you pass away at an early age or, alternatively, if you live a long life and run through your savings. We've already discussed it above in the context of special needs planning where life insurance can be vital to being fair to all your children while still funding a trust for a child or grandchild with special needs. Before the threshold for federal estate taxes began its rise from $600,000 to $11.4 million today, life insurance and life insurance trusts were often used to reduce estate taxes or to have funds available to pay the tax, or both. They are still used for this purpose today, but such high-end estate tax planning is outside of the purview of this book.

Instead, I'll provide a basic framework for understanding the different types of life insurance available on the market:

1. TERM

Term life insurance is similar in structure to homeowners or auto insurance. You're insured only as long as you continue to pay premiums. The premiums are based on your age, health and gender and are often quite low, increasing with age as your likelihood of dying within a year increases. In order to keep the premiums the same from year to year, you have the option of purchasing a term policy with level premiums for a period of time, often 10 or 20 years. This means that you'll pay a bit more during the first few years, but you'll know what the cost is for the period of the level term.

Premiums generally increase substantially after the end of the term and most people then drop the policies at that time. With proper planning, the need for the insurance will be much less at the end of the term. For instance, you might purchase a policy to make sure that your spouse and children are financially secure through your children's graduation from college. After that, they should be more independent and your need for insurance will diminish significantly. The one circumstance where you might pay the steep premiums offered to maintain the policy at the end of the term is if you have a medical condition that would preclude purchasing a new term policy, but would make it worth the cost of continuing to maintain the old one.

2. WHOLE LIFE

Whole life policies are often referred to as "permanent" because the intent is for you to hold the policy for the rest of your life. This means that the insurance company will have to pay out on most policies, even if that event is likely to occur long in the future. Whole life policies build up a cash reserve over time, which the insurance company invests. Often, the earnings on the cash reserve fund are sufficient in later years to cover the annual premium. The policy owner may also borrow funds in the reserve if he needs cash in the future. The amount borrowed plus interest will then be deducted from the future death benefit.

Insurance brokers often sell whole life policies in part as investments since the value of the cash reserve grows income tax free, similar to an IRA. In addition, the death benefit grows over time. It's only taxed if you liquidate the policy during your life and cash out the reserve fund. Instead, it's usually better to borrow the funds, as mentioned above, which is not a taxable event. I don't know whether investment professionals who are not insurance brokers would recommend purchasing a whole life policy, but I own one that should serve as an example of how this works.

I purchased the $500,000 policy when I was 53. The premium is about $16,000 a year, including the cost of a disability waiver, meaning I can stop paying if I become disabled. There are minimum cash surrender values, but the company also provides estimates of what they will be based on projected returns of the company's investments. Using its midpoint projection provided in 2016, here's how the numbers look:

When I am 70, after paying in about $270,000, the cash reserve will be just over $240,000 and the death benefit will be just under $590,000.

When I am 80, after paying in about $430,000, the cash reserve will be $440,000 and the death benefit about $675,000.

If I outlive my actuarial life expectancy and make it to 90, at that time the cash reserve is expected to be $680,000 and the death benefit $815,000, after paying in about $590,000.

After age 100, they waive the premiums.

I have no idea whether I (or rather my heirs) would be better or worse off if instead of purchasing this policy I were to invest the premiums in the stock market or a balanced portfolio. At least this has the benefit of a forced savings plan since I have to pay in each year or risk losing the policy.

3. UNIVERSAL LIFE

Universal life policies are similar to whole life policies in structure, the main difference being the treatment of the cash reserve. While the cash reserve in the whole life policy grows at a rate that is determined when the policy is purchased, universal life reserves are invested in a bucket of securities growing when the market goes up and declining if the market drops. The owner can choose from a variety of investment options. The hope with universal life policies is that the investments will do better than the predetermined return in a whole life policy. Universal life policies were more popular in the past when the market seemed stronger. But many owners were "burned" when the investments failed to perform as expected. They found that their policies were "under water" and they had to put additional funds in to maintain them.

4. SECOND-TO-DIE

In some instances, it makes sense for two spouses to purchase life insurance that doesn't pay out until the second spouse passes away, especially if the purpose of the policy is to leave an inheritance for the next generation rather than for the surviving spouse. This type of policy is often used to fund special needs trusts. Depending on the spouses' ages and health, the premiums can be substantially less than those insuring a single life since statistically there's a greater chance that one of the two spouses will live longer than her actuarial life expectancy. But work with an insurance agent to make sure that your savings are sufficient to justify giving up funds for the surviving spouse. For instance, are you better off buying one second-to-die policy for $500,000 or insuring each spouse for $250,000? The larger policy will likely be cheaper than the two individual policies, but will the surviving spouse need the extra $250,000?

5. INSURANCE REVIEW

If you already have an insurance policy, have it reviewed. An insurance agent can have the insurance company provide a statement of the policy's terms and, if it's a universal policy, advise you whether your current premium payments are sufficient to support the policy. You might need to change your premiums or your benefit level. The agent will also be able to advise whether there might be a better policy available to you at the same price. While low interest rates have been pushing premiums up, greater longevity has been pushing them down. It might be that you can get the same coverage at a lower premium or more coverage at the same premium. Even if no better alternative is available, it can't hurt to take a look.

And while you're at it, review your beneficiary designations and make sure that they are what you want and are consistent with the rest of your estate plan.

6. SELLING YOUR POLICY

If you are considering dropping your life insurance policy because you can no longer afford the premiums or no longer need to provide the money for your heirs, first check out whether you would be better off selling it. There is an aftermarket for life insurance policies fueled by investors who have calculated that they will make money by buying insurance policies, paying the premiums and ultimately receiving the death benefits.

Don't be worried that the buyer will decide to enhance its investment by taking steps to accelerate its collection date. This only works because the investment pools buy up thousands of policies and have calculated the actuarial odds based on large numbers. Your own longevity is only one statistical point in their data.

Of course, the insurance companies have also studied the actuarial records and have set the premiums accordingly. The reason investor-purchased life insurance works is that in setting their premium levels the life insurance companies have calculated that a certain percentage of policyholders will drop their policies before they die. The investors are taking advantage of this by upending that assumption.

Over time, if a lot of policies are sold to investors rather than being dropped, insurance companies will have to raise their premiums. This will make the purchase of policies less profitable and eliminate this secondary market. Nevertheless, in the meantime, you might benefit from the market if you're considering permitting a policy to lapse. It's at least worth checking out.

About 10 years ago, many investment pools were even more aggressive, paying for healthy older individuals to take out NEW life insurance policies, which they would subsequently sell to the investors. These were referred to as STOLI policies for "stranger-originated life insurance." Often they were large policies in order to make the numbers work for the investors, and because of their size were of great concern to insurance companies. Fortunately for the insurance companies, and perhaps for the health of the insurance market, the insurance industry was successful in denying payment on these policies under the doctrine that life insurance may only be sold to those with an insurable interest—meaning the individual whose life is being insured, his family members, or his business associates. The success of these challenges in court put an end to the STOLI gambit.

CHAPTER 21

STEPS FOR THE NEXT GENERATION

Every baby boomer needs an estate plan, But what about their children and grandchildren? With death and disability much less likely for younger people than for older ones, they are much less likely to need to have their plans in place. In addition, they are less likely to have assets to plan for or family members dependent upon them.

On the other hand, all of this makes it much easier to set up an estate plan. Everyone over the age of 18 needs to appoint agents to represent them on financial matters through a durable power of attorney and on health care matters through a health care directive. Anyone with children needs to name a guardian in the event of the parents' death or disability and a trustee to manage whatever assets they may leave to their children.

The financial cost of setting up a relatively simple plan and the time involved are quite low when compared to the possible effects of not having a plan in place when and if it is needed. A parent or grandparent may facilitate their children and grandchildren taking these steps by offering to pay the legal fees or the cost of an online program. Of course, nagging or scheduling an appointment can also help.

PART 3
CREATING A PLAN

Now that we've covered the importance of having an estate plan, and many of the considerations and special situations that might apply, we turn to the actual process of creating the legal blueprint that will carry out your goals and wishes, provide for your family or other beneficiaries, and prevent undue stress to your loved ones when the time comes.

CHAPTER 22

DO YOU NEED AN ATTORNEY?

I hope by now you agree that you need an estate plan. But how should you proceed—with a do-it-yourself online program or by hiring an attorney? The information in this book can support both options. They both have their advantages and disadvantages:

1. ADVANTAGES OF DIY PLANS

- They're cheap.

- You can work on them when convenient or inspired, even at 3:00 in the morning.

- They're private—you don't have other people knowing your business.

2. ADVANTAGES OF WORKING WITH AN ATTORNEY

The attorney will:

- answer your questions.

- advise you about pitfalls for the unwary that apply to you.

- know about specific state laws that might affect your situation.

- use his experience to help you make any difficult decisions.

- prod you along to complete the process.

- modify her standard forms to suit your situation and goals.

- help resolve and plan for complex situations, whether having to do with taxes, businesses, long-term care planning or family situations.

- help with follow-up issues, like properly titling accounts.

- be connected to other qualified professionals you might need, such as accountants, financial planners, and geriatric care managers.

3. DISADVANTAGES OF DIY PLANS

Essentially, the disadvantages of DIY plans are that they are missing the advantages of working with an attorney. Recognizing this, some online services (including the largest, LegalZoom) now offer consultations with lawyers through its Legal Plan. This might work if you simply need answers to a few questions, but not if you require more complex planning—and as far as I can tell, working with their lawyers does not give you the ability to revise and tailor the DIY forms to suit your particular goals and situations. Finally, you have no ability to control for the quality or experience of the lawyer you are assigned to consult with if your DIY option includes this feature.

CASE STUDY
RISKS OF DOING IT YOURSELF

My firm was engaged to probate the estate of a man—a professor—who died earlier in the year. His estate plan consisted of a trust he had drafted himself and a letter of instructions. It was unfortunate, as you'll see below, that his plan did not include a will. The well-drafted trust and letter of instructions, written with verve, were consistent. They directed that his home pass to his partner of many years, that his vacation home in another state go to his daughter, who lived there, and that the rest of his property go to his other three children in equal shares after paying off the mortgage of about $50,000 on his home.

Here are the glitches: First, when the professor drew up the plan, his savings and investments totaled

---

approximately $950,000. At the time of his death, these had been depleted to approximately $350,000 through spending, a decline in the value of his portfolio that was heavily invested in gold (whether someone in their 80s should be investing in gold is another story), and annual gifts to his children. If the mortgage were to be paid off with these remaining funds, the three children not receiving real estate would get about $100,000 each rather than the $300,000 each contemplated when the plan was created.

The second glitch is that the professor never transferred any of his property into the trust or executed a will. Whenever estate planners create plans centered on trusts as the primary estate planning document, they also prepare so-called "pour over" wills that simply state that all of the probate property owned by the decedent passes to the trust. Funding the trust during life avoids probate. Executing a pour over will doesn't avoid probate, but does make sure that the property will be distributed according to the terms of the trust. With no property titled in the name of the trust and no will, the laws of intestacy take over. These say that the entire estate passes equally to the professor's four children with nothing going to his partner of many years. (If they had married, she would have had rights to a portion of the estate. And in our state she cannot claim to be a "common law" spouse.)

The child who contacted our office wanted to follow his father's wishes, but he was not sure all of his siblings would agree, especially the two others who would not receive the vacation house. And who knows whether the professor's plan would have been exactly the same had he made it knowing that he had only $350,000 in savings and investments rather than the $950,000 he had when he drew up his documents. Further, in conveying the house to their father's partner, the children would incur taxable gifts. While given the current estate and gift tax threshold this is probably academic, it might not be for all of the children.

While this example illustrates one of many things that can happen, I would argue that this was not a true DIY situation. The professor had a complicated plan in mind, one that involved specific instructions with respect to two pieces of real estate, property in two states, and a major beneficiary who was not his child or spouse. While the attorney might not have improved on the drafting of the trust and almost certainly would not have written a better explanatory letter, she would have made certain that a pour over will was part of the plan. She also probably would have asked the professor if he would want a different distribution scheme if his assets were depleted in any way, perhaps eliminating the requirement that the mortgage be paid off before the savings and investments were distributed. While the professor avoided legal fees in drawing up the plan himself, his children paid more in resolving the problems their father left behind.

4. DISADVANTAGES OF WORKING WITH AN ATTORNEY

They're expensive. This is the result of a few factors:

a. **Limited competition.** Though numbers have fluctuated way up and then slightly down in the past 50-plus years (expanding due to increased numbers of law schools and contracting following the Great Recession), there were still more than double the number of first year law students in 2010 compared to 1964. To the extent that bar rules continue to restrict the numbers, there remains less competition and lawyers can set higher fees.

b. **Value of legal work.** Lawyers have expensive training and experience, which makes their work valuable and they charge accordingly. Caveat: there is not always a *direct* correlation between a lawyer's experience and expertise and their fees. Due to marketing and sales savvy, some relatively inexperienced attorneys charge more than some more experienced and thoughtful ones.

c. **Individualized work is time-consuming.** Good attorneys spend time learning their clients' particular situations and goals to work out an individualized plan. They also spend time implementing that plan, including drafting documents, explaining terms, educating clients, revising documents, and often helping retitle assets. The amount of time spent is highly variable depending on the complexity of the client's estate and goals.

d. **Inefficiency.** In part because of the mom-and-pop nature of law firms, few have the wherewithal to develop efficient systems that bring down the cost of doing business and the time involved.

A second potential disadvantage of working with an attorney is that she might move you towards a more complicated plan for two reasons: First, the more she does, the more she can charge. This is where the interests of the lawyer and the client diverge. Second, while the simpler plan might work out in nine cases out of ten, the lawyer may well have seen and experienced that tenth case and be seeking to avoid it both to protect the client and to avoid any future malpractice claim if the avoidable problem develops.

This concern also, in large part, explains why many estate planning documents are very long and contain many seemingly extraneous provisions. Each has been added to prevent the occurrence in the future of something that went wrong in the past. Over the years, these provisions accrete and the documents get longer and longer.

Some lawyers are more efficient and responsive than others. Some have a better bedside manner than others. Some listen better than others. Unless you have already worked with your attorney in the past, you might have no idea and have significant apprehension about what the experience will be like. For a large litigation or corporate matter, you may interview a number of attorneys before choosing the one to represent you. But for a smaller estate planning matter, a number of in-person interviews might take more time than the work itself and the attorneys might be reluctant to take the time to meet with a prospective client as opposed to a committed one. The resulting uncertainty can deter clients from working with attorneys. (See below for advice on selecting an estate planning attorney.)

Another reason many consumers avoid or put off estate planning is that traveling to the lawyer's office might be inconvenient, especially compared to doing a DIY plan in your pajamas in the comfort of your own home.

There is no one right answer for everyone. Whether you choose to work with an attorney or use a DIY plan should depend on the complexity of your situation, the goals you hope to achieve, your comfort level with computers on the one hand and with lawyers on the other, and your ability to pay legal fees.

CHAPTER 23

FINDING THE RIGHT ATTORNEY

If you do choose to work with a lawyer for your estate planning, retaining the right attorney or law firm will be very important to the process and the results. Factors that might influence your choice may include:

- Price sensitivity

- Ability to travel

- The complexity of your situation

- Desire for anonymity

- Preference of a smaller or larger firm

- Your timeframe
- Your location

The more complex your situation, the more likely you will need a specialist rather than a generalist. If you have a small business it could be important that you work with a lawyer who is familiar with family business succession planning. If you are concerned about long-term care costs, it will be important that you work with an experienced elder law attorney. In terms of the size of the firm, with a smaller firm you might be more likely to work with the principal attorney. A larger firm may have a broader and deeper level of expertise since it handles more cases and its attorneys can specialize. In addition, there's backup in the event your attorney is unavailable, whether due to vacation or illness or, in the worst case, can no longer work due to death or disability. The latter issue might be more important if you are seeking a long-term relationship than if you are hiring the lawyer for a single transaction.

In selecting the right attorney for you, there are three overlapping steps: First, creating a list of candidates. Second, narrowing the field based on what you learn about the options and the criteria that are most important to you. And, third, making your choice.

To both make your initial list and to research your candidates, good sources for leads include:

1. **Family and friends.** Your family, friends and neighbors should be able to tell you about their experiences with various attorneys. Of course, there might be instances where you don't want to mention that you are consulting with a lawyer, for instance if you needed to consult with a divorce attorney. But this is less likely to be an impediment when seeking an estate planning lawyer.

2. **Professional advisors.** Your accountant or financial planner is likely to know qualified attorneys and to be familiar with their reputation and work product. Lawyers in other fields can usually recommend colleagues with the expertise you need. If you are seeking an elder law or special needs planning attorney, social workers, doctors and teachers who are working with your family might be able to recommend qualified attorneys.

3. **The Internet.** The Internet is useful both in finding potential candidates for your list and in researching those already on the list. You can simply Google "Topeka estate planning attorney," "Baltimore business succession lawyer," or "San Antonio elder law attorney." Your results will include advertisements for lawyers and lawyer referral groups, individual lawyer and law firm listings, and directories of law firms. Some might include websites devoted to their

field of law, which provide substantive information as well as lawyer listings. (I'm the founder of www.elderlawanswers.com, which does this for the field of elder law and of www.specialneedsanswers.com, which performs the same function for attorneys focusing their practices on special needs planning.)

Once you have created your list of candidates, begin researching them by checking them out online and by asking friends, family members and professional advisors what they know about the lawyers you're considering. Online, you can look at the attorneys' own websites and see what they say about themselves, what they emphasize, how much experience they have, and whether their approach meshes well with what you are seeking. You can see what they've written, if anything, and where they speak publicly, whether to consumers or to other attorneys and professionals. You can also check out the attorney rating service at www.avvo.com. Similarly, other businesses such as www.superlawyers.com and www.bestlawfirms.com give their picks of the best lawyers and firms (locally and nationally) based on their criteria. Take these ratings services with a grain of salt, though, because they are in large part popularity contests. The lawyer who devotes all of his time and energy to best representing his clients might not have as high a rating as the one who spends more time speaking, writing and attending bar conferences.

Consider all of the information you have collected about your candidates in light of the criteria that are important to you, and narrow your field to two to four finalists. This should be a gestalt of all the information you receive—those who feel to you like the best possible fits. Weigh the impressions of people who have worked with the attorneys in question more than anything else. The glossy website might simply indicate that the law firm hired a great marketing person and the old site that hasn't been updated in years might indicate that the attorney doesn't need to market because she's in such high demand due to her compassion and results.

Once you have your finalists, call their offices and learn how they work. Here are a few questions you can ask:

- Do they charge for the first visit?
- Can they provide you with an estimate of what the total costs will be?
- Do they charge by the hour or flat fee?
- Do they do home visits (if necessary)?
- Do they prefer to communicate by telephone or by email?
- Who does the work: the lead attorney or associates and paralegals?
- Do they have experience with your particular legal challenge?

- Do they perform the whole range of legal services you might need? For instance, if your application for Medicaid is denied, will they represent you on the appeal?

- How long will the process take?

- Will the attorney talk with you on the phone? As I suggested above, estate planning attorneys are unlikely to meet with you for an interview, but most will talk with you on the phone in advance of your scheduling a meeting.

There's no right or wrong answer to these questions. Or rather, there's no right answer for everyone, but there may be for you. Based on the information about your final candidates that you obtain over the phone, as well as everything else you have learned before you call, you can trust that your decision will be a good one.

CHAPTER 24

ONLINE DIY OPTIONS

There are many online estate planning services available at low cost, ranging from the behemoth of online legal services, www.legalzoom.com, to the granddaddy of DIY legal services, www.nolo.com, which started as a publisher of legal manuals for lay people. They are all good, and far better than no plan at all. Above, we discussed some of the pros and cons of doing estate planning on your own or working with an attorney. The main problems with DIY programs are that you cannot know what you do not know, you don't have anyone to ask questions of, and the forms might not be tailored for your state. Some online services, such as LegalZoom and RocketLawyer, offer low-cost legal services along with their forms, but it appears the two are not connected. The consumer must still complete her own forms even if she can call a licensed attorney with her questions.

In addition to using a DIY program, it always makes sense to do a quick online search to see if your state has statutory forms for durable powers of attorney and health care directives. You might be able to download and execute these free of charge, and they might have a better chance of being accepted by banks and other financial institutions in states that are familiar with these forms. Along those lines, it's always a good idea to see if your financial institutions have their own durable power of attorney forms and to execute those as well as a general power of attorney. Finally, when using a DIY program, be clear to read all of the instructions very carefully. You don't want a document to be invalid because, for instance, a signature wasn't notarized or an interested party served as a witness.

One of the questions I have with online estate planning programs is how many consumers actually complete them. Do they get started, come across a question they can't answer or a decision they can't make right then and there and not get back to completing the process? Do they complete the forms and never get around to bringing them to a notary to witness their signatures? One of the advantages of working with an attorney is that the attorney will push to get the work completed. In our office, we schedule the meeting for the document execution as soon as we're hired so that there's a clear deadline for everyone involved.

Here's a thumbnail sketch of the most popular DIY online programs.

1. NOLO

Nolo.com is a wonderful website full of clear information about estate planning and other consumer-oriented legal fields. It sells individual documents including wills and trusts, each for $59.99.

The sample will on the website is well-written and comprehensive, permitting specific bequests of specific items and even creating continuing trusts for minor children. Nolo seems to offer only a limited power of attorney and selected state living will forms online. It does, however, sell the Quicken Willmaker Plus program for $79.99, which rather than being online is a downloadable document assembly system that is also available on CD. It includes a will, durable power of attorney and health care directive. Its purchase also includes a one-year subscription to Nolo's online trust package and it may be used for all family members.

Given Nolo's resources and experience, users should be confident that it offers well-drafted forms. But it is a bit confusing that some forms are offered online, while others require downloading Nolo's Willmaker forms system. In addition, while Nolo provides great consumer-oriented information both online and in its many downloadable manuals, their FAQ page and other links could do a better job of directly providing guidelines as to when and when not to use the system.

The bottom line is that if you determine based on the guidance in this book that a DIY system makes sense for you, then you should feel comfortable using Nolo's Willmaker system. You will need to use that system rather than the online forms because it's the only one that includes a durable power of attorney and a health care directive. If you choose to use a trust, you will then need to combine this with Nolo's online trust (at no additional charge).

2. LEGALZOOM

LegalZoom.com offers a will for $69, the software available for just 30 days (though this limitation might be useful in getting users to follow through and complete their planning). For just $10 more, the user can consult with an attorney. A $149 bundle also includes a financial durable power of attorney and health care directive and a year of access to both the software and to unlimited 30-minute consultations with attorneys. A revocable trust costs $249 with access for 30 days, $269 with a 30-minute legal consultation, and just $30 for a package that includes a financial durable power of attorney, a health care directive, a year of access to both the software, and unlimited 30-minute consultations with attorneys. It does not appear to include a will.

The low cost of the services that include legal consultations likely reflects that fact that few of those who sign up actually take advantage of them. It does not appear that the independent lawyers in its legal network edit documents, instead providing answers, advice and guidance over the telephone.

If you use the services, this could be an excellent deal. The caveats are the experience of the attorneys who participate on the panel. While they are supposed to have at least five years of experience, a spot check on the biographies of a few panel lawyers shows that many have less time in practice. They might work at firms where senior attorneys can assist with questions the junior attorneys cannot answer. It's also not clear whether the clients are eligible for a refund, or what happens next, if they are advised that due to their circumstances the LegalZoom forms won't meet their estate planning goals.

3. SUZE ORMAN

The television financial planner, Suze Orman, tells her viewers not to go to a lawyer for their estate planning but instead to buy her $90 online package of four "must have" documents (which she claims has a $2,500 value—the amount she says a lawyer would charge). You can do so at this link: www.suzeorman.com/books-kits/collections-and-kits/must-have-documents/

It's a good, comprehensive program that includes explanations of those "must have" documents:

- Will
- Revocable trust
- Financial durable power of attorney
- Health care power of attorney and advance directive

One problem with the program is that the user only learns after he buys it that perhaps he should see a lawyer. Within the program, Orman advises anyone who has a child with special needs or an estate over $1 million to go see a lawyer instead. This is because she recognizes that the options for such consumers are too complicated and too unique to be handled by a DIY program. Orman developed the program with California attorney Janet L. Dobrovolny, which results in the documents being somewhat California oriented, which may or may not present a problem outside of the state. I also found that in attempting to create a highly tailored end product, the program becomes quite complex in a way that many users might find daunting.

4. WILLING.COM

Willing.com is a relatively new easy-to-use site for making your estate plan. Unfortunately, it's pricing is less than transparent. It quotes a $69 fee for a will, but then discusses a package that includes a durable power of attorney, health care directive and revocable trust as well without mentioning the price or whether it's included in the $69. On the other hand, the site appears to have the best user interface of all the options I've reviewed, so the user might not mind spending some time interacting with the program before finding out the ultimate cost.

5. ROCKETLAWYER.COM

RocketLawyer.com, like LegalZoom, provides online legal forms in a variety of legal fields, all of which are free for the first seven days. After that, RocketLawyer charges $39.99 per document. Users can subscribe at a rate of $39.99 a month for unlimited use of forms and free 30-minute attorney consultations for each new legal matter. (This pricing structure is somewhat different from what they offered when I reviewed the site a few years ago, so it looks like they're still trying to figure out the best pricing model.)

I tested out the will creation software and found it easy to use and comprehensive, but too comprehensive for my patience. It asks many of the questions that in our practice we simply assume answers for our clients in order not to get too bogged down in ancillary details. For instance, should the trustee who would manage a trust for your children if you were to die while they are minors have to purchase a bond? What about the successor trustee in the event the first trustee can't serve or stops serving for any reason? Bonds are expensive and require reporting, which otherwise is usually not necessary. Presumably, you are appointing someone you trust who is unlikely to abscond with the funds. We don't require bonds in our documents and never ask our clients whether one should be required. So far, we've never had a problem with this (knock on wood), but we've saved countless hours of mostly irrelevant discussion and decisionmaking. Overall, I feel confident recommending their service with the caveat that their will-creation questionnaire needs streamlining.

6. FREEWILL.COM

On this new site you can indeed create a new will for free. Its funding model is supported by charities. In exchange, after asking for personal information it invites the user to include a charitable gift in her plan. It provides buttons for nine charities and then allows the user to name others. Users can give the charities a percentage of their estate or a specific amount. They are not, however, required to make any charitable gifts.

The online interface is very easy to use. After the user has filled in her information and wishes, she can choose to have the document finalized or simply printed out as information to bring to an attorney. If the user chooses the latter option, the site provides her with links to AVVO, Google, Yelp and the American Bar Association. If she chooses to create the will, the program provides it as a pdf that she can print out and sign. It comes with straightforward instructions on signing and storing the will.

FreeWill.com produces a perfectly adequate simple will with few bells and whistles. I'd use some different language, but that's mostly a matter of taste. Of course, I feel strongly that durable powers of attorney and health care proxies are at least as important as wills. It would be great if FreeWill.com also produced these for free.

CHAPTER 25

WORKSHEETS AND FORMS

This chapter contains several worksheets and forms that you should find useful in organizing your affairs, thoughts and goals. Use them to prepare your own estate plan, get ready for a meeting with your lawyer, or to guide those who need to take over in the event of your incapacity or death.

1. ESTATE PLANNING WORKSHEET, UNMARRIED

ESTATE PLANNING WORKSHEET (SINGLE)

Name: _____

Address: _____

_____

Telephone: (h)_____

(w) _____

(cell) _____

Email:_____

Are you a United States citizen? _____ yes _____ no

CHILDREN

Name: _____

Birth Date: _____

Name: _____

Birth Date: _____

Name: _____

Birth Date: _____

Name: _____

Birth Date: _____

Do any of your children have any special needs?

_____ yes _____ no

If so, please describe:

_____

_____

_____

_____

PROPERTY

Does the value of all of your property total:

_____ less than $1 million.

_____ more than $1 million.

If you would like any of your property (including tangible property such as jewelry, artwork or furniture) to go to specific individuals, please describe the property and who you would like to receive it on the following lines.

_____

_____

_____

_____

While it's an unpleasant thought, who would you like to receive your estate should both you and your children pass away?

_____

_____

_____

_____

If your children or grandchildren are minors when they are due to inherit, the funds may be held in trust until they are old enough to responsibly manage it themselves. Please choose among the following ages for the ultimate distribution to them:

25

30

35

The following options are only available if you are choosing a plan that includes a revocable trust.

Half at 25, half at 30

Half at 30, half at 35

One third at 25, 30 and 35

Other. Please describe: _____

_____

_____

GUARDIANS

Please indicate who you would like to serve as guardian of your minor children (if any) should you become incapacitated or pass away, along with an alternate in case the first person cannot serve:

Guardian's name:

_____

Address: _____

_____

Telephone: (h)_____

(w) _____

(cell) _____

Email:_____

Alternate's name:

_____

Address: _____

_____

Telephone: (h)_____

(w) _____

(cell) _____

Email:_____

AGENTS

In addition to naming a guardian for your children, you will need to name agents on your powers of attorney, health care proxies, and wills. You can appoint the same person or different people for the various roles. And—except for your agent under the health care proxy—you may name a single person for each role or two people to share the responsibilities.

Using the form below, you may list the people you intend to appoint and indicate their role or roles on each of your documents by circling all that apply:

Principal Agent

Agent on durable power of attorney

Health care agent

Personal representative on will

Trustee

Alternate

Durable power of attorney

Health care agent

Personal representative on will

Trustee

Name:_____

Address: _____

_____

Telephone: (h)_____

(w) _____

(cell) _____

Email:_____

Principal Agent	**Alternate**
Agent on durable power of attorney	Durable power of attorney
Health care agent	Health care agent
Personal representative on will	Personal representative on will
Trustee	Trustee

Name:_____

Address: _____

_____

Telephone: (h)_____

(w) _____

(cell) _____

Email:_____

Principal Agent

Agent on durable power of attorney

Health care agent

Personal representative on will

Trustee

Alternate

Durable power of attorney

Health care agent

Personal representative on will

Trustee

Name:_____

Address: _____

_____

Telephone: (h)_____

(w) _____

(cell) _____

Email:_____

Principal Agent

Agent on durable power of attorney

Health care agent

Personal representative on will

Trustee

Alternate

Durable power of attorney

Health care agent

Personal representative on will

Trustee

Name:_____

Address: _____

_____

Telephone: (h)_____

(w) _____

(cell) _____

Email:_____

2. ESTATE PLANNING WORKSHEET, MARRIED COUPLE

ESTATE PLANNING WORKSHEET (COUPLE)

Names: _____

Address: _____

_____

Telephone: (h)_____

(w)_____ (w)_____

(cell) _____ (cell) _____

Email:_____ Email:_____

Are you both United States citizens?

_____ yes _____ no

CHILDREN

Name: _____

Birth Date: _____

Name: _____

Birth Date: _____

Name: _____

Birth Date: _____

Name: _____

Birth Date: _____

Do any of your children have any special needs?

_____ yes _____ no

If so, please describe:

_____

_____

_____

_____

PROPERTY

A few states impose taxes on estates exceeding $1 million and larger estates in any case might involve more complex estate planning considerations. So it's important to know whether the value of your property (including real estate, savings, investments and retirement plans, but not including life insurance) totals less than $1 million. Please confirm:

_____ Our property totals less than $1 million.

_____ Our property totals more than $1 million.

This planning document also assumes that you would like all of your property to pass to one another and then on to your children. If you would like a different distribution of some or all of your property (including tangible property such as jewelry, artwork or furniture), please describe the property and who you would like to receive it:

_____

_____

_____

_____

While it's an unpleasant thought, who would you like to receive your estate should both of you and your children pass away?

_____One half to each of our next of kin.

_____Other (this can include charities). Please describe:

_____

_____

_____

_____

If any of your children are minors when they are due to inherit, their funds will be held in trust. Please choose among the following ages for the ultimate distribution to them:

25

30

35

The following options are only available if you are choosing a plan that includes a revocable trust.

Half at 25, half at 30

Half at 30, half at 35

One third at 25, 30 and 35

Other. Please describe: _____

GUARDIANS

Please indicate who you would like to serve as guardian of your minor children (if any) should you become incapacitated or pass away, along with an alternate in case the first person cannot serve:

Guardian's name:

_____

Address: _____

_____

Telephone: (h)_____

(w) _____

(cell) _____

Email:_____

Alternate's name:

_____

Address: _____

_____

Telephone: (h)_____

(w) _____

(cell) _____

Email:_____

AGENTS

In addition to naming a guardian for your children, you will need to name agents on your powers of attorney, health care proxies, and wills. We assume that you will appoint one another as your principal agents on all documents, but it's important to name alternates in case either of you is unavailable for any reason when needed. You can appoint the same person or different people for the various roles. And—except for your agent under the health care proxy— you may name a single person for each role or two people to share the responsibilities.

Using the form below, you may list the people you intend to appoint and indicate their role or roles on each of your documents by circling all that apply:

For Spouse 1

Agent on durable power of attorney

Health care agent

Personal representative on will

Trustee

For Spouse 2

Agent on durable power of attorney

Health care agent

Personal representative on will

Trustee

Name:_____

Address: _____

Telephone: (h)_____

(w) _____

(cell) _____

Email:_____

For Spouse 1

Agent on durable power of attorney

Health care agent

Personal representative on will

Trustee

For Spouse 2

Agent on durable power of attorney

Health care agent

Personal representative on will

Trustee

Name:_____

Address: _____

_____

Telephone: (h)_____

(w) _____

(cell) _____

Email:_____

For Spouse 1

Agent on durable power of attorney

Health care agent

Personal representative on will

Trustee

For Spouse 2

Agent on durable power of attorney

Health care agent

Personal representative on will

Trustee

Name:_____

Address: _____

_____

Telephone: (h)_____

(w) _____

(cell) _____

Email:_____

For Spouse 1

Agent on durable power of attorney

Health care agent

Personal representative on will

Trustee

For Spouse 2

Agent on durable power of attorney

Health care agent

Personal representative on will

Trustee

Name:_____

Address: _____

_____

Telephone: (h)_____

(w) _____

(cell) _____

Email:_____

3. DIGITAL ASSETS

While there's no foolproof way of keeping track of all your online accounts, usernames and passwords (and making sure that your agents have access when needed), this form is a helpful start. Fill it out and keep it with your important documents. Choosing to keep passwords recorded by hand has the advantage of being very clear and simple to use for any of your agents, but this method has two drawbacks: First, it is difficult to keep up-to-date as you open new accounts or change passwords. And second, it's not entirely secure, as anyone going through your physical papers will have access. We recommend keeping it securely locked but making sure your agents have an easy method of access.

Another approach to keeping track of your passwords is to develop three strong passwords. You should be able to remember three. Then, if necessary, you can run through all three when trying to access an account without going over any limit on attempts. Again, make sure your agents know those three passwords.

A newer way to store the many passwords required in our increasingly digital lives is to use a secure password manager. 1Password, LastPass, and Dashlane are examples of these programs, of which there are many. For $20 to $40 a year, they allow you to store all of your passwords and logins (and even credit cards, bank account info, or anything else you want to store) secured by one single master password. These programs are easy to keep updated, and can even help you generate unique and complex passwords for each account, which can be entered directly from the program into your online logins so that you don't have to remember them or spend time trying to type them perfectly. While the downside is that *all* of your sensitive information is guarded by just one password, it is far easier to generate and remember one very secure password to protect your information, which you can share with your trusted agent for her use when needed.

My Digital Assets

Name: _____

Date: _____

E-mail Address: _____

_____

[The purpose of the following form is to make it convenient for you to keep a record of your usernames and passwords both so that you will remember them and also in case you become incapacitated so your agent or agents can gain access as needed. This has the benefit of convenience and can save you and your loved ones a lot of time and trouble. But it also has risks, since if anyone who shouldn't gain access to this list finds it, you could lose your privacy or be defrauded. So keep this list in

a safe place, and let your agent or agents know where to find it. Also, update it periodically as you add accounts or change passwords.]

Desktop

Computer: _____

Username: _____

Password: _____

Excel: _____

Username: _____

Password: _____

Quicken: _____

Username: _____

Password: _____

Program: _____

Username: _____

Password: _____

Program: _____

Username: _____

Password: _____

Facebook: _____

Username: _____

Password: _____

Google: _____

Username: _____

Password: _____

LinkedIn _____

Username: _____

Password: _____

Twitter _____

Username: _____

Password: _____

Other Internet Accounts

Platform: _____

Username: _____

Password: _____

Platform: _____

Username: _____

Password: _____

Platform: _____

Username: _____

Password: _____

Platform: _____

Username: _____

Password: _____

Platform: _____

Username: _____

Password: _____

Financial Accounts:

Bank: _____

Username: _____

Password: _____

Bank: _____

Username: _____

Password: _____

Investments: _____

Username: _____

Password: _____

Investments: _____

Username: _____

Password: _____

Retirement: _____

Username: _____

Password: _____

Retirement: _____

Username: _____

Password: _____

Other:

Company: _____

Username: _____

Password: _____

Company: _____

Username: _____

Password: _____

Company: _____

Username: _____

Password: _____

Company: _____

Username: _____

Password: _____

4. PET INSTRUCTIONS

While you can create a trust for the benefit of a pet or provide instructions in your will, we find that most clients do not do so—assuming either that they will outlive their pets or that family members will take care of them in due course. However, clients who do not have family members in a position to do so, or who have especially long-lived pets, are more likely to include them in their estate plans. Those who do not make formal arrangements for their pets may choose to do so in a less formal way, simply leaving instructions for their personal representative in the form of a letter, as in the example here.

PET INSTRUCTIONS LETTER

Dear _____:

In the event that I, _____, am incapacitated and unable to make my wishes known regarding my (cat, dog, other), or I pass away, please honor the following requests: (emergency contact person) is to be contacted as soon as possible at (phone number). All expenses for my (cat, dog, other), (pet's name), will be guaranteed by them. If (pet's name) is not injured and (emergency contact) cannot be reached, my pet is to be cared for by my veterinarian listed below or the nearest reputable boarding kennel, and kept in the best possible manner until arrangements can be made to get (pet's name) home.

I prefer that my veterinarian, (vet's name and contact), be contacted regarding decisions on (pet's name) care and treatment. If my pet is injured beyond all hope of recovery, he or she is to be humanely euthanized. (Pet's name) is a (male/female), (breed), (colors) and list any identity markings). (Pet's name)'s shots are all up to date. The welfare of (pet's name) is my primary consideration.

Sincerely,

Veterinarian

Name:_____

Address: _____

_____

Telephone: _____

CHAPTER 26

WHAT TO DO WITH YOUR DOCUMENTS

So you've gotten your act together and executed your estate plan. What should you do with the documents? Should originals go into your safe deposit box? Should copies be sent to your children, agents and heirs? The answer is . . . yes. Or, to put it differently, there are many right answers.

If a law firm prepared your plan, it may be willing to hold the originals. Some prefer to do so. Historically, law firms saw this as a great way to ensure repeat business. The thinking was that if the law firm had your documents, you would be more likely to return to it if you have questions or want revisions. And if you became incapacitated or after your death, your children or other agents would come to the law firm for the original documents and presumably would hire it for representation. Some law firms went so far as to include provisions in their form wills directing that the firm be hired.

Often, the result is that law firms have multiple fireproof file cabinets full of the original documents for clients with whom they have long lost touch. I've been practicing law for three decades and have some documents just as old. Being responsible for and keeping track of all of these originals can be a significant burden. As a result, more and more firms are refusing to keep originals, instead giving them to their clients to take with them.

My firm's practice is to continue to keep one set of originals despite the cost involved. We have found that clients often misplace originals or family members can't put their hands on them when needed. However, we have instituted a policy (added to our fee agreements) that we may destroy documents after 10 years if we have made diligent efforts to locate the client and cannot do so. This avoids ongoing storage of original documents belonging to misplaced clients. For all documents except for the will (of which there can be only one), we have our clients sign multiple originals. Then, we keep one set (if the client allows, as all documents belong to them) and give clients the others.

Then the client has the same issue with her set of originals, whether she created them herself through a DIY program or has originals prepared by an attorney: Where to store them? The answer depends in large part on whether she cares if anyone sees the documents. If this is not a big concern, they may be kept in a file cabinet or desk drawer and she may simply let her agents know where they are. We usually recommend that they not be kept in a safe deposit box at a bank because this can make it difficult for others to get the documents when needed. But this might be the best course if she is concerned about security and privacy. In that case, she must make sure that her agent or agents have access to the safe deposit box. If the client has the *only* originals their safety is more important, meaning that they should be stored—where possible—in a box that is fireproof and waterproof.

We also provide our clients with copies of their documents on paper and, if they wish, as electronic files. These don't need the same security as originals unless the client wishes to protect them from prying eyes. The client or her attorney can send paper or electronic copies to children and other designated agents if the client wishes. But what about giving originals to agents, especially with respect to the durable power of attorney and health care directive? We generally don't do so, advising that it's better to keep all the originals in one place and simply let the designated agents know where to locate them when necessary. But sometimes when it's clear that an agent is better organized or living in a more secure setting than the client, it can make more sense for the agent to hold a set of originals. This can be the case when the client is showing early signs of dementia (but is still sufficiently competent to execute estate planning instruments).

CHAPTER 27

REVIEWING AND UPDATING YOUR PLAN

How often we should all update our estate plans always depends on the circumstances. At age 18, everyone should have a durable power of attorney, health care proxy and HIPAA release, just in case an accident occurs. These should then be updated upon marriage, having children or accumulating significant assets—adding a will and perhaps a trust. Frequently the people one would appoint as agents at 18—parents or siblings—are not those one would appoint at 28 or 38. After this base plan is put in place, a new plan may not be necessary for decades absent a change in circumstances. A divorce, death in the family, or move to a new state would indicate the need to at least review your plan.

As we have discussed earlier in the book, unfortunately for us baby boomers, after age 55 the chances of dying or becoming disabled increase significantly as every year goes by. It is important to review your plan at age 55 and then to do so again every five years. (Unfortunately, this sounds a bit like advice about colonoscopies.) Circumstances often change in these later years—retirement, moving to a new state, disability of oneself or beneficiaries—as do tax and public benefit laws. For reasons that make no logical sense, some financial institutions will only honor recently executed durable powers of attorney. So it can be useful to sign new ones every five years. The rest of your plan might not need to be changed, but a review is useful just in case. Think of it as your annual medical checkup, except that you only have to do it every five years.

A case in our office shows the need to review your estate plan—if not every five years, at least every few decades.

CASE STUDY
THE IMPORTANCE OF UPDATING

John executed a will in 1988. He was not married and did not have children and he split his estate among his three siblings. When he died 27 years later in 2015, at the age of 82, he was still unmarried and childless—his circumstances had not changed. But those of his siblings had. One was living in a nursing home; one in assisted living; and one had passed away leaving five children. The will provided that the children of a deceased sibling would receive his share.

Unfortunately, one of those five nieces and nephews, who was to receive a 1/15th share of John's estate (about $80,000 in this case), was drug addicted and homeless. His siblings were afraid that when he received these funds he would spend the money on drugs, the quantity of which then available to him might kill him.

The brother who was living in a nursing home was covered by Medicaid. The receipt of funds— about $400,000—would make him ineligible for further benefits. At current rates, the inheritance would have been completely depleted in three years and if he passed away before he spent it all down, the state would have a claim against his estate for reimbursement of past expenses. It is also possible that the third sibling, who was then in assisted living, might need nursing home care in the future with her inheritance being spent down in a similar way.

Due to the situations of these beneficiaries, this was a case that cried out for a trust that would have permitted John's siblings and nieces and nephews to benefit from his generosity, but for his brother in a nursing home to continue to receive Medicaid-covered care and his nephew to receive some benefit from his share without it going into his arm in days or weeks. Of course, John could not know this in 1988, which is why periodic reviews are necessary.

CONCLUSION

Writing this book has helped me refine my thoughts about estate planning. Here are a few of my conclusions:

First, everyone needs an estate plan. Of course the very word "estate" in estate plan is unfortunate because most people don't feel they have an "estate," so they don't feel that they need any estate planning. But estate planning involves planning for life as well as death, and durable powers of attorney and health care directives can be more important than wills and trusts. Let me know if you have a better word for the process.

Second, while the United States is full of experienced and caring estate planning lawyers who provide great service, advice, and drafting for their clients, the reservation of estate planning to attorneys causes many people not to plan their estates. Many people are afraid of attorneys because of their cost, because they don't want to open up their private affairs to someone they don't know well, and because lawyers often seem to complicate simple situations. As discussed above, often simple situations aren't as simple as clients think. But just as often lawyers are concerned about planning for the one-in-a-hundred possible outcome, while the client may be less concerned about the unlikely event. The result is that most people who should have estate plans avoid attorneys.

Third, for most people online DIY programs are far better than no plan at all. But they're also dangerous if they're used in the wrong circumstances or misused, such as examples we've seen in our practice where clients did not fund perfectly good trusts they created on their own. I hope this book will help you choose the right solution for your situation and avoid these mistakes.

Finally, it's time for baby boomers to plan. It can make all the difference for your family. Don't wait. Enjoy the process.

ACKNOWLEDGMENTS

A lot of people helped me get this book written and published, starting with my law partners, Jeffrey Bloom and Patricia D'Agostino, who kept our clients represented and our firm prospering as I cut back my practice to devote time to this project. Similarly, my life partner, Susan, and our children, Maya and Jeremy, suffered my distraction and preoccupation as I focused on the book rather than more communal entertainments, especially during vacations. Susan also came up with the name of our publishing company, Ducks in a Row Publishing.

Many people at the firm, lawyers, legal assistants, and law clerks, read and commented on early versions of chapters and looked up fine points of law or statistics to make sure the book is accurate and up-to-date, including: Judy Carnes, Marie Posey, Patricia Flynn, Patricia D'Agostino, Rebecca Benson, Karen Mariscal, Jasmine Eberhard and Kimberly Smith. I'm sure I left some people out and if so, I apologize to them.

A few people were instrumental in moving the book from manuscript to actual publication, especially Julie Hills, who copyedited and polished the rough text to make it readable and comprehensible to those not immersed in the topics every day, and Janica Smith, who shepherded the book from manuscript to publication.

Of course, if there are any errors or lack of clarity in the book despite all this help, the buck stops with me. But I need your assistance too. If anything is wrong or confusing, please let me know by posting your question or comment on my AskHarry.info website. The beauty of websites and on-demand printing is that corrections and improvements do not have to stop with publication; they can continue indefinitely.

ABOUT THE AUTHOR

A passionate advocate for seniors, individuals with special needs and their families, Harry S. Margolis has been practicing elder law and estate planning for more than 30 years. Through his initial firm, ElderLawServices, and his current firm Margolis & Bloom, he has helped thousands of clients pay for long-term care, grapple with the incapacity of a family member, and secure the futures of their children and grandchildren.

Harry edited The ElderLaw Report, a monthly newsletter for attorneys, for three decades. He has been selected as a Fellow of both the National Academy of Elder Law Attorneys and the American College of Trust & Estate Counsel, has been named a "Super Lawyer" since 2005, recognized as one of the top 100 "Super Lawyers" in New England, and named Elder Law Attorney of the Year by Best Lawyers.

The founder of the websites www.elderlawanswers.com and www.specialneedsanswers.com, Harry recently began answering consumer questions online at www.askharry. info, demonstrating his commitment to empowering everyday people with the knowledge they need to achieve the best legal solutions. He has served as an elected town meeting member in Brookline, Massachusetts, and on the town's bicycle advisory committee. Mr. Margolis resides in Brookline with his wife, college-age twins (when they're home) and dog of uncertain breed. He loves biking and traveling, both in the US and abroad.

INDEX

PAGE NUMBERS WITH TABLES ARE INDICATED IN BOLD.

public benefits programs, 204–205,
212, 215–216, 219, 222–223
See also Medicaid; SSI

R

real estate, 17, 69–70, 87, 128–
129, 133, 268–269, 271, 337,
344–345
documents, 34
irrevocable trusts, 174
life estates, 172–174
Medicaid, 156, 164, 171–172
mortgages, 101, 322
shielding, 267–268
transfers, 33
See also real property; vacation
homes
real property, 59–60
See also intangible personal
property; real estate;
tangible personal property
required minimum distributions,
110, 246, 248, 250–253,
258–262
residue, 65, 69–70, 103
retirement, and estate planning,
16–17
retirement plans, 108–110,
243–246, 248, 250, 256–257,
269–270, 329–330
revocable trusts, 21, 35, 81, 97–98,
101–102, 106–107, 257, 386
documents, 98, 100
and retirement funds, 108
See also trusts
Roth IRAs, 243, 330

S

Shenkman, Martin, *Powers of
Attorney: The Essential Guide
to Protecting Your Family's
Wealth*, 28
Simpson, O.J., 269
spending down, and Medicaid,
149–150, 178
spouses, 250
as agents/representatives/
executors, 30, 33, 71, 93
as beneficiaries, 110
and citizenship, 303–305, 307
and gifts, 92, 123, 125
HIPAA regulations, 53
immediate annuities, 179–180
and life expectancies, 248
and Medicaid, 147, 151, 153,
156, 161, 238
right of refusal, 183–184
traditional planning, 125–127
and trusts, 33, 82
and veterans benefits, 142–143
wills/intestacy, 77–78, 81
"springing" power of attorney,
30–31
See also current power of
attorney
states, 81, 85, 90, 174, 310–312,
324
conservatorship/guardianship,
26, 226–227
durable power of attorney,
27–28, 31, 38, 40

Made in the USA
San Bernardino, CA
11 September 2019